Praise for Transforn

"Buchheit and Schamber's long-awaited master [illegible]
and evolution of the most effective personal [illegible]
planet. As a former student and client of Carl, I saw a significant [illegible] in my personal life and my ability to help others. Every change agent and student of personal growth will want to read this book, refer to it, keep it close by!" **–Christine Comaford, executive coach to peak performers, presidential advisor, and best-selling author of *Smart Tribes: How Teams Become Brilliant Together***

"*Transformational NLP* is one of the most important books to be written in our time. Carl Buchheit has synthesized the breakthrough psychology and consciousness achievements of the previous century with his own brilliant version of Neuro-Linguistic Programming. The result is a body of knowledge as well as practical tools that contribute effectively to our ongoing task to understand why and how we are the way we are. More importantly, because this new psychology is founded in NLP, Buchheit shows us how to use these tools to live more creatively, respectfully, and peacefully with ourselves and with each other." **–Irving S. Katz, Ph.D., Chancellor of International University for Professional Studies**

"Carl Buchheit is a remarkable person. It was my great good fortune to be one of his students and clients. I have known and been a student or a mentor of several Nobel Prize winners. Carl is certainly of their caliber or beyond them in his depth of conceptual thinking and revolutionary thought. Through his genius, I have become a happier and more fulfilled individual. This book is a wonderful introduction to his genius. It describes step by step the concepts behind his change work, which can appear to be like magic. I am convinced that *Transformational NLP* is a significant contribution to the field of psychology and to the world." **–From the Foreword by Carl Pennypacker, Ph.D., astrophysicist at the University of California, Berkeley and Lawrence Berkeley National Laboratory**

"In this groundbreaking book, Carl Buchheit has given us the pieces that have been missing from the world of spiritual and mind-body practices. His discoveries of how spirit, mind, and body can be brought into alignment open the way for us to become who we truly want to be and to work with one another with new depth and respect for the experience of being human. I believe that Buchheit's work is essential for all practitioners in the fields of consciousness and wellbeing—and for anyone who aspires to live with inner fulfillment and contribute to planetary peace." **–Debra Poneman, motivational speaker, founder and president of *Yes to Success!* seminars, and author of *Chicken Soup for the American Idol Soul***

"In my life I have crossed the paths of a handful of teachers and mentors who were offering something so useful and powerful that it forever changed what was possible for me in my life. Carl Buchheit is at the top of my very short list of such mentors. From studying Transformational NLP with Carl for many years, my existing coaching practice got better by leaps and bounds and light years. And I personally shifted into the person I had been trying to become for my entire life, at ease with myself and the world. If you have the chance to learn from this teacher, do it! *Transformational NLP* is a life-affirming, life-changing gift to the world!" **–LiYana Silver, coach and author of *Feminine Genius: The Provocative Path to Waking Up and Turning On the Wisdom of Being a Woman***

"Carl Buchheit is a one-of-a-kind loveable genius who speaks to the heart of transformation. He is one of the true elders of transformational work, the Nicola Tesla of change work! Carl's work has profoundly touched my life as well as the lives of countless others. In addition to helping me personally, his teachings have added greater depth to my own teachings and trainings. I have deep, deep gratitude to this exceptional teacher. *Transformational NLP* explains the innovative concepts underlying Carl's methods." **–Jeffrey Slayter, motivational speaker, executive leadership trainer, and best-selling author of *Imagine: Start a Revolution in Your Life and Business***

"Carl Buchheit started to change my life even before I met him, because several of my mentors had already been Carl's students and clients. They guided me to change patterns of working too hard, losing money, being overweight, and not living in happiness. The changes in my life were so profound that I decided to study with Carl himself. Now my life has achieved much higher levels of fulfillment and my effectiveness with clients has greatly increased. I am so grateful to have found this new approach to change work. Through all of us who have learned so much from him, Carl's work is changing the world. I highly recommend this landmark book." **–Steve Napolitan, motivational speaker, business coach, and author of *Capture Clients, Close Deals***

"Carl Buchheit is a modern-day magician. How can you achieve the ambitious goals you set for yourself? By having rapport with yourself! Carl shows you how. In this wonderful book, he shares all of the tools and new perspectives at the root of his remarkable work." **–Katia Verresen, CEO of KVA Leadership**

"Carl Buchheit's *Transformational NLP* offers a new perspective on why we humans have limiting beliefs and behavior patterns. His approaches and methods enable people to have more choice over their lives, thus providing the potential for them to achieve fulfillment and inner peace." **–Sharon Tennison, founder of Center for Citizen Initiatives and author of *The Power of Impossible Ideas***

A New Psychology

Transformational NLP

Carl Buchheit, Ph.D.
Ellie Schamber, Ph.D.

Transformational NLP Press
San Rafael, California

Cover and Interior Design by Christy Collins, C Book Services

Printed in the United States
First edition: 2017
Second edition: 2024
16 17 18 19 20   10 9 8 7 6 5 4 3 2 1
Library of Congress Cataloging-in-Publication Data

Contents

Introduction. 1

Chapter I: Humans Have Four Brains 7
The Reptilian Brain. 8
The Paleomammalian (Old Mammal) Brain. 8
The Neomammalian (New Mammal) Brain 9
The Modern Human (Fourth) Brain. 11
Conflicts Among Our Four Brains 12

Chapter II: The Intellectual Background of NLP 20
New Developments in the Field of Psychology. 20
Alfred Korzybski 21
Noam Chomsky 25

Chapter III: History and Literature of Early NLP 28
The Founders: John Grinder and Richard Bandler 28
The Beginning of NLP: The Meta Model. 31
Further Developments in NLP 34
Milton Erickson. 37
Virginia Satir 39

Chapter IV: NLP After 1976. 40
NLP in 1976. 40
Robert Dilts 40
Byron Lewis and Frank Pucelik 41
Steve Andreas 42
Parting of the Ways 45
John Grinder After 1978. 46
Richard Bandler After 1978 47
Robert Dilts After 1978 49
More Recent Schools of NLP 50
Tad James 51
Michael Hall 52

Chapter V: Jonathan Rice 54
Background of Jonathan Rice and NLP 54
Differences Between Mainstream NLP and Jonathan Rice's NLP . 57
NLP as Techniques versus NLP within Psychotherapy . . . 58
Standing versus Seated Interaction 59
Eye-Accessing Cues 61
Changing Limiting Beliefs. 67
The Ecology of Personal Change 68
Re-Imprinting 69

Chapter VI: Transformational NLP. 76
The Influence of Jonathan Rice. 76
Transformational NLP compared with
Mainstream Psychotherapy 79
Content versus Structure of Experience. 79
Transference 80
Attention to Personal History and Family Dynamics 81
Completing the Experience 82
Transformational NLP compared with Mainstream NLP . . . 84
Techniques versus Transformative Conversation 84
Intended Positive Outcomes. 86
Working with Ecology. 87
Re-imprinting 89
Metaphorical Timeline 91

Chapter VII: Unique Perspectives of Transformational NLP. . . . 93
Rapport 93
Practitioner Stance 97
Practitioner Desired Outcomes. 99
Respecting All Experience 101
Perception of the Nature and Meaning of the Past. 102
Hope for a Better Past 105
Consenting to the Past 109
The Client is the Source of the Experience. 111

Chapter VIII: Alignment with Quantum Physics. 113
The Nature of Reality and Consciousness 113
The Future Influences the Past 118

Chapter IX: The Family System 122
Influences on Transformational NLP 122
Anne Ancelin Schutzenberger 122
Rupert Sheldrake 124
David Bohm 126
Ervin Laszlo 126
Bert Hellinger 127
Family and Systemic Constellations at NLP Marin 133

Chapter X: Manifesting Alternative Realities 142
Influence of Carlos Castaneda's Don Juan 142
Change of Life Version as well as Life Vision 144

Chapter XI: Can People Re-Program Themselves? 151

Conclusion 158

Appendixes 167
A: Research on NLP 167
B: Survival Equivalence 170
C: Alfred Korzybski 172
D: A Metaphorical Timeline: Temporal/Spatial Sorting. . . . 174
E: How Transformational NLP Promotes
Personal Transformation 176
F: The Hellinger Family Constellation 178
G: The Influence of Kaskafayet on Transformational NLP . . 180
H: The Teaching Programs of Carlos Castaneda 182
I: Strategies in Our Neural Programming 184

Definitions of Key Terms 187
Endnotes 201
References 210

Foreword

I am a scientist, a specialist in experimental astrophysics and science education, working at the Lawrence Berkeley National Laboratory of the University of California. I was the principal researcher for the *Hands-On Universe* project in the 1990s, and received the *Prix Jules Janssen* of the French Astronomical Society. I have dedicated much of my career as an astrophysicist to the study of supernovae, the deaths of stars, which happened unimaginably long ago and far away. I helped start the Berkeley supernova searches, which led to the discovery of Dark Energy and numerous international prizes for the team.

For me, understanding and getting along with the natural processes of the universe has always been both challenging and rewarding. I have always had the tools necessary to figure things out, and when I haven't had those tools, I've known where to go to find them or how to invent some of my own. For a scientist like me, learning about the universe is very fulfilling. Even the occasional experience of being completely wrong has had its own kind of reward.

In science, not making progress is part of making progress, but in life, not making progress is just being stuck. It is profoundly painful. In science, if what we do isn't working, we try doing something else. It's pretty straightforward. But in being human, no matter what happens we usually continue to operate with the same emotions and behaviors that are proven, through our own experience, to be somewhere between less-than-optimal and completely disastrous. Why are we like this? While my professional career advanced nicely, it was always the inability to understand and get along with *myself* that was confusing and dispiriting.

Approximately eight years ago, I realized that I had been making some bad life choices over and over again. Although my career in science was progressing well and was very fulfilling, my personal life was becoming increasingly frustrating and painful. I could not find the tools to make the changes I wanted and needed. I investigated a number of schools and systems that promised personal transformation, but none of the therapies I tried provided me with any insight into my behaviors, let alone helped me to change them.

Eventually, I mentioned this to a friend. She had heard of a teaching organization called NLP Marin, founded and directed by Carl Buchheit, in the San Francisco Bay Area. Ever the curious scientist, I went to an introductory seminar. Wow! What I learned during those few hours that morning was amazingly eye-opening and encouraging. Carl spoke about and demonstrated some of the basic tools of Neuro-Linguistic Programming. He showed us, actually *showed* us, right on the spot, some entirely new things about *how* humans create and maintain their experience of themselves and the larger world. He *showed* us *how* feelings and meanings that seem fixed and immutable in day-to-day life are in fact adjustable, and are actually far more easily changed than anyone thought. He introduced everyone in that room, that morning, to some of the discoveries made by the founders and originators of NLP in the 1970s, and I am sure that no one's life was entirely the same after that. I certainly know that mine was not.

I enrolled in the beginning-level class and, over the next few months, as I allowed the changes I was making to integrate, I daily felt an increasing calm that always seemed to keep pace with an equivalently improving sense of my strength and capability. The wonderful thing was, I did not have to repeat processes or maintain practices. I was simply and directly changing how my brain interacted with my life, so that what I truly wanted in life began to unfold and what I no longer wanted, such as persistent feelings of shame and guilt, began to disappear. I was changing in ways I had always wanted. The changes were real and confirmable, and I did not have to exert effort for them to happen. As Carl underlined repeatedly, with good NLP, when we revise the programming and patterns that give rise to our experience, then our experience changes and we do not have to remember to be different—we just are different, and then our attention can naturally move on to the next upgrade in the quality of our lives.

Carl insisted on letting his students know that what we were learning in NLP had a history; while it is a new field, it has a long intellectual lineage. Carl acknowledged his teachers and his teachers' teachers, and always gave credit to the remarkable people who came before him. I think that this is one of Carl's main intentions for the present volume. He wants to make sure there is a solid record of where NLP came from, and its original true power and beauty. NLP has been maligned and discounted as superficial and distorted expressions of it have become commonplace. It has also been endlessly copied and appropriated without attribution. Carl wants to set things right, and this volume does that beautifully.

After Carl describes the history of the "real NLP" and fully acknowledges his primary teacher, Dr. Jonathan Rice, he outlines the stunning originality of his own work. As much as it is founded in and brilliantly infused with 1970s NLP, Carl's Transformational NLP is nothing like its progenitors. Both a synthesis and an explosion into new territory, Carl's work takes NLP's remarkable, practical power to make changes in human patterning and combines it with the respectful perspective on human nature that comes from humanistic psychology and much of what was best in the human potential movement of the last thirty years of the twentieth century. Carl's teachings and healing magic are ultimately about making sure we have abundant awareness of our true nature and purpose, combined with just the right tools to dissolve resistance to old pain. He offers solid, easy access to amazing methods that allow us to reach for better future experience without having to blame ourselves—or anyone or anything else, for that matter—for what has been going on in our lives before now.

In addition, Carl introduces some practical applications of the amazing implications of quantum mechanics, or the so-called New Physics. As Carl and the quantum physicists note, we can never separate the observer from the system, and by changing our inner states and beliefs we can influence other individuals, society at large, and even the universe itself. He also explains, as do the quantum physicists, that all sorts of tendrils and paths exist through space-time connecting pasts and futures. Understanding this on a psychological, emotional, and intellectual level was very important in my own growth.

Carl is a remarkable person. It was my great good fortune to be one of his students and clients. I have known and been a student of or a mentor of several Nobel Prize winners. Carl is certainly of their caliber or beyond them in his depth of conceptual thinking and revolutionary thought. Through his genius, I have become a happier and more fulfilled individual. This book is a wonderful introduction to his genius. It describes step by step the concepts behind his change work, which can appear to be like magic. I am convinced that *Transformational NLP* is a significant contribution to the field of psychology and to the world.

–Carl Pennypacker, Astrophysicist at the University of California, Berkeley and Lawrence Berkeley National Laboratory

Introduction

Neuro-Linguistic Programming is a dynamic and fast-growing new field that was born of the coupling of the fields of linguistics and psychology and yet is not recognized by either of these disciplines as its legitimate offspring. While it was originally touted as a way to improve the practice of psychotherapy, since the mid-1980s it has been most popular in applications outside the boundaries of conventional psychotherapy. The techniques of NLP are widely used to increase skills in such fields as sales, sports, education, and public speaking, as well as in life and executive coaching. Yet, there is widespread confusion and disagreement about what NLP actually is, how (and even whether) it works, and which approach of the many versions is most useful.

Part of the problem seems to be that there is little awareness of the intellectual roots of this discipline. Many people seem to believe that NLP sprang into existence, like Botticelli's Venus, fully grown from the brains of John Grinder and Richard Bandler. There is little written about the background, history, and evolution of NLP, and what is written is fragmented. The information that is available is often taken out of historical context and is therefore limited in value.

The study of intellectual history is vital to understanding where we come from, how, and why. Our identities are tied to our history. If we do not understand the background and evolution of our ideas, we lose the context for their rationale and decrease our ability to update them appropriately according to new information and understanding. Although the works of scientist/philosopher Alfred Korzybski and linguist Noam Chomsky paved the way for the discoveries of NLP, they would probably not recognize some of their NLP great-grandchildren as being in their lineage. If NLP practitioners understand where their ideas come from, they will be able to more consciously and effectively choose in which direction they want to go. As Isaac Newton famously declared, "If I have seen a little further it is by standing on the shoulders of Giants."

As an NLP practitioner and trainer for more than thirty years, I have been eager to understand how my own ideas and practices fit into the historical context and evolution of NLP. This work accordingly addresses the following questions:

1. What were the philosophical and other intellectual roots of NLP? What were the contemporary as well as past intellectual influences on the founders and developers of NLP?
2. What were the motives and goals of the founders of NLP? How and in what way did the field of NLP evolve?
3. What were (and are) the controversies about NLP?
4. How did the NLP movement become fragmented, and what are the differences in the approaches of each group?
5. How did my own work in Transformational NLP evolve? What new information, perspectives, and methodologies does my work contribute to the field of NLP?

This book investigates the intellectual history and evolution of NLP. It describes how the brilliant scholar Alfred Korzybski, informed by the new worldview of quantum physics, pointed to an innovative way to perceive human nature and potential. He devoted his life to constructing a new method of psychotherapy that would allow people to transcend their programming and achieve fulfillment of their desires and their highest human potential. Korzybski's innovations formed the foundation of the new thinking that led to NLP.

Neuro-Linguistic Programming has been a major, albeit controversial, force in the fields of psychology and communication since the early 1970s. The famous family therapist Virginia Satir and the renowned anthropologist Gregory Bateson applauded the founders of NLP for making groundbreaking discoveries in the theory and practice of communication that could profoundly assist psychotherapists in helping clients to change (Bandler & Grinder, 1975b, pp. ix-xi).

From the middle 1980s, however, a number of researchers and

established psychotherapists declared that scientific evidence did not support the claims of NLP. (See Appendix A for a detailed discussion of this research and the controversy.) Thereafter, most NLP practitioners were careful to avoid any suggestion that what they were doing with clients might be a form of psychotherapy, while most psychologists and psychotherapists of all types either never heard of NLP or regarded it as mind-control trickery practiced by charlatans.[1]

Nevertheless, there continued to be a plethora of applications for NLP techniques (often re-branded) outside the boundaries of conventional, formal psychotherapy. Anthony Robbins popularized some aspects of NLP in his motivational seminars, and Wayne Dyer sometimes referred to concepts from NLP in his transformational consciousness work. L. Michael Hall presented Neuro-Semantics, and more recently Sharon Pearson promulgated Meta-Dynamics, both of which are offshoots of NLP. A main use of NLP in recent years has been in the relatively new domains of executive and personal coaching. Also, techniques taken from NLP are often used to increase sales and promote business goals and strategies. There are also numerous groups in the realms of both self-help and professional counseling which incorporate some form of NLP. For example, cognitive behavioral therapy (CBT), eye movement desensitization and reprogramming (EMDR), acceptance and commitment therapy, solution-focused brief therapy, and narrative therapy have borrowed much from NLP.

Alfred Korzybski had looked for techniques that could be used in the context of psychotherapy. However, the founders of NLP and most of their students became more interested in the techniques as standalone procedures rather than as part of psychotherapy. After several years, NLP developed into two approaches: One group focused on individual techniques and the other incorporated the techniques into psychotherapy. It is my opinion that to the extent that NLP diverged from the original intent of its forebears it became less effective than its original potential in creating powerful methods for psychological change. In contrast, those practitioners who did continue in the intellectual tradition that led to NLP and incorporated NLP techniques into psychotherapy, have been able to be extremely effective in helping clients to achieve the personal transformation that they truly desire. I believe that Korzybski's vision and goals were lost in the development of mainstream NLP, but were fulfilled by the legacy of Jonathan Rice that forms the basis of the school of Transformational NLP. My own innovations in the field of NLP, which I have labeled Transformational NLP, are based on the work that came before, through the legacy of Jonathan Rice, and the new scientific knowledge that we have only recently acquired.

Utilizing a combination of historical and heuristic methodologies, this work provides a comprehensive history of NLP, along with its intellectual antecedents and contemporary influences on its development. For this volume I have almost entirely used primary sources and interviews, as secondary sources for most of this investigation are not available. This study reviews the literary works that were milestones along the path of development of NLP, and explains the process by which the field evolved. Then this work compares and contrasts the two main strands of development of NLP by the second generation of practitioners. Finally, it shows my own work as based on one of those lines of development, and illustrates how I have taken NLP to another level that is based on the most recent knowledge of quantum physics.

This work, like all others, has limitations. The main limitation is my personal bias. As a third-generation teacher and practitioner, I had to make many decisions over the years about which path among several divergent ones to follow. Although in this study I made every attempt to present all points of view fairly, I recognize that I sometimes became overly passionate about one course of action as compared to the others. Another limitation is the lack of information from surveys regarding the effectiveness of one type of change work over others. Instead, during the more than thirty years that I have been practicing and teaching NLP, I have relied on the personal communications of clients and students. Clearly, forgetfulness over time and personal bias can influence the results.

Nonetheless, I hope that this work will have value in increasing people's understanding about this very significant development in the field of psychology. I also trust that it will be useful in spreading the word about the beneficial effects of this new form of NLP, with the result of helping more clients, teaching more practitioners, and informing the wider public that is so eagerly searching for happiness and fulfillment.

CHAPTER I

Humans Have Four Brains

As far back as recorded history will allow us to look, people have always considered suffering an inevitable and inescapable fact of life. It is an unfortunate aspect of being human that people frequently continue to experience what they do not want and are not able to experience that which they really do want. It seems that the main reason for this anomaly is that all of our most stuck patterns of experience are generated by our brain's ongoing efforts to keep us well and safe. All of our thought and behavior patterns that do not work are actually the consequence of our brain's patterning to make sure that we survive.

Most neuroscientists agree that as a product of the evolutionary process we humans all have more than one brain, and each of our brains has a different set of instructions and descriptions about what wellbeing is. In his seminal work *The Triune Brain* (1990), neuroscientist Paul MacLean writes that nature builds new brain components and functions on top of (rather than in place of) whatever has already evolved over eons of time. As a result, humans have several co-existing brains, and each of them seems to have its own goals and indicators for success. While the different brains are not completely autonomous, and they each get information from the others, they can nevertheless operate somewhat independently.

As MacLean describes:

> A comparison of the brains of existing vertebrates, together with an examination of the fossil record, indicates that the human forebrain has evolved and expanded to its great size while retaining the features of three basic evolutionary formations that reflect an ancestral relationship to reptiles, early mammals, and recent mammals. . . . Radically different in chemistry and

> structure and in an evolutionary sense countless generations apart, the three neural assemblies constitute a hierarchy of three-brains-in-one, a triune brain. Based on these features alone, it might be surmised that psychological and behavioral functions depend on the interplay of three quite different mentalities. . . .[T]he three evolutionary formations might be imagined as three interconnected biological computers, with each having its own special intelligence, its own subjectivity, its own sense of time and space, and its own memory, motor, and other functions. (MacLean, 1990, pp. 8-9)[1]

More recent investigations point to four, rather than three, co-existing brains, which as often compete against as cooperate with one another (Cummings & Miller, 2007; Joseph, 2001; Massey, 2001; Miller, 2007).

The Reptilian Brain

The first and oldest brain is our reptilian brain, which includes the brainstem and cerebellum. It appears that it has not changed much in function from the brain of the contemporary lizard. It regulates the basics of physical survival such as respiration, heartbeat, and blood pressure. This is the brain that governs instinctual behaviors such as fear, hunger, the fight-or-flight response at times of danger, and the struggle for power, territoriality, and sex. Incorporating learning from its previous life-threatening mistakes, this brain then automatically generates the same adaptive behaviors again and again, over and over, with neither the impetus nor the wherewithal to revise and update its earlier learning (MacLean, 1990).

The Paleomammalian (Old Mammal) Brain

The middle part of the brain is called the paleomammalian (old mammal) brain, or the limbic system. This brain, which developed during the early evolution of mammals, augments primitive reptilian responses such as fear and adds the capacity to experience strong primary emotions such as rage, pleasure, pain, and joy (MacLean, 1990). As psychiatrist Bessel van der Kolk (2014) succinctly describes, "It is the seat of the emotions, the monitor of danger, the judge of what is pleasurable or scary, the arbiter of what is or is not important for survival purposes" (p. 56).

The paleomammalian brain also provides the ability to remember past experiences along with their associated emotions. The emotions and the memory of the emotions provide stronger motivations to move toward or away from conditions that affect survival. Thus, this brain links emotions and memory with behavior. Since the limbic system enables the memory of ongoing experience along with the associated emotions, it provides the mammal with a sense of individual continuation. The limbic system is also responsible for the motivation and emotions involved in bonding with others, such as during reproductive behavior and parental care. The primate brain adds the ability to feel a part of, and participate in, multifarious social relationships (MacLean, 1990; Van der Kolk, 2014).

The Neomammalian (New Mammal) Brain

Our third brain is the neomammalian (new mammal) brain, the cerebral neocortex, which is the largest part of the brain of primate mammals, including humans. As mammals evolved, around 150 million years ago, the neocortex developed to increasingly refine its visual, auditory, and tactile information processing. This provided mammals, and especially primates, with far greater ability to analyze sensory input and store information, thereby increasing their cognitive abilities (Joseph, 2001).

Humans developed from the same ancestor as monkeys and apes. Pre-humans separated from monkeys and apes around five or six million years ago. Over the course of several million years, these pre-humans learned to stand on their hind legs and walk upright. They developed the opposable thumb, which enabled them to grasp and hold objects and thereby explore and manipulate them (Joseph, 2001; MacLean, 1990).

About 500,000 years ago, the brain of Homo erectus greatly enlarged to about twice the size of the brain of earlier hominids. They also developed more flexibility in the hands. These were the first archaic (primitive) *Homo sapiens*, who originally appeared in Africa and Asia. Then, about 250,000-300,000 years ago, Neanderthals appeared in Europe and the Middle East (Joseph, 2001).

Until recently, the prevailing theory among scientists and linguists was that archaic pre-humans and Neanderthals did not have the capacity for speech. According to this view, the language of these pre-humans was largely a combination of guttural sounds, facial expressions, and gesticulations connected with the social-emotional expressions of the limbic system, similar to the vocalizations, facial expressions, and gestures of apes. They were only capable of making the same simple tools, which served only a single purpose, over and over again. They eventually learned to wear animal skins, but they used only very simplistic methods to prepare them to wear (rather than bone sewing needles, for example, which were developed much later). Yet, the limbic system in conjunction with the evolving neocortex enabled these pre-humans and Neanderthals to develop a primitive cultural and social life that included burying their dead with ritual offerings such as animal bones. This indicates that these primitive people were capable of intense emotions, including love and spiritual feelings. Such emotions are a function of the limbic system and inferior temporal lobe, and were the same as in modern humans (Joseph, 2001).

In the last two decades, new findings have led to the theory that an East African pre-human, called *Homo heidelbergensis*, was the common ancestor of Neanderthals, Denisovans, and modern humans. The new evidence indicates that the *Homo heidelbergensis* did have the basic anatomy and cranial capacity for modern speech. According to this theory, between 300,000 and 400,000 years ago a group of this species left Africa. Some of them went north into Europe and the Middle East and became the Neanderthals. Others traveled east and became the Denisovans. The findings indicate that the Neanderthals and Denisovans had a much more complex stone tool technology, culture, and social life than previously realized, and such advances would have necessitated a high level of cognition and motor control and the ability to communicate verbally. They hunted large game, controlled and used fire, built shelters and camps, created ornaments with pierced beads and shells, used earth pigments for cosmetic or artistic purposes, buried their dead with ritual offerings, looked after their wounded and ill, and apparently used medicinal herbs. They seemed to live in small family groups and communities (Dediu & Levinson, 2013; National Geographic, 2016; Nowell, et al., 2016).

The Homo heidelbergensis who remained in Africa evolved into Homo sapiens around 200,000-150,000 years ago. Although there is evidence for migrations out of Africa as early as 120,000 years ago, those non-African early humans became extinct. Modern non-Africans are almost entirely, with the exception of trace amounts of DNA from Neanderthals and earlier migrations, descended from a mass migration from Africa through Egypt and into the Arabian Peninsula that took place 60,000 years ago (National Geographic, 2016; Rincon, 2016).

In Homo sapiens, the frontal and parietal lobes had greatly expanded in size and function. There were huge differences in the brain anatomy and cognitive functioning between the archaic and the early modern human (Joseph, 2001; Massey, 2001; National Geographic, 2016). This set the stage for the appearance of the Fourth Brain.

The Modern Human (Fourth) Brain

Around 35,000 years ago, there was an abrupt leap in evolution that resulted in the development of the Fourth Brain.[2] The first fully modern human (*Homo sapiens sapiens*), known as Cro-Magnon, suddenly and mysteriously appeared in Africa, Europe, and the Middle East (Cummings & Miller, 2007; Joseph, 2001; Massey, 2001; Miller, 2007). The appearance of the Cro-Magnons came at the same time as the rapid extinction of the Neanderthals and archaic humans. The early modern humans had co-existed (and, according to DNA analysis, sometimes even mated) with the Neanderthals and archaic humans for about 5,000 years. It seems that either the more evolved Homo sapiens successfully competed against them for resources (and Neanderthals consequently gradually died off), or the early modern humans actually killed off the Neanderthals and archaic humans, or they "made love, not war" and merged into the larger population of *Homo sapiens*. Similarly, modern humans in the Far East and Asia who had evolved from archaic pre-humans either successfully competed against, killed off, or absorbed the remaining primitive humans (Joseph, 2001; National Geographic, 2016).[3]

The Cro-Magnons had greatly increased brain volume, increased versatility in use of the hands, and more highly evolved anatomy and function of the frontal cortex. As neuroscientist Bruce Miller writes, "The human frontal lobes mediate the behaviors that most distinguish man from animals" (Cummins & Miller, 2007, p. 12). These modern *Homo sapiens* also had an evolved angular gyrus, which is the part of the brain that is connected to processing language, mathematics, and other cognitive skills. This corresponded to more complex tool construction, cognitive development, language, and artistic achievement (Joseph, 2001; Massey, 2001). In addition to speech and language abilities, the larger size and qualitative development of the left prefrontal cortex provided the ability to plan for the future, organize resources to achieve goals, develop problem-solving strategies, think abstractly, create values, and develop social skills to live in complex social networks (Joseph, 2001).

Conflicts Among Our Four Brains

All of our four brains are operating constantly and are frequently well coordinated. However, there are some inevitable conflicts among them as a result of opposing directions in the programming. What MacLean designates as the reptile and mammal brains are sometimes referred to together as the *emotional brain* in contrast to the *rational brain* (Van der Kolk, 2014). I prefer to refer to it as the *creature brain* in contrast to the more highly evolved *human brain.*

The main driver for the creature brain is fear, with the goal of survival. It does not want to change anything that has become associated with the experience of having survived. In contrast, as humanistic psychologists describe, the primary impulsion in the human brain is the desire to receive and extend love, along with the impetus to continue learning and pursuing the changes involved in self-development. This creates a huge inner conflict. The human is always imagining things being different and better; simultaneously, our creature brain insists that things remain as they are (because, after all, the way things have been has successfully resulted in surviving until now). Also, the creature brain does not have a sense of time as humans do. The creature functions only in the eternal present: There is meal time and sleep time, but not a life time. Consequently, the creature brain creates and stabilizes patterning that may be obsolete, unproductive, and painful as long as it associates this behavior with survival.

The creature brain creates associations rather than meanings. It generalizes and jumps to conclusions based on rough similarities, initiating preprogrammed and automatic muscular and physiological reactions such as the fight-or-flight response (Van der Kolk, 2014). In its natural processing, it learns to associate survival with situations and conditions that threatened survival but did not actually lead to death. This association has ironic and tragic implications for human beings.

In my work with clients I have found that the conditions that we learn to survive become the template for the experiences upon which our continued surviving will depend. When a young child's survival is threatened—or is perceived by the child to be threatened, regardless of what is actually happening in the life situation—then the very presence of the threat becomes part of a gestalt of survival. From the moments when these associations are first created in the child's creature neurology, the threat and the creature brain-mediated survival of the threat become forever linked. They become part of the child's survival patterning. From those moments forward, in the child's creature neurology, any experiences that involve the threat have survival value, and any situations that do *not* include perception of the threat do *not* carry survival value. Non-threatening contexts and situations are thus experienced as being "not survivable" precisely because they are not dangerous!

A common example of such survival patterning is what happens when a child is is raised in a household in which one or both parents frequently use shame as a way to control the child. The child frequently experiences feeling "shamed to death," although of course s/he does not actually die. Because the child does not perish, the experience of being shamed to death becomes strongly associated in the creature neurology with the experience of not perishing. This is what I term *survival equivalence*—a situation in which survival in general becomes linked (in this case) with the survival of overwhelming shame in particular.

It is important to remember that this equivalence is formed and held at the level of creature neurology—a level of the mind/brain that does not make meaning. However, countless meanings will be generated higher in the mind/brain, and probably throughout the person's life, as s/he seeks to explain his/her experience to him/herself—a severely limited experience that is generated almost timelessly by the tenacious, error-free operation of this unhappy equivalence of survival with survival of shame.

When the child matures and is able to leave home and move away from the apparent sources of the shaming experience, the link between shame and surviving continues in the neurology. Typically, the now-mature person goes into a relationship with, or accepts employment with, or otherwise creates a close and dependent connection with someone who has essentially the same patterning to shame others that the parents had. In fact, if we watch the person's life and choices unfold over time, we find that the individual continually attracts and is attracted to people who are also impelled to participate in shame-based relationships. It is not just that the relationship is based on the experience of shame—it is that, for the creature-self, continuing shame actually *equals* continuing survival.[4] (See Appendix B for more discussion of Survival Equivalence.)

Of course, the person's human-level consciousness is confused and upset about these repeating developments and is desperately trying to make sense out of them. With his or her family and friends in despair, with counselors and coaches offering more and more advice about making better job and relationship choices, and with his/her own self-trust and self-esteem reaching new lows, s/he continues to move toward situations s/he definitely does not want to be experiencing, apparently without the common sense or the personal will to make things better. The bewildered human finds it necessary to create limiting beliefs about him/herself and the world, just to have what keeps happening make some sense. A "limiting belief" is a belief about reality (which works to structure that very reality) that is in conflict with what the human aspect of the person now wants to experience.[5] In this case, as a simple example, the person has come to believe that there must be something shameful about him/herself.

Painful as this is for the human, the person's creature neurology is operating perfectly to fulfill its imperative to survive. Such survival patterning is the result of millions of years of creature brain evolution. This creature brain learns very fast and well, but it is not equipped to "unlearn" anything. While it can learn any number of new things, it will always have to add them to what it already knows instead of substitute them for old patterns. This creates ongoing, extremely painful conflict in the human psyche.

Additional sources of conflict for humans are the dichotomy in the functioning of the neocortical and limbic systems and the divide between the two hemispheres of the neocortex itself. As neuroscientist Rhawn Joseph (2001) explains:

> Over the course of evolution, the limbic system and each half of the brain have developed their own unique strategies for perceiving, processing, and expressing information, as well as specialized neuro-anatomical interconnections that assist in mediating these functions. . . . Indeed, whereas the limbic system mediates the more primitive aspects of social-emotional intelligence, the neocortex and the cerebral hemispheres are organized such that two potentially independent mental systems coexist, literally side by side. (p. 75)

Although humans have the newer brain of the neocortex, we remain creatures of the primary emotions governed by the limbic system. While the limbic system is the source of the emotions, it does not "think" like a human, nor can it comprehend speech or communicate verbally. The emotions connected with and sustaining our beliefs arise in the limbic system, which is why verbal arguments usually do not greatly impact them (MacLean, 1990; Van der Kolk, 2014). Joseph (2001) elucidates:

> The old limbic brain has not been replaced, and is not only predominant in regard to all aspects of motivational and emotional functioning but is capable of completely overwhelming 'the rational mind'. . . . this schism between the rational and the

> emotional is real, and is due to the raw energy of emotion having its source in the nuclei of the ancient limbic lobe . . . [which appeared] long before humans walked upon this earth and that continue to control and direct human behavior. (p. 162)

The difference in function between the right and left hemispheres of the neocortex adds to the confusion. The two halves of the brain speak different languages. The left hemisphere organizes information into temporal units and logical sequences, making it possible for humans to identify cause and effect and thereby plan for the future. It enables humans to translate our feelings and perceptions into words. It controls linguistic thought and speech including grammar, syntax, reading, writing, verbal comprehension, and memory, and it is associated with mathematical and analytical reasoning (Joseph, 2001).

The right cerebral hemisphere is associated with the more subtle forms of human social and emotional intelligence, including the perception of emotional feelings and nuances of expression in others and the ability for facial recognition. It is also the source of our potential for empathy. It mediates our sense of humor, our understanding of metaphors and symbols, our spiritual feelings, and all of our imaginative and intuitive processes (McGilchrist, 2009; Joseph, 2001; Miller, 2007). In many ways, "the mental system maintained by the right cerebral hemisphere is . . . dominant over the temporal-sequential, language-dependent half of the cerebrum. Indeed, the right cerebrum . . . is fully capable of motivating, initiating, as well as controlling behavioral expression—often without the aid or even active (reflective) participation of the left half of the brain" (Joseph, 2001, p. 117).

Throughout our lives, human beings experience a bewildering discord among the experiences provided by combinations of multiple-brain activity. We are all familiar with the experience of doing and being what we *do not* want to do and be, and of conversely *not* being and doing what we apparently *do* want. Everyday life is a continuing stream of these conflicts—from our complicated struggles in interpersonal relationships to forcing ourselves to select the low-carbohydrate, gluten-free option on the lunch menu.

In Western Civilization, there is a common assumption that reason and emotions are constantly at odds with each other. This is illustrated in the conflict between Apollo, the god of reason and logic, and Dionysus, the god of passion and instincts, in ancient Greek mythology. The preponderance of Western literature and philosophy is based on the conflict and tenuous balance between these two themes. From Plato to Descartes and Kant, Western philosophers have taught that the body and mind are separate and distinct entities, and that decisions should be based on rational thinking and logic rather than emotions.

However, all thoughts involve having feelings. Neurologist Antonio Damasio, in his brilliant book *Descartes' Error* (1994), shows that emotions and feelings are necessary for the functioning of reason. There is a strong neurological connection between reason and emotion. Emotions profoundly influence both what people reason about and *how* they reason. Our rationality relies on our having good access to our feelings, and our emotions always have their own life-sustaining intentions. However, these feelings may be totally outside of conscious awareness, and simply be in the form of a "gut feeling" or "hunch."

In fact, what we call "thinking" is actually a process of internal and external representational events. If a client is having "painful thoughts," I am going to be very curious about the pictures, sounds, and feelings that comprise what that person experiences as a "thought." All thoughts are complex combinations of internal and external pictures, sounds, feelings, smells, and tastes, in some sequence, with some kind of bias or weighting toward one or two of the five senses more than the others. So, the issue is not "thinking" versus "feeling." The real issue is: where are the feelings in your thoughts coming from? Are they "reptile feelings," "primate feelings," "human spiritual feelings," or a mixture of these? As humans, what makes the difference is not whether we are thinking or feeling, but which feelings our programming prioritizes to give weight to the visual and auditory components of our experience. Are the emotions appropriate for the situation? For example, "creature feelings" are likely to be inappropriate in the context of performing complicated dental surgery, just as "spiritual feelings" will probably provide inadequate driver states for professional football players and their fans during a game.

Inappropriate emotions can cause great pain in humans. Neuroscientist Joseph Le Doux discovered that sensory signals travel first to the amygdala, which is the seat of the emotions, before they travel to the neocortex, the thinking brain. Hence the amygdala responds before the neocortex does, which explains the power of emotions to overwhelm rationality. To make matters even more complex, the brain has two memory systems, one for ordinary facts, controlled by the hippocampus, and one for emotionally charged situations, monitored by the amygdala. When the amygdala is aroused, it imprints in memory the emotional arousal more strongly than other memories (Goleman, 1995). As psychologist Daniel Goleman (1995) writes, the amygdala "frantically commands that we react to the present in ways that were imprinted long ago, with thoughts, emotions, reactions learned in response to events perhaps only dimly similar, but close enough to alarm the amygdala" (p. 21). However, emotional memories are not always appropriate guides to present situations. When someone "pushes our buttons" we are most often experiencing the incongruous association between a past experience and a present event. For example, a person who, as a child, experienced harsh criticism from a parent may overreact emotionally to constructive feedback from his/her boss.

The prevailing approach that most well-meaning psychotherapists take to address their patients' emotional pain and apparently self-defeating behaviors, aside from medication, is some form of talk therapy that is predominantly about life's content. Psychologist Daniel Goleman explains that when the client retells the story of the trauma in the safety of the therapist's office, the painful memories "are brought more under control of the neocortex, where the reactions they kindle can be rendered more understandable and so more manageable. . . . This begins to impart a telling lesson to the emotional circuitry—that security, rather than unremitting terror, can be experienced in tandem with the trauma memories" (Goleman, 1995, pp. 211-12). Even in cases of severe trauma and PTSD, such talk therapy, along with the support system and education it provides, can be helpful.

However, there are limitations to how far such therapy can go. Most therapists mainly depend on what clients recall consciously and are able to disclose about the content of the memories that cause pain. This usually does not work to either reveal or revise the deeper levels of representations in automated programming. Psychiatrist Bessel Van der Kolk (2014) explains that, "The rational, executive brain is good at helping us understand where feelings come from. . . . However, the rational brain cannot *abolish* emotions, sensations, or thoughts. . . . Understanding *why* you feel a certain way does not change *how* you feel" (p. 205). Since the creature brain does not understand English (or any other human language, for that matter), discussion and analysis of past traumas achieve only limited results in helping people create desired life experiences.

Neuro-Linguistic Programming, in contrast, is a methodology for helping us to both understand and change the actual structure and internal events of human experience. Instead of the *why* asked by most psychotherapists, the NLP founders became more concerned with *how* the client creates his or her experience through the structural building blocks of sensory representational systems. Good NLP change work includes locating and revising the creature-level/human-level communication problems that generate almost all of our unwanted experiences, and that heretofore have been considered impossible to stop or change. Now we are able to *re-imprint* or re-potentiate neural pathways so that the way is cleared for new learning and needed resources can be transferred or created to achieve the desired state.

The goal of the proficient NLP practitioner is to assist the client to have what s/he wants, based on his or her most truly human desires and values. This can usually be accomplished in a short time. NLP can achieve this outcome because it speaks not only to the human brain, but also to the creature brain. It speaks to the creature part of us in the programming language of creature neurology: This is a language not of words, but of pictures, sounds, feelings, smells, and tastes. When we re-program the creature brain by using its own programming language, it accepts updates easily and permanently. Hence, we can describe NLP as a methodology to assist our creature neurology to better support our most human and spiritual goals.

CHAPTER II

The Intellectual Background of NLP

Neuro-Linguistic Programming was the child of two movements that had reached young maturity in the early 1970s: the Human Potential movement and the Cognitive Psychology movement. The two main figures in these movements who strongly influenced the founders of NLP were Alfred Korzybski and Noam Chomsky.

New Developments in the Field of Psychology

In the early twentieth century, Sigmund Freud, the father of psychoanalysis, believed that he had discovered the science of the mind. He argued that human thoughts and behavior are determined by largely unconscious mental states that spring from our basic instincts. For Freud, human emotions, ideas, and actions could be explained as results that came from hidden causes that can be discovered and explored (Thornton, n.d.).

Later, the behaviorism of John Watson and B. F. Skinner strove to make psychology even more "scientific" by focusing only on observable behavior rather than theories of the unconscious. In this view, people's thoughts and behavior are a function of the external stimuli they receive. Behaviorism was the dominant school of thought in psychology from the 1920s through the 1950s (Miller, 2003).

In the later 1950s, the rise of humanistic psychology, also known as the Human Potential movement, became a new and third force in the world of psychology. The works of Alfred Korzybski in the earlier part of the century laid the foundation for this new worldview. The pioneers of the Human Potential movement were Abraham Maslow and Carl Rogers. Unlike behaviorism, humanistic psychology is interested in self-actualization and the problems of human existence such as values, personal responsibility, human potential, creativity, love, and spirituality. Instead of studying pathology and neuroses, the Human Potential movement explores how people can achieve their highest potential.

The founders of NLP were deeply affected by the Human Potential movement. Gregory Bateson, Fritz Perls, and Virginia Satir worked together at Esalen in the 1960s as key pioneers of this movement. Their influence on John Grinder and Richard Bandler was key in forming the conceptual framework that gave rise to NLP (Hall, 2010a, 2010b).

In the mid-1950s, a related revolution in thought took place in the cognitive sciences. the Cognitive Revolution was an intellectual interdisciplinary movement that included the fields of experimental psychology and linguistics.[1] In contrast to behaviorism, which focuses only on observable behaviors, cognitive psychology is more interested in internal mental processes, such as how people think, perceive, remember, learn, and solve problems. The famous linguist Noam Chomsky, who considered linguistics a branch of psychology, was a key figure in this movement. He launched the Cognitive Revolution in 1956 when he espoused his transformational generative grammar in a paper leading to his 1957 monograph *Syntactic Structures* (Miller, 2003).

Chomsky's influence on John Grinder was basic to the mindset that informed the language model of NLP, the Meta Model, described in *Structures, I.* Chomsky also strongly influenced psychologists George Miller, Eugene Galanter, and Karl Pribram, who wrote *Plans and the Structure of Behavior* (1960). Grinder was especially influenced by the work of George Miller, for whom he worked as a guest researcher in 1969–1970. Miller's TOTE model formed the basis for Robert Dilts's work on strategies (Bostic St. Clair & Grinder, 2001; Dilts, 1980, 1999a; Grinder & Pucelik, 2013; Miller, 2003).

Thus, NLP erupted from the combination of the Human Potential movement, anchored in the conceptual framework of Alfred Korzybski, and the Cognitive Psychology movement, based largely on the work of Noam Chomsky. We cannot even begin to appreciate the intellectual roots of NLP without paying our respects to the worldviews and work of these two extraordinary scholars.

Alfred Korzybski

In the first half of the twentieth century the brilliant scholar, scientist, and philosopher Alfred Korzybski (1879–1950) laid the foundation for the thinking that brought about the development of NLP. Korzybski's philosophy of language, which he called General Semantics, formed the basis of NLP (Dilts, 1999a). In fact, Korzybski is the one who (in the preface to the 1941 edition of *Science and Sanity*) coined the term "neuro-linguistic" (Korzybski, 1994).

Korzybski's work is scarcely known and his influence on NLP is barely acknowledged, but he was a stunningly original thinker who worked with an amazing range of curiosity. He formulated most of the conceptual framework that made the development of NLP possible. Yet, neither John Grinder nor Richard Bandler, the acknowledged founders of NLP, mentions him in any of their works in more than a passing manner.[2] In 1999, more than a quarter of a century after the inception of NLP at the University of California in Santa Cruz, one of the original group, Robert Dilts, briefly nodded to Korzybski's influence (1999a). In 2013, James Eicher, another member of the group, mentioned in passing that the philosophical premise of NLP was based on Korzybski's work (Grinder & Pucelik, 2013).

Korzybski is the key to understanding the presuppositions and most of the basic principles of NLP. While Grinder and Bandler constructed a methodology for NLP, it was Korzybski who had previously conceived and developed the worldview that provided the rationale and pointed the way. If Grinder and Bandler fathered this new field of psychology, we must consider Korzybski the grandfather who made their work possible.

Korzybski was greatly influenced by the ideas of the eighteenth-century philosopher Immanuel Kant. Like Kant, Korzybski (1994) argued that we are limited in what we can know by the structure of the human nervous system. People can never experience the world directly—instead, they make abstractions from their sense perceptions. However, these abstractions do not necessarily have a structure that is similar to whatever is actually happening. Different people have different neurological responses to, and make different generalizations about, their neurological responses to the same external stimuli. As Korzybski explained, the new science shows that "what we label 'objects' or 'objective' are mere nervous constructs inside of our skulls which our nervous systems have abstracted... from the actual world of electronic processes on the sub-microscopic level" (p. lii).

In addition to being influenced by Kant, Korzybski was affected by the burgeoning new field of quantum physics. He dedicated *Science and Sanity*, originally published in 1933, to quantum physicists Werner Heisenberg and Niels Bohr, and declared that he was intellectually indebted to Albert Einstein, Ernst Mach, and Werner Heisenberg as well as to the philosopher of Skepticism, Bertrand Russell. Korzybski based much of his philosophy on Heisenberg's uncertainty principle, which is that the reality that is being observed is modified by the very act of observing. Thus, Korzybski explained, Heisenberg shows us that reality is in some way created by the observer (Korzybski, 1994).

Like Heisenberg, Korzybski argued that logically we can never assume that one thing causes another, since all we know is that the two things often appear one after the other (1994, pp. 93, 218). This principle of relativity is a cornerstone of Korzybski's theory of semantics. He developed a brilliant hypothesis concerning the relationship between people's conceptual frameworks and the structure of language. He arrived at his theory of linguistics independently of other linguistic theorists who were just beginning to publish their works at the time but were not yet known. He was, for example, not aware of the works of Franz Boas, Edward Sapir, or Benjamin Whorf (Read, 1990).

Korzybski (1994) wrote that people are limited in their knowledge by the structure of their language. The language itself determines one's perception of the world. Humans create in their minds abstractions of the reality that they perceive through their senses, then they create further abstractions of their sensory abstractions through language. Korzybski's transformational grammar explores the changes that occur between a person's perception and how s/he describes it.

In his seminal work, Korzybski (1994) argued that the languages that we inherited from our primitive ancestors are based on outdated perceptions of the structure of reality. Parents and teachers teach the child the structure of language along with the socially acceptable habits of thought and behavior. These behavior patterns are based on unconscious assumptions and presuppositions. If the unconscious presuppositions are factually false, one's entire mindset is impacted and the presuppositions can result in harmful thinking and behavior, and even lead to insanity. Korzybski concluded that it is necessary for us to modify the structure of our language so that it corresponds to our new understanding of the structure of the world and the nervous system.

Korzybski blamed much of modern psychopathology on presuppositions derived from the misunderstanding about and perversion of Aristotle's scientific method. This obsolete model of Aristotle views the world and human nervous systems as objective and fixed. Korzybski argued that we should discard this outdated worldview of reality being objective and unchangeable. Instead, in accordance with the new discoveries of physics, we should think of the world in terms of relative processes (Korzybski, 1994).

According to Korzybski, many people are in psychological pain because they do not distinguish between their experience (their linguistic representations of reality) and reality itself. In other words, widespread human misery occurs mostly because, as he explained, people confuse the map with the territory. He wrote that "if we reflect upon our languages, we find that at best they must be considered *only as maps*. . . . A map is *not* the territory it represents, but, if correct, it has a similar structure to the territory, which accounts for its usefulness. . . . [Similarly] a word is *not* the same as the object it represents" (Korzybski, 1994, p. 58). Thus he brilliantly coined the famous phrases used in NLP: "A map is not the territory" and "A word is not what it represents."

Korzybski concluded that just as the world is not fixed, also human nature is not fixed. What we consider *human nature* is largely a product not only of heredity but also of environment, especially the structure of our language, which contains within it dogmas, prejudices, misunderstandings, fears, and other pathological presuppositions. The great innovator wrote the startling statement, "'Human nature' *can be changed*, once we know how" (Korzybski, 1994, p. xciii). The old habits of thought are not inevitable—they can be changed by training. Korzybski discussed a new functional definition of *man* based on an analysis of human *potentialities* as contrasted to fixed characteristics. He urged linguists and psychologists to follow in the footsteps of the quantum physicists: We "must abandon permanently the use of the [fixed] 'is' of identity" (Korzybski, 1994, p. 60).

This pioneering thinker provided a methodology to accomplish this goal. He claimed that human nature could be changed through both education of the masses of people and one-to-one therapy with individuals. For the public, Korzybski constructed a new transformational grammar that focuses more on processes than fixed identities. For individuals, Korzybski created a therapy that taught people to distinguish between words about reality and the actual reality (1994, p. 695). (See Appendix C for a description of Korzybski's psychotherapy.) Korzybski believed that this would develop a critical attitude in people which would lead to psychological health as well as increased creativity and productivity. By such training, "making ourselves conscious of abstracting we prevent the animalistic unconsciousness of abstracting" and allow the individual to find more appropriate evaluations and generalizations about reality (1994, p. 501).

Science and Sanity reveals the wide scope of Korzybski's genius. He opened new doors in the field of psychotherapy. Brilliant and innovative as his conceptual framework was, however, his method of disciplining the mind was extremely laborious and difficult.

Nonetheless, this does not diminish its importance in our cultural history. Korzybski's work provides the basis for the development of the much more direct and simple, not to mention far more effective, methods of NLP. A major part of NLP is based on what are called "Meta Model challenges" of language. These "challenges" are processes that are derived from Korzybski's transformational grammar. The NLP concept of the Meta Model (discussed in the following chapter) is based on Korzybski's exploration of the changes that take place between sensory perceptions and our thoughts and language about them. Like Korzybski, NLP seeks to change the client's thinking process by questioning the language s/he uses that reveals his or her views about reality.

Noam Chomsky

Another important influence on Grinder was the linguist Noam Chomsky, who is especially famous for his theories about the syntax of language. Chomsky's most important contribution to NLP is his syntactic theory of transformational grammar (Bostic St. Clair & Grinder, 2001; Dilts, 1999a).

Chomsky can best be understood against the background of the work of several earlier great linguists. Franz Boas (1848–1942), a student of Kant, is considered the founder of anthropology in the United States in the late nineteenth century. He was deeply influenced by Kant's view that we can never know external reality, but rather understand it only by interpreting sensations via certain "categories of understanding." In opposition to the contemporary mainstream mindset among anthropologists that viewed human cultures as shaped by biological propensity and the stage of evolution of a race, Boas pointed to cultural relativism. He taught that learning and habit, rather than race and heredity, are the basis for the diversity in human cultures. Studying the different linguistic families of diverse Native American tribes, Boas maintained that the culture, world view, and ways of life of a people are reflected in the structure of their language (Boas, n.d.; Kemmer, 2008b; McCall, 2006).

A student of Boas in the early twentieth century, Edward Sapir (1884–1939), expanded on Boas' argument. He declared that language does not merely reflect the culture and habit patterns of a people, but rather language and thought influence each other. In other words, habits of thought are themselves influenced by the structure of a language (Ash, 1999; Kemmer, 2008a; Sapir, 1997).

Benjamin Whorf (1897–1941) took this idea further by examining the grammatical processes by which language affects thought. Whorf (1940) argued that thoughts and actions are influenced by language and culture. He wrote that:

> We dissect nature along lines laid down by our native languages. . . . the world is presented in a kaleidoscopic flux of impressions which has to be organized by our minds—and this means large-

> ly by the linguistic systems in our minds. . . . we are parties to an agreement to organize it in this way—an [implicit] agreement that holds throughout our speech community and is codified in the patterns of our language. The agreement is, of course, an implicit and unstated one, but its terms are absolutely obligatory; we cannot talk at all except by subscribing to the organization and classification of data which the agreement decrees. (As cited in Ash, 1999)

There has been considerable controversy among linguists as well as anthropologists during the past century about the validity of the Sapir-Whorf Hypothesis.[3] Noam Chomsky (1957) argued against Sapir and Whorf, claiming that all language is universal and innate rather than simply a function of our culture and activities. In his book *Syntactic Structures*, published in 1957, he described his theory of Transformational Grammar. He argued that a universal, internal grammar underlies all language. The *deep structure* of a sentence is the meaning, which is universal. The *surface structure* refers to the sounds (e.g. pronunciation) and words in the sentence, which differ among languages. The *deep structure* is converted into the *surface structure* in accordance with an ordered set of rules. According to Chomsky, all human children in every culture on earth are born with the knowledge of the same principles of the grammatical structure of all languages, and this inborn knowledge explains the success and speed with which children learn language. (Bostic St. Clair & Grinder, 2001).

Chomsky's work in linguistics had major implications for psychology, providing new insights into the nature of mental processing and human psychology. His critique of Skinner's view (that language could be explained as a stimulus-response process) signaled the decline of interest in behaviorism in American psychology and stimulated much more interest in the cognitive processes in all aspects of human psychology. Chomsky's view of how the mind works and his theory of linguistics greatly influenced John Grinder and the development of NLP (Bostic St. Clair & Grinder, 2001).

CHAPTER III

The History and Literature of Early NLP

The Founders: John Grinder and Richard Bandler

The writings of Korzybski and Chomsky greatly affected the study of linguistics in the 1960s and 1970s. In 1971 John Grinder, at thirty-one years old, received a Ph.D. in linguistics from the University of California, San Diego, and was hired as an assistant professor in the Linguistics Department at the University of California in Santa Cruz. He worked with Noam Chomsky, and his research focused on Chomsky's theories of transformational grammar (Dilts & Hallbom, 2009).

Richard Bandler was a brilliant twenty-one-year-old senior in 1971, majoring in psychology at UCSC. At that time, students were allowed to direct seminars that were supervised by a professor, and in 1972 Bandler asked Grinder to oversee the Gestalt therapy groups that he was leading (Grinder & Pucelik, 2013; McClendon, 1989). Grinder's consent to supervise the seminars was one of those decisive moments that change history.[1]

Bandler was especially interested in the Gestalt therapy of Frederick (Fritz) Perls (1893–1970). He began studying the work of Perls in 1972 when he was hired by a publishing company, Science and Behavior Books, to produce transcripts of videos of Perls' lectures and workshops for the books *The Gestalt Approach* and *Eyewitness to Therapy* (Grinder & Pucelik, 2013; McClendon, 1989).

Perls' Gestalt therapy focuses on experience, specifically the present moment, and the precision of language. It emphasizes the role of language in creating a person's experience and expression of reality. Like Grinder, Perls had been strongly influenced by Alfred Korzybski (Bowman & Brownell, n.d.; Dilts, 1999a; Grinder & Pucelik, 2013; Wysong, n.d.).

Bandler had excellent behavioral modeling skills: he had a remarkable capability to mimic other people's behavior and the way they spoke. He also had an extensive knowledge of the new contemporary systems of psychotherapy. As he worked with Perls' papers and numerous video and audio tapes, Bandler found that he was able to imitate Perls' therapeutic language patterns. In 1973 Dr. Robert Sptizer, the owner of Science and Behavior Books, asked Bandler to also audio tape and transcribe a month-long workshop done by the famous family therapist Virginia Satir. Bandler was able to effectively reproduce her voice and behavioral mannerisms as well. Soon Bandler was able to run Gestalt groups and effect change like Perls and Satir (Dilts & Hallbom, 2009; Grinder & Pucelik, 2013; Hall, 2010a; McClendon, 1989).

However, Bandler felt frustrated that he was not very successful in teaching others to do what he did. He asked Grinder to help him figure out what he was doing (the meta-patterns) so he could teach his skills to others. Grinder had acquired brilliant modeling skills from his study of linguistics. He told Bandler that if he would teach Grinder the behavioral skills, Grinder would help him to reproduce them. He said, "If you teach me to do what you're doing, I'll tell you what you're doing" (Dilts & Hallbom, 2009). This collaboration was the beginning of the new field of NLP (Grinder & Pucelik, 2013; McClendon, 1989).

Both Grinder and Bandler were unhappy with the theories and talk therapy of psychotherapists and psychoanalysts. Bandler's initial creative impetus came from his dissatisfaction with the models of psychology he was studying at UCSC and his fascination with the practical results he saw from the Gestalt therapy of Fritz Perls and the family therapy of Virginia Satir (Grinder & Pucelik, 2013; McClendon, 1989). Grinder was influenced by the left-wing political views of his mentor, Noam Chomsky, and had himself become involved in leftist politics. He considered psychotherapy the self-indulgence of the bourgeoisie who were wallowing in their problems. He wanted a more practical way of effecting change. Hence, like Chomsky, he was interested in the more practical cognitive psychology, which explored how information is processed (Dilts & Hallbom, 2009; Grinder & Pucelik, 2013; Miller, 2003).

The early 1970s was also the time when computer programming, and the concepts behind it, began to be available for the non-specialist. Increasingly, people made parallels between the mind and computers (Miller, 2003). The NLP founders were not interested in psychological theories—they wanted to know how, not why (Dilts & Hallbom, 2009).

As Grinder phrased it, "the core question . . . in NLP modeling is: Given some genius, what are the differences that make the difference between his or her behavior and the behavior of [merely] competent performers in the same field?" (Bostic St. Clair & Grinder, 2001, p. 83). Grinder and Bandler chose as models some contemporary geniuses in behavioral communications and therapy. Because of Grinder's background in linguistics, they started with verbal communication. Together they listened to audio tapes and watched video tapes of Fritz Perls and Virginia Satir (McClendon, 1989).

During this period, Bandler and Grinder were neighbors and friends of the renowned anthropologist and social scientist Gregory Bateson and his famous wife, Margaret Mead. Bateson viewed the mind as similar to a biological ecosystem, in which all living organisms as well as all components of the physical environment interact with one another and function together as a unit. In his concept of the "ecology of mind" he emphasized the importance of understanding how ideas interact with one another in society. Bateson's systems theory greatly influenced the NLP founders in the development of their concept of the "ecology" of change, an inquiry that involved assessing how a change in a person's model of the world may affect other aspects of his or her life. Bateson wrote the Foreword to the first volume of Grinder and Bandler's landmark first book, *The Structure of Magic* (Bandler & Grinder, 1975b).

In late 1974, Gregory Bateson told Grinder about the hypnotic techniques of his long-time friend, psychiatrist Milton Erickson. On Bateson's recommendation, in 1975 Grinder and Bandler traveled to Phoenix, Arizona to participate in Erickson's seminars and observe his work with patients. Their experience of Erickson profoundly affected all of their subsequent work (Bostic St. Clair & Grinder, 2001; Grinder & Pucelik, 2013; McClendon, 1989).

Thus, NLP was built on the foundation of the conceptual framework constructed by Alfred Korzybski and Noam Chomsky. It developed from a combination of the Human Potential movement pioneered by Abraham Maslow and Carl Rogers; the Cognitive Psychology movement catalyzed by Noam Chomsky and developed by George Miller, Eugene Gallanter, and Karl Pribram; the Gestalt therapy of Fritz Perls; and the family systems therapy of Virginia Satir. To these influences were added the systems theory of Gregory Bateson and the hypnotherapy of Milton Erickson.

The Beginning of NLP: The Meta Model

From the beginning of their collaboration in 1972, Grinder and Bandler noticed that language patterns were key to the success of the highly accomplished psychotherapists whose competence they were modeling. Intrigued by the therapeutic brilliance of Fritz Perls and Virginia Satir (and later Milton Erickson), the two young men sought to replicate these language patterns in their own workshops. They did not understand how they themselves were using behavior and language that affected change in their clients, so they began to analyze their language patterns and formalize them so other therapists could utilize them successfully. Bandler had an uncanny ability to imitate these linguistic structures, and Grinder discovered that the analytical tools of Chomsky's transformational grammar could be directly applied to explicate just how the patterns worked to produce marvelous results for clients (Bandler & Thomson, 2011; Grinder & Pucelik, 2013; McClendon, 1989).

Grinder and Bandler also learned that if they could properly challenge the words that a client used to talk about his or her experience, this had the effect of also challenging the presuppositions behind the words. They found that when people changed their language patterns they experienced change in their lives. This work led to their first book, *The Structure of Magic*, volume I, published in 1974 (Bandler & Thomson, 2011; McClendon, 1989).

The name of this work, *The Structure of Magic*, implies that the "magic" that occurs in change work done by great therapists can be understood and communicated to others by analyzing the structure—

not just the content—of their communications (Grinder & Pucelik, 2013). As Virginia Satir writes in the first paragraph of the Foreword to *The Structure of Magic, I*: "Grinder and Bandler have come up with a description of the predictable elements that make change happen in a transaction between two people. Knowing what these elements are makes it possible to use them consciously and, thus, to have useful methods for inducing change" (Bandler & Grinder, 1975b, p. vii).

The Introduction was written by the famous anthropologist Gregory Bateson, who declares that he and his colleagues had attempted "something similar" about twenty years earlier. He explains that, like the two authors, he had endeavored "to create the beginnings of an appropriate theoretical base for the describing of human interaction … [including] not only the event sequences of successful communication but also the patterns of misunderstanding and the pathogenic" (Bandler & Grinder, 1975b, p. ix). However, as Bateson describes, he and his colleagues had used cultural contrasts and psychosis as a starting point rather than neurology and linguistics. Bateson writes that the two founders of NLP "have succeeded in making linguistics into a base for theory and simultaneously into a tool for therapy …. *[They] have succeeded in making explicit the syntax of how people avoid change and, therefore, how to assist them in changing*" [emphasis added] (Bandler & Grinder, 1975b, p. x).

In *The Structure of Magic, I*, Grinder and Bandler use Korzybski's and Chomsky's concepts and terminology to explain how language not only represents and communicates, but actually creates, people's maps and models of the world. They describe what they call a Meta Model of language. The Meta Model is a series of categories of processes based on transformational grammar. These processes investigate the transformations that take place between our perceptions and experiences and how we talk about them. The language we use in our internal talk to ourselves, as well as the language we use to communicate with others, is a function of and represents our model of the world (Bandler & Grinder, 1979, p. 68; Bostic St. Clair & Grinder, 2001, pp. 148-49).

The writers explain that the three major processes in the ways that people construct their maps of the world, are generalization, deletion, and distortion.[2] "A person's generalizations or expectations filter out and distort his experience to make it consistent with those expectations" (Bandler & Grinder, 1975b, p. 16). They clarify that:

> Human beings live in a real world. We do not, however, operate directly or immediately upon that world, but rather we operate with a map or a series of maps, which we use to guide our behavior. These maps, or representational systems, necessarily differ from the territory that they model by the three universal processes of human modeling: Generalization, Deletion, and Distortion. When people come to us in therapy expressing pain and dissatisfaction, the limitations that they experience are typically in their *representation* of the world, not in the world itself. The most thoroughly studied and best understood of the representational systems of maps is human language. The most explicit and complete model of natural language is transformational grammar. Transformational grammar is, therefore, a Metal Model—a representation of the structure of human language—itself a representation of the world of experience. (Bandler & Grinder, 1975b, p. 179)

The founders expound on how the therapist can use knowledge about the structural operation of a shared language as a toolset within the psychotherapeutic interaction. They emphasize that since people create maps of the world and use these maps to guide their behavior, effective therapy must assist the clients in changing their maps. They provide a Meta Model for language-based therapy, proposing Meta Model challenges to contest the client's model, so that s/he will have alternative ways to view the world and therefore more choice in behavior (Bandler & Grinder, 1975b).[3]

The Structure of Magic, volume I, is based on the work of Korzybski and Chomsky. Korzybski's concept that the map is not the territory is the cornerstone of this book, as are his ideas about the ways in which language both represents and influences our map of the world. Chomsky's transformational grammar is the basis of the Meta Model. The authors went beyond Korzybski and Chomsky, however, in clarifying the processes of linguistic representation and by demonstrating how the therapist can use the structure of language itself to change the experiences of the client (Bandler & Grinder, 1975b).

Structure I brilliantly poses some of the basic questions of what would later be called NLP, and lays the foundation for the subsequent work in the field. However, it is very dense and difficult to read. Its jargon, drawn from linguistics, continues to haunt NLP today. The terms used in the Meta Model, such as *lost performatives* and *unspecified referential index*, are derived from complex linguistic terminology and obscure the usefulness of understanding and mastering the processes to which they refer. A simpler, less insistently technical language and style would perhaps have induced more therapists and other students to engage with these concepts and tools, to their very great benefit.[4]

Further Developments in NLP

The class taught by Bandler and supervised by Grinder in the spring of 1972 expanded into several training workshops and programs. The first Metal Model study groups met at the house of Frank Pucelik, Leslie Cameron, and Judith Delozier in 1972. The group included David Gordon, Stephen Gilligan, Terence McClendon, Byron Lewis, and (later) James Eicher and Robert Dilts (Grinder & Pucelik, 2013; McClendon, 1989). In the period between the study of Perls and the emulation of Satir, the focus shifted from Gestalt therapy on themselves to exploring each new linguistic pattern: first of Perls, then Satir, then Erickson (Grinder & Pucelik, 2013).

Bandler met Virginia Satir at a cocktail party during this period and was intrigued by her very effective communication techniques in her system of family psychotherapy. In these early NLP gatherings, Bandler conducted many of what Satir called parts parties and family reconstructions. Some classic NLP techniques, such as reframing (changing the client's view of the meaning of an event), developed during this period (McClendon, 1989).

In 1974 Bandler and Grinder developed the concept of the 4-tuple, which refers to the ongoing flow (outside of conscious awareness) of multiple sensory representational systems: V (visual), A (auditory),

K (kinesthetic), and O/G (olfactory/gustatory). Then they noticed that people had individual processing biases toward one or more of these representational systems, and that these biases are evident in people's use of verbal predicates. For example, if a person says, "I see what you mean" rather than "I hear you," this often indicates that s/he is oriented more toward visual processing than auditory, at least at that moment. Later on, they also found that so-called sub-modality changes (changes in representational sub-distinctions) significantly affect people's experience. For example, if a client changes a visual representation—an internal picture—from color to black and white, this usually immediately changes his or her experience of the situation (McClendon, 1989).

Also in 1974 Bandler and Grinder experimented with a unique application of Ivan Pavlov's classical conditioning process, by which a desired response becomes reliably associated with a specific stimulus (McClendon, 1989). Around the turn of the century Pavlov had discovered that, by ringing a bell while he offered food to a dog, he could create a direct association between the dog hearing a bell and food. The dog eventually salivated when it heard the bell even without the food being present. Pavlov's finding was extrapolated to pertain to human learning and was the foundation of the behaviorist school of psychology, led by John B. Watson and B.F. Skinner, that was predominant in the United States between 1920 and the mid-1950s. In 1949, the Canadian neuropsychologist Donald O. Hebb demonstrated that the human brain can change (i.e., it has neuroplasticity) because neurons form interconnections when they are activated at the same time. As psychiatrists Jeffrey Schwartz and Rebecca Gladding (2012) explain, "When groups of nerve cells (or brain regions) are repeatedly activated at the same time, they form a circuit and are essentially 'locked in' together" (p. 63). Hebb's theory is frequently summed up in the paraphrase, *Neurons that fire together wire together* (Doidge, 2007, p. 63; Schwartz & Gladding, 2012). Thus, neuronal structure can be altered by experience. Experience changes the brain, and ultimately our genes (Doidge, 2007).[5]

Building on these discoveries, the NLP founders developed an application of conditioning that they called "anchoring." This technique facilitates change in people by associating a kinesthetic, auditory or spatial trigger with a desired internal response. They learned to use anchoring in a variety of ways, especially to assist clients to eliminate unwanted emotional reactions and to have more access to positive resources. Eventually the group was anchoring entire 4-tuples and portions of 4-tuples and their relevant sub-modalities, and applying this new methodology to outcomes such as pain control and the permanent interruption of negative behavior patterns (McClendon, 1989).

Perhaps the most remarkable discovery, also in 1974, was what these brilliant innovators called patterns of eye-accessing cues. Grinder and Bandler noticed that there is a correlation between eye movements and internal representations. The eye movements are correlated with specific internal sensory events that are the basis of all cognitive and emotional experience (Grinder & Pucelik, 2013; McClendon, 1989). This was an original discovery of momentous proportions—a foundational leap in the evolution of NLP.

In 1976, Grinder and Bandler published *The Structure of Magic,* volume II. While in volume I they focus on verbal communication, in the second volume they discuss a model of communication and change involving the other modes of communication that people use to represent and communicate their experience. The book continues the discussion of VAKOG from volume I. It also describes how to identify and match the client's preferred representational system by matching his or her preferred verbal predicates (Grinder & Bandler, 1976). For example, to convey the meaning, "I understand you," a kinesthetic person may say, "What you are saying feels right to me," a visual person may say, "I see what you are saying," and an auditory person may say, "I hear you clearly."

Then the authors explain the process of switching or adding representational systems as part of therapy, and they address the issue of incongruity between what the person says and the body posture, gestures, tone of voice, etc. There is also a discussion of lack of semantic "well-formedness" in which the speaker places responsibility for his or her feelings on an external source (for example, "You make me angry") or assumes that s/he knows what others are thinking (e.g., "He thinks I'm ugly"). Finally, there is a discussion of how family therapy applies all of these procedures to the family system (Grinder & Bandler, 1976).

Structure II is a more comprehensive work than *Structure I*, since it discusses the five representational systems rather than only language. Also, it contains a number of illustrations of how to use the techniques. Brilliant as this work is, like volume I, it is difficult to read. The language is complex and not easy to navigate, and as a result this work is rarely read, even by students and teachers of NLP.

Milton Erickson

In 1975, Bandler and Grinder wrote *Patterns of the Hypnotic Techniques of Milton H. Erickson, M.D.*, volume I (Bandler & Grinder, 1975a). This book centers on identification of the voice and language patterns used by Erickson in his hypnotic therapy. In the Introduction, the authors reiterate that the map is not the territory and review the concepts of deletion, distortion, and generalization, as well as the various sensory representational systems. They then show how Erickson works with these patterns within the context of his hypnotherapy (Bandler & Grinder, 1975a).

In *Patterns of the Hypnotic Techniques of Milton H. Erickson, M.D.*, volume II, published in 1977 (Grinder et al.), there is an in-depth description of Erickson's patterns of hypnotic communication, such as trance induction and embedded questions and commands. According to Erickson, hypnosis interrupts unconscious patterns in behavior by means of a confusion technique. This renders the subject available for (vulnerable to) new learning. Erickson persuaded the NLP founders that it is not possible to successfully coerce the unconscious mind, since authoritarian suggestions are usually resisted. Instead, Erickson offered his model of what may be called "permissive" hypnosis, in which the unconscious mind is invited to allow itself to change through techniques involving artful vagueness, questions, suggestions and metaphors (Grinder et al., 1977).

Grinder and Bandler noticed that Erickson's hypnotic language model is the inverse of the NLP Meta Model that was based on the techniques of Perls and Satir. Instead of challenging the client's model of the world by requiring that the verbal description of it be made more specific (Meta Model challenges), Erickson uses deliberately vague and general language to enable the client to work at an unconscious level. This method has the effect of distracting the conscious mind, thus allowing easy access to the unconscious in order to gather information from deeper levels of mind or lead the client into a more deeply altered state of consciousness. The practitioner is thus able to speak directly to the unconscious mind without interference from the conscious mind, with all of its attachments to "reality" and the rules that govern the scope and speed of change within it.

Thus, while the Meta Model worked with the conscious mind in developing a fuller linguistic map by questioning generalizations, deletions, and distortions, the Milton model, in contrast, allowed highly effective communication with the unconscious by actually emphasizing and utilizing this lack of specificity (Grinder & Pucelik, 2013; McClendon, 1989). As Stephen Gilligan explains:

> A main purpose of the Meta Model was to develop a more complete mapping of experience. The idea . . . was that the deletions, distortions, and generalizations made (typically without awareness) in a representational process, resulted in an impoverished map that led to limited choices. The implication of the Meta Model was that developing more complete and less distorted maps would allow other choices and thus superior experience and performance .... But a second, equally prominent emphasis of the early days was learning to navigate without fixed maps .... [an Ericksonian] hypnotic induction is a set of communications that de-frames or dissolves fixed maps, thereby allowing new experiences unhindered by the map bias. (Grinder & Pucelik, 2013, p. 84)

The two volumes describing the work of Milton Erickson contain very insightful analyses of Milton Erickson's therapeutic method and show its profound influence on the two writers. NLP had now become a combination of Meta Model maneuvers and Ericksonian hypnotic techniques.

Virginia Satir

In 1975, in *Structures I*, Grinder and Bandler had attempted to provide a model of the competence of successful therapists such as Virgina Satir. In 1976 Grinder and Bandler worked with Satir directly, seeking to apply their new discoveries about communication process to her work in the field of family systems and family therapy. Satir had been quite frustrated that she did not know how to communicate her methods and the internal processes behind them so that others could replicate her know-how. She wrote the book *Changing with Families* with the two NLP founders, to enable them to model and communicate her techniques (Bandler, Grinder, & Satir, 1976).

In this work, Satir uses some of Grinder's and Bandler's concepts and language to describe her process. For example, she refers to their concepts of map, referential index, Meta Model challenges, complex equivalence, and so on. However the book as a whole is written in much clearer language than *Structures I* and *II*, describing and clearly illustrating her thinking and processes without the encumbrances of specialized complex linguistic terminology.

CHAPTER IV

NLP After 1976

NLP in 1976

By the end of 1976, Grinder and Bandler had combined Satir's and Perls' language patterns and Erickson's hypnotic language and use of metaphor with anchoring to create new processes that they called collapsing anchors, trans-derivational search, changing personal history, and reframing. By 1976 they had also had more experience using eye-accessing cues, and this became a major tool in the practice of NLP. Another major breakthrough that occurred during this period was the discovery of the need to build rapport with their clients, so that the clients felt safe enough to allow themselves to participate fully in the therapeutic interaction. This was accomplished through a variety of techniques involving physical and auditory mirroring and matching. The name "Neuro-Linguistic Programming" was coined in early 1976, inspired by the older field of neuro-linguistics, which explores the neurological basis of language (Dilts, 2008; Grinder & Pucelik, 2013; McClendon, 1989).

ROBERT DILTS

In 1977 a young member of the Santa Cruz NLP group, Robert Dilts, was commissioned by Grinder and Bandler to write *Neuro-Linguistic Programming: The Study of the Structure of Subjective Experience. NLP,* vol. I was first published in 1978. In the Introduction, Dilts discusses the concept of modeling (emulating others) in general as well as the Meta Model and the various representational systems. Here, finally, is a readable explanation of these concepts.

The new contribution that this work adds to the NLP menu is a clarification of the process of "cognitive strategies"—the sequences of sensory representations that lead to particular outcomes of experience.[1] Dilts shows how the NLP practitioner can elicit and make explicit a heretofore unconscious "strategy" that a client has to achieve a specific outcome. Then he illustrates how to interrupt an existing dysfunctional strategy to make way for a revised programming sequence that can actually deliver the original desired outcome. He discusses the procedures for installing a new strategy in the client's patterning, primarily through the use of anchoring (Dilts, 1980).

This is a well-written and clear explanation of the various techniques of NLP extant at the time. Dilts describes very lucidly the process and utilization of Meta Model challenges, representational systems, eye-accessing cues, and strategies, as well as anchoring, reframing, pacing, and rapport-building.

BYRON LEWIS AND FRANK PUCELIK

In 1978 two more members of the NLP core group in Santa Cruz, Byron Lewis and Frank Pucelik, also took on the project of writing a clear exposition of NLP. *Magic Demystified* was first published in 1980. The preface and introduction reiterate the theme that NLP views personality and communication as processes, not as part of a static model. The authors describe in very clear terms the argument of *Structure I* concerning the role of the three unconscious processes of generalization, deletion, and distortion in constructing our models of the world (Lewis & Pucelik, 1982).

The authors pose the question: If the map is not the territory, what causes the differences in the maps of different people? They discuss the neural constraints (4-tuple, or VAKOG), the social constraints (language, the acceptability of eye contact, etc.), and individual constraints (personal history and genetic make-up) that constitute the maps of individuals. This brings the writers to a discussion of how these three constraints overlap, for example in complex equivalents. The meanings associated with words are based on the individual's "model of the world which is also subject to the processes of generalization, deletion, and distortion, as well as to neurological, social, and individual constraints" (Lewis & Pucelik, 1982, p. 28). Hence, one person's understanding of a word is not necessarily the same as that of another person.

The authors make the interesting point that all behavior is communication. There are observable patterns of interaction, primarily through speech and overt gestures. In addition there is internal communication, which also affects us in externally observable ways. Some of this communication is conscious, but much of it is outside of our conscious awareness (Lewis & Pucelik, 1982). The practitioner can take note of external behavioral cues, such as verbal predicate preferences, breathing, body posture, and eye-accessing, in order to externally track these otherwise entirely internal occurrences.

Lewis and Pucelik clarify the Meta Model that Bandler and Grinder had outlined in *Structure of Magic* I. They explain that the Meta Model is the overview of how humans use language to make sense of their world that is presented through the senses. Like Noam Chomsky and the founders of NLP, these authors argue that the rules of language are innate and that a person's use of language reveals the generalizations, deletions, and distortions that participate in generating and stabilizing his or her map of reality. A self-fulfilling and self-confirming process of reality creation continues indefinitely. These unavoidable constraints, which occur naturally as a consequence of any use of language, are called " Meta Model violations." By challenging these "violations," the therapist can assist the client to reassess and re-imagine many aspects of his or her life experience. The authors offer detailed descriptions of methods to elicit a client's unconscious Meta Model violations and how to challenge them.

This thin volume is a clearly written and very readable summary of NLP concepts and procedures. It explains the complex concepts of *Structures* in terms that the reader can easily understand. In addition, the authors outline the advances that had been made since that book was written. For example, they go into detailed explanation of eye-accessing cues, and they explain why building rapport and trust with the client is crucial. This work is an excellent introduction to NLP.

STEVE ANDREAS

Another landmark work was published in 1978. John Stevens, who later changed his name to Steve Andreas, edited some transcripts of a live seminar presented by Bandler and Grinder. This collection of transcripts became the book called *Frogs into Princes*. The seminar was for therapists, to show how applications of NLP techniques can improve therapeutic communication with patients.

In the preface, Andreas proudly describes how NLP can cure phobias, overcome learning disabilities, eliminate most unwanted habits (smoking, drinking, over-eating, insomnia, and so on), make changes in couple, family, and organizational interactions so they function in more satisfying and productive ways, and cure many physiological problems. Additionally, Andreas writes, NLP can determine the structure (key patterns and sequences of behavior) of talent so that it can be taught to others (Bandler & Grinder, 1979).

The book, like the seminar from which it is derived, is divided into the three main sections that were presented on three separate days in the original workshop. The first section discusses sensory experience: representational systems, and accessing cues. The speakers discussed how to create rapport with the client by using language to match the client's representational patterns, and by adjusting one's own body positions and movements to match those of the client. This section also includes discussion about noticing visual and other sensory-accessing cues in order to help the client to bring unconscious internal representations into conscious awareness.

The authors explain that the process begins by asking for specification of an "unspecified verb." The combination of verb specification ("What does [*verb you are using*] mean, specifically?") and non-verbal specification (by noting eye movements and body shifts) will tell the practitioner the process by which the client creates his/her experience. They offer an example of a client saying, "My father scares me." The practitioner might then ask, "How, specifically, does your father scare you?" or "How do you know that you are scared?" While the client is trying to answer such questions, his/her eyes and head may move up and to the left, where the nervous system stores images of the past, or they may move down and to the right to access feelings. (Meanwhile, his/her face may become pale, the eyes may water, breathing may become labored, and the shoulders may hunch over.) As Bandler describes, "The combination of the unspecified verbs that the person is using and the quite elegant non-verbal specification by eye movements and body shifts will give you the answer to the question, whether they ever become conscious of it or not." (Bandler & Grinder, 1979, p. 69).

In Section I there are also discussions about communication and modeling that contain some of the most famous sayings in NLP. For example, regarding modeling, we read that, "if any human can do anything, so can you" (Bandler & Grinder, 1979, p. 36). Concerning communication, we encounter the now-famous brilliant insight that "the meaning of your communication is the response that you get" (Bandler & Grinder, 1979, p. 61).

This lecture clarifies the point that most perception is outside of conscious awareness. The therapist should investigate the processes, not just the content, of the client's problems. If we know the sequences of sensory events that cause the difficulties, we can scramble them to interrupt the unwanted patterns. We also find in this section Erickson's hypnotic language for trance induction and discussion of some of the key concepts in *Structure I* (Bandler & Grinder, 1979).

In section II we have discussion of the technique called "changing personal history" and clarification of the process of anchoring. The book discusses classical conditioning and the capacity to deliberately associate certain intentional stimuli, mostly external kinesthetic (touch), with specific responses in the form of emotions and thoughts. Then we learn how to anchor the problem state and use resources to change the meaning the client makes and the emotions s/he associates with his or her personal history. When we collapse anchors, integrating new possibilities into the patterning that produces the present limitations, the client's system then has more choice about which feelings to experience in relation to the painful past event. The authors specify that choice means having alternative multiple responses to the same stimulus. We discover in this work that anchoring can be used in therapy to overcome fear and change the meanings associated with painful memories so that they no longer affect our experience in the present. This capacity to revise internal processes also enables us to eliminate phobias in a mere matter of minutes (although, in terms of technique, the phobia fix process is usually carried out without the use of explicit kinesthetic anchors).

The book explains that the therapist must "join" the client's model of the world to gain rapport, as a prelude to helping him or her find new possible choices in behavior. We do this by mirroring: matching the client's behavior, both verbally and non-verbally. The therapist mirrors speech predicates and syntax, body posture, breathing, voice tone and tempo, facial expression, and so on. S/he paces the client so s/he can then lead him or her to new alternatives. The book also describes the process of "future pacing." In this work, we find brilliant insights such as the statement "We believe that *all* communication is hypnosis. That's the function of every conversation" (Bandler & Grinder, 1979, p. 100).

In section III, the presenters discuss new techniques, such as reframing. Reframing changes the way a person perceives or gives meaning to an event. The presenters claim that reframing is the best treatment for any psychosomatic symptom, and that the therapist should assume that any physiological symptom is psychosomatic. Also in this section we learn how to communicate with the different parts of the unconscious (Bandler & Grinder, 1979).

Although the book consists of transcripts from a three-day seminar for therapists, it was intended to be a simple explanation of NLP "for the layman who knows nothing about psychology or therapy" (McClendon, 1989, p. 115). This work is much easier to read than anything Bandler and Grinder had done previously. The discussion in *Frogs* of the concepts in *Structure* is much easier to understand than the discussion in *Structure* itself. In addition to clarifying the basic tenets and practices of NLP, this work adds the techniques of body and facial calibration and eye accessing which Bandler, Grinder, and the Santa Cruz group had not discovered until after *Structure* was written. In 1978, NLP was a compilation of the Meta Model, representational systems, eye-accessing cues, anchoring, reframing, strategies, hypnotic language, and techniques to create and adjust rapport.

Parting of the Ways

In late 1978, as a result of increasing tension between John Grinder and Richard Bandler, the two founders of NLP decided to go their separate ways. Bandler and Grinder had previously formed a partnership called The Society of Neuro-Linguistic Programming. Bandler bought John Grinder out and continued to promote The Society of NLP, asserting that it alone was the valid authority in the new field.[2] Grinder partnered with Judith DeLozier to form Grinder, Delozier and Associates (McClendon, 1989).

From 1981 through 2000 Bandler filed a series of intellectual property lawsuits against Grinder. They finally settled the dispute in an agreement that acknowledged them both as co-creators and co-founders of NLP. Bandler continued working through The Society of Neuro-Linguistic Programming, and Grinder worked with The International Trainers Academy of Neuro-Linguistic Programming. While Bandler continued developing and teaching change patterns, Grinder focused on the business marketing applications of NLP (McClendon, 1989).

JOHN GRINDER AFTER 1978

In 1994, Grinder wrote a book with Michael McMaster called *Precision: A New Approach to Communication* that shows how to improve business communication in the areas of negotiation, meetings, and interview skills (McMaster, 1980). Grinder then created *Precision* workshops across the United States (McClendon, 1989).

In 2001 Grinder co-authored *Whispering in the Wind* with Carmen Bostic St. Clair. In this work Grinder expounds on what he calls the "New Code of NLP," which claims to provide a much more systematic approach to NLP. The authors discuss the fundamental principles of NLP in its historical context in order to enable the reader to distinguish "true" NLP from some of the more superficial distortions. The book emphasizes the primary importance of modeling. It also underlines the critical distinction between content and the structure of experience in NLP therapy. While most talk therapy works with the *content* of human experience (*what* happens in our lives, and *why* it happens), NLP therapy focuses on *how* the brain is generating thoughts and feelings in the client's life. This work also suggests a rigorous methodology for doing NLP research and comments on the possible applications in business and other non-therapeutic modalities (Bostic St. Clair & Grinder, 2001).

Unfortunately for the layperson, the language in this book is almost as specialized and difficult to understand as *Structure*. Nonetheless, this work made an important contribution by opening new doors regarding a methodology for research in the field of NLP and the possible applications of NLP in the wider social context.[3]

RICHARD BANDLER AFTER 1978

After 1978, Bandler focused on developing patterns to change clients' limiting beliefs that prevent them from achieving their goals. He taught this material around the world in NLP training programs. This work was presented in two books published in the mid-1980s. The books were actually transcripts of Bandler's therapy sessions, edited by Steve Andreas: *Magic in Action* (1984) and *Using Your Brain for a Change* (1985).

Magic in Action provides edited transcripts of Bandler working directly with people and their problems. The first five chapters are demonstrations to psychologists of how he works with people who have phobias. Chapters six and seven illustrate his ground-breaking work with seminar participants on changing beliefs. However Bandler includes very little commentary about or explanation of the techniques he uses, so the first seven chapters are more an exhibition of Bandler's expertise than a tool to educate others (Bandler, 1984).

Chapter eight is written in an entirely different style. This chapter is a research study that seems to have been tacked on at the last minute. It is a transcript of a case study with commentary by a different person, Peter Gregory, of several sessions using NLP to cure a Vietnam War veteran's PTSD. This section is written in a much more formal, academic style than the other chapters, and is the only section that discusses the methodology (Bandler, 1984).

Using Your Brain for a Change is an edited version of the transcripts of several seminars for therapists that Bandler conducted in 1982. The main thrust of these seminars is that since most of our experience is subjective, we can radically change that experience by reprogramming (revising) those portions of it that we do not like. In this work Bandler shows how to use the basic tools of NLP to accomplish this kind of change. To prove Bandler's points, the book interweaves descriptions and commentary with entertaining snippets of his interactions with clients. However, in contrast to *Magic*, there are no full patient case histories, so the reader may wonder how well these techniques would work in the real world (Bandler, 1985). A combination of the approaches used in the two books would make for more informative reading.

In 2008 Bandler published *Guide to Trance-Formation,* also an edited transcript of a seminar for therapists. Here he explains the concepts and processes described in *Structure I* and *Patterns I* over thirty years earlier, but in much clearer language. It contains much material included in a work he published with Grinder in 1981, called *Trance-Formations: Neuro-Linguistic Programming and the Structure of Hypnosis.* However there are some new insights and techniques in the later version.

In *Guide to Trance-Formation* (2008), Bandler describes his use of hypnosis in change work. He maintains that all thoughts and behaviors are hypnotic trances, in that they are patterned, repetitive, and habitual. "People are not simply in or out of trance but are moving from one trance to another. They have their work trances, their relationship trances, their driving trances, their parenting trances, and a whole collection of problem trances" (p. 2). He explains that our brains quickly learn how to automate all behavior, including limiting, negative, and even self-destructive patterns. However, the brain can as quickly learn how to change these patterns of behavior and thinking. We can use our conscious mind to direct and re-direct our unconscious activity. Bandler writes that, "Neuro-Linguistic Programming, sometimes described as the study of subjective experience and what can be predicted from it, demystified hypnosis and brought its underlying structure into conscious awareness" (Bandler, 2008, p. 294).

In this work, Bandler discusses how to use NLP to elicit thought patterns, induce hypnotic trance, and use hypnosis to generate change. For example, the author repeats the point made in *Structure* that challenging Meta Model violations not only gives the practitioner information, but also allows the client's conscious mind to access the unconscious process. What are the generalizations, deletions, and distortions in the client's speech? This is the first step to revising the undesired program. Bandler provides more than thirty self-teaching exercises and four "trance-scripts" of his actual work with clients with comments in the margins about the techniques he is using. This is a clearly written, very readable book. It clarifies existing information about NLP as well as offers new perspectives.

ROBERT DILTS AFTER 1978

Robert Dilts found value in the approaches of both Grinder and Bandler, so he straddled both worlds. He wrote about applications of NLP, but he also increasingly focused on changing beliefs as a way of changing one's life—and sometimes he combined the two approaches. For example, he taught NLP training programs with an emphasis on the way our beliefs affect health, and on methods to change beliefs to improve health (McClendon, 1989).

In his writing, Dilts, like Grinder, now focused more on new applications outside of the therapeutic framework. In 1981, Dilts wrote a book entitled *Applications of NLP* (published in 1983). After providing a synopsis of the history, concepts, and techniques of NLP, he shows how the processes he outlines can be used in business communication, sales, family therapy, interpersonal negotiation, health, education, and creative writing (Dilts, 1983). This book seems to consist of a series of articles written at different times, and the order is sometimes confusing. Nevertheless, it is clearly written and provides an excellent explanation of how NLP can be used to achieve desired outcomes in different venues.

Dilts also increasingly explored how to change unwanted beliefs by using NLP. In 1990 Dilts wrote *Beliefs: Pathways to Health and Well-Being* (1990) and *Changing Belief Systems with NLP* (1990). These works describe how he uses NLP to change unwanted, limiting beliefs as part of supporting better goal-achievement and more fulfilling life experience. In these books, Dilts presents the technique of re-imprinting and the process of installing new beliefs (See Dilts, 1980b, pp. viii–ix).

Dilts's books that followed, *Tools for Dreamers* (1991) and *Skills for the Future* (1993), focus on using applications of NLP to enhance creativity. *Strategies of Genius*, vol.1-3 (1994) shows how to use NLP to model the way several great geniuses and historical figures thought and acted. Dilts continues with this theme when he explores leadership in *Visionary Leadership Skills* (1996c) and in *Modeling with NLP* (1998a).

In 1999 Dilts wrote *Sleight of Mouth: The Magic of Conversational Belief Change* (1999a). In this work, Dilts explains that what he calls sleight-of-mouth patterns are his attempt to encode some of the key linguistic mechanisms that charismatic individuals use to persuade others and to influence social as well as individual belief systems.[4] He points to a common, fundamental set of patterns in the language of people who have shaped and influenced powerful social change in human history—people such as Jesus of Nazareth, Karl Marx, Abraham Lincoln, Albert Einstein, Mohandas Gandhi, Martin Luther King, and others. Dilts explains, "these 'Sleight of Mouth' patterns are made up of verbal categories and distinctions by which key beliefs can be established, shifted, or transformed through language. They can be characterized as 'verbal reframes' which influence beliefs and the mental maps from which beliefs have been formed" (Dilts, 1999a, pp. x-xi).

In 2003 Dilts wrote *From Coach to Awakener.* This work is based on the neurological levels model of the renowned contemporary anthropologist, Gregory Bateson, who had been a strong influence on Grinder and Bandler in the earliest days of NLP. This model postulates that there is a hierarchy of levels of learning and change. Dilts argues that we need different types of support for change at each level. The Coach works on improving behavioral competencies. The Teacher targets new cognitive capabilities. The Mentor empowers people to acquire new beliefs and values. The Sponsor fosters growth at the identity level. The Awakener raises people's awareness of the (quantum) field, which is the source for desired change (Dilts, 2003). Dilts thus brilliantly differentiates among the diverse ways that NLP can stimulate change in accordance with an individual's needs and level of personal evolution.

More Recent Schools of NLP

In the late 1970s, there was a turning point in the development of the field of NLP. As John Grinder complains, there was a movement away from the creative exploratory spirit of the early days to a focus on coding what had already been discovered. NLP was taken over by people who paid "primary attention to their content (fixed content models) typically [resulting] in confusing the maps as the territory, while also favoring the development of technocrats over creative thinkers" (Grinder & Pucelik, 2013, pp. 90, 102). However, there were some new schools of NLP that emerged in the 1980s and after that did offer innovative contributions to the field. Two of the better-known schools were formed by Tad James and L. Michael Hall.

TAD JAMES

Tad James' system is a combination of basic NLP tools, hypnotherapy, and an innovation that James calls Time Line Therapy. The NLP and hypnotherapy aspects of his work are well presented but do not appear to offer anything original. However James's time line therapy, in which he incorporates several existing NLP methods and hypnotic language patterns, is innovative.

In *Time Line Therapy and the Basis of Personality,* written in 1985 with Wyatt Woodsmall, James elaborates on a technique that uses a metaphorical timeline to regress the subject to events that appear to have occurred in childhood or—depending on the client's beliefs—in literal past lives. These events are understood to be root-decision causes for negative conditions affecting the person's present experience. From a point of view floating above the timeline, the client is afforded a dissociated view of events preceding and resulting in crucially limiting decisions. Through the use of an innovative representational shift, the client is invited to discover that the apparent past choices are available for revision. James claims that the result of these timeline changes is the amelioration or outright elimination of all subsequent negative or limiting effects of the original decision. The second and third parts of the book, which are mostly written by co-author Wyatt Woodsmall, are about conventional NLP meta-programs and values elicitation, with not much that is new other than a profiling system entitled Meta Program and Values Inventory (James & Woodsmall, 1988). In sum, while much of Tad James' work seems to consist of previously offered methods of NLP and hypnotherapy, the notion and practice of the timeline—notwithstanding extravagant claims for the technique's efficacy—do provide a valuable contribution to the toolkit of NLP change work.

MICHAEL HALL

L. Michael Hall is the founder of what he calls Neuro-Semantics, which he first introduced in 1997 in his book *Mind-Lines: Lines that Change Minds.* Hall explains that he and co-author Rev. Bobby Bodenhamer created the school of Neuro-Semantics as an advanced development of NLP. They developed a number of new patterns using what Hall calls the Meta-States Model. On his website, Hall writes that "Neuro-Semantics highlights much more fully and extensively the existence of multiple meta-levels . . . than does NLP" (Hall, 2007a). He claims to be guided by Korzybski in his focus on self-reflexivity "about how we evaluate and then evaluate our evaluations and by that create higher levels of 'mind'" (Hall, 2007a).

Hall concedes that NLP was a meta-discipline from its inception, and has always taught and used meta-level information (for example, the Meta Model and Meta Programs). Also, he admits that, "co-developer Robert Dilts has contributed numerous meta-level models" (Hall, 2007a). However, Hall claims that his own meta-states model is the most fully descriptive and comprehensive model about meta-levels. He says that in his meta-states model, the focus on self-reflexivity provides a way to track thoughts-about-thoughts, feelings-about-feelings, and other states-about-states (meta-states). According to Hall, "the system that emerges from the meta-levels that govern the lower levels brings about an overall gestalt (or configuration of interactive parts) which in turn, define the character of the whole." He explains that, "we set up a higher level frame-of-reference that will take over. The power to identify a frame enables us to step aside from a frame and to set a whole new frame" (Hall, 2007a). When we reframe meanings, we can improve our performance in life. Hence, this new frame empowers us to present a new "strategy of excellence" (Hall, 2007a; Hall, 2007b).

Hall's *Mind-Lines* (1997) essentially focuses on challenging limiting beliefs through the art of reframing conversations. Despite Hall's claims, the material in this work does not appear to offer techniques that are qualitatively different from the meta-programs model in NLP, the books on reframing by Grinder and Bandler, and the works by Robert Dilts such as *Changing Belief Systems With NLP* and *Sleight of Mouth. Mind-Lines* directs us to analyze our map of the world, so we can change what does not serve us. However, Hall's focus on self-reflexivity leads one to wonder about the extent to which just thinking about an issue and reframing it verbally can change its meaning for us. It seems that Hall thoughtfully greatly elaborated on one aspect of NLP to the exclusion of the many other valuable techniques developed by the founders of NLP.

CHAPTER V
Jonathan Rice

Background of Jonathan Rice and NLP

In the mid-eighties a new branch of NLP sprouted and developed in a very different way from the other schools of NLP. This new iteration was organized around the work and teaching of Jonathan Rice. By 1985 the philosophy and methodology of the NLP taught by Rice had developed in a substantially different direction from that of mainstream NLP.

The founders of NLP were not interested in the field of psychology. As described above, Richard Bandler and John Grinder developed the new field of NLP largely in reaction against the theories and contemporary practices of psychology (Dilts & Hallbom, 2009; Grinder & Pucelik, 2013; McClendon, 1989). They taught their students that they did not have to study the field of psychology or have a degree in it in order to excel in NLP. Grinder told his students that, "graduate school is where the limitations of one generation are passed on to another" (Dilts & Hallbom, 2009). John Grinder later said: "I believe it was very useful that neither [Richard Bandler nor I] were qualified in the field . . . [of] psychology and in particular, its therapeutic application" (Collingwood, 1996). The students who gathered around the founders therefore believed that the more expertise a person had in a subject, the more his knowledge was archaic. The new field of NLP could best progress with people who were not contaminated with the old ideas (Dilts & Hallbom, 2009).

Jonathan Rice joined the NLP group around Bandler and Grinder in 1975. In contrast to the other members of the group, most of whom were undergraduates at the time, Rice was an academically trained and licensed psychotherapist with a Ph.D. He managed a community mental health clinic in Monterey and maintained a private psychotherapy practice in the nearby town of Carmel. Rice had attended a seminar given by the renowned family therapist Virginia Satir and was intrigued by her excellent results. In the course of reviewing ways of spending what little remained of his annual training budget, Rice came across a flyer for a seminar to be given by Grinder and Bandler. The flyer described definite behavioral outcomes that would occur for all workshop attendees. For example, the flyer promised that each person attending would acquire the ability to immediately "fix" phobias. Rice was struck by the specificity of the claimed good results since, as a conventionally trained psychotherapist, he was entirely unaccustomed to training outcomes ever being stated in precise, behaviorally measurable terms (J. Rice, personal communication, June 2011).

Most psychotherapists at that time relied on a process-oriented approach to change and healing rather than one that centered on the accomplishment of specific outcomes for the client. The then-predominant therapeutic paradigm was humanistic psychology, which had been developed in the 1950s in reaction to both murky, unending psychoanalysis and mechanistic behaviorism. As exemplified in the work of masters such as Carl Rogers, the humanistic approach emphasized the primacy of the therapist/client relationship. The nature, quality, and dynamics of this relationship were the major determining factors in whether the client got well.

However, along with many others at the time, Dr. Rice noticed that since the psychotherapeutic experience was so dependent on the on-going presence of the therapist, what good changes did occur did not necessarily stabilize and continue after the client left therapy. Also, he saw that frequently the psychotherapist projected his/her own issues onto the client, with all involved then becoming entangled in the conflicts and mysteries of transference/counter-transference dynamics. At that point in his career as a clinician, Rice was looking for more practical ways of doing therapy, with the goal of creating tangible and measurable behavioral outcomes that could endure without his continuing presence in his clients' lives (J. Rice, personal communication, June 2011). At the time, this was a tall order.

In the fall of 1975, Rice went to the abovementioned weekend seminar taught by Grinder and Bandler in Santa Cruz. Then he went to another three weekend seminars and a ten-day workshop. In these trainings, he said, "I saw them doing things that I didn't know how to do" to achieve profound and permanent behavioral changes, such as eliminating the experience of phobias. The trainers used procedures that Rice had never seen before, and then showed the audience how they accomplished their remarkable results. Thus, Rice saw that the NLP techniques were replicable and could accomplish changes in clients that he knew he could not achieve with talking psychotherapy alone (J. Rice, personal communication, June 2011).

These trainings were aimed toward and attended mostly by psychotherapists. However, in the course of their presentations Grindler and Bandler frequently ridiculed the current theories and methodologies of psychology (J. Rice, personal communication, June 2011). They did not call themselves therapists or coaches or scientists. Instead, they called themselves "modelers." Their goal was to make and teach a model of how to do something that works. They were focused on the practical uses of specific techniques that actually worked to effect change in people (Dilts & Hallbom, 2009).

Increasingly, because of the power and effectiveness of the tools they were evolving, Bandler and Grinder's focus became centered on NLP techniques purported to be rapid cures for nearly every life problem or challenge. The techniques were more and more presented as stand-alone events, formulas for change that could be combined or chained in sequence with other techniques to produce a variety of outcomes for the client (J. Rice, personal communication, June 2011). Bandler and Grinder had developed an entirely new field, but their work increasingly took on a quick-fix orientation that, although brilliantly innovative, was—from Rice's perspective as a psychotherapist—superficial and limiting.

During the late 1970s, Rice was apprehensive that Bandler and Grinder's cavalier iconoclasm and emphasis on formulaic techniques allowed for little real attention to the broader ecology and emotional well-being of their students and clients. The founders often used their students as guinea pigs to test their methods, sometimes with devastating emotional consequences for the youngsters. Rice was troubled by his perception that the NLP founders had discarded compassion along with many of the outdated theories and methodologies of conventional process-focused psychotherapy (J. Rice, personal communication, June 2011).

Rice was concerned that NLP, which had developed out of the fields of linguistics, psychology, and Ericksonian hypnosis, had become divorced from these roots. It had become simply an aggregation of techniques, and had failed to develop into the more comprehensive system of effective and practical psychotherapy that Rice had been seeking for his own practice. Therefore, even while he learned as much as he possibly could from them from 1975 to 1978, he was content to remain on the outskirts of the primary Bandler-Grinder group. At the end of 1978, when the relationship between Grinder and Bandler disintegrated, Rice completely disconnected himself from the NLP founding circle. He never rejoined the original group, and his work proceeded to develop along a very separate track (J. Rice, personal communication, June 2011).

Working from the perspective of his formal academic background in psychology and his need to respond creatively to the demands of a daily clinical practice, Jonathan Rice himself developed that which he had been seeking. By the middle 1980s he had extended the NLP of the 1970s into his own evolution of it: a cohesive psychotherapy that combined the fundamental core of developmental psychology with the perceptual tools and powerful interventions of NLP. It was this synthesis, of the mid-1980s, that Rice then taught to his students. Transformational NLP evolved from the teachings of Jonathan Rice.

Differences between Mainstream NLP and Jonathan Rice's NLP

There are some key differences between the NLP developed by Jonathan Rice and taught to his students, and the way that most NLP is practiced today. Perhaps the most significant dissimilarity is the practice of NLP as a combination of discrete techniques (in conventional NLP) as compared to applying NLP methodologies within the larger psychological context of a person's life. There are numerous other differences in style and technique. In Rice's approach, eye-accessing and other physiology cues are vastly more important than in conventional NLP. He pays constant attention to questions of belief and ecology, and rather than working from a script, he customizes all re-imprinting activity for each client individually. Also, Rice's work is conducted conversationally, while seated facing the client, and makes little use of spatial anchors arrayed along the floor such as used in conventional NLP changework.

NLP AS TECHNIQUES VERSUS NLP WITHIN PSYCHOTHERAPY

As described above, Grinder and Bandler were fascinated with techniques for quick as well as powerful change; they largely ignored the contexts of their clients' problems and experiences. Indeed, they often denigrated traditional psychotherapy's common practice of paying attention to past events and childhood issues (J. Rice, personal communication, June 2011). Most of their students reflected and in turn taught this approach, and it became standard as the basis for NLP practice up to the present time. One of the remarkable things about these techniques is that this material is highly effective much of the time. Many students of conventional NLP become adept technicians of change and healing without focusing on the childhood traumas that formed the basis of present patterns of belief and behavior.

There is much to be said for any transformation modality that can open the way to a better future so quickly and directly, without having to pay attention to one's painful past experience. However, without respectful acknowledgment of the strength and dignity that have come through such hard-won past learning, this process can fall short of providing a stable basis for future growth. In his work as a psychotherapist, Rice found that acknowledging and reframing the past is almost always the best way to create good rapport with the future.

Jonathan Rice worked with conventional NLP methodologies as part of an internally consistent psychotherapy that was inclusive of the client's entire experience. He used the information-gathering and behavior re-patterning techniques of NLP only when they were appropriate and useful within his model of one-to-one psychotherapy, a model that emphasized attention to childhood developmental stages and traumas—subjects in which most conventional NLP practitioners were at that time not interested (J. Rice, personal communication, November 2011).

In Rice's view, people who came to his office were usually stuck in self-limiting patterns of thought and behavior developed in response to childhood trauma. If these issues were not resolved, the client would stay stuck in these patterns. Even if isolated NLP techniques were able to change a bit of behavior, the patterns would likely manifest in another form that would be equally self-limiting. Therefore, Rice focused on revealing and resolving childhood traumatic events that were the basis of the adult client's problems in the present. He paid more attention than other NLP practitioners to the client's physiology as it was correlated with internal representations, since it offered clues to the origins of the imprints of childhood trauma (J. Rice, personal communications, January 2015).[1]

Rice was oriented toward flexibility and creativity in addressing what the client presented rather than proceeding with specific, pre-packaged techniques (J. Rice, personal communication, January 2015). While his client work may have included one or more of the standardized, procedural change formats, such as the phobia fix or changing personal history, he used such techniques mainly to specify and stabilize changes that had been set in motion through his conversational interaction with the client. Rice gradually extended and refined the NLP toolbox specifically for this purpose (J. Rice, personal communication, November 2011).

STANDING VERSUS SEATED INTERACTION

The dissimilarity between NLP as a series of techniques as compared to NLP methodologies incorporated into psychotherapy is exemplified by the difference between standing while performing a specific technique and sitting while having a conversational interaction. Robert Dilts and most mainstream NLP practitioners use "walking timelines" as their primary means of effecting change in clients. The client physically stands and steps from one spatial anchor to another. S/he walks on specific locations on the floor that have been intentionally associated with a current problem state that the client wants to change, such as a belief that s/he is unworthy or not capable of success, and the desired resource state, such as a feeling of confidence and self-respect and a belief in one's capabilities. The clients walk on a physically marked out (although imaginary) timeline that connects the spatial anchors on the floor (Dilts, 1990).

This walking timeline format has a number of benefits. It assists clients to become more aware of their unconscious experience. Also, this format can often supply important information about significant ecology issues, albeit at a conscious-mind level (since the walking timeline relies primarily on the client's conscious experience and capacity to accurately self-report). Additionally, the process of actual physical movement onto and off anchored locations on the timeline allows for effective association and dissociation, representational maneuvers that are an essential part of reorganizing almost any neuro-linguistic patterning. Dilts believes that the walking timeline, because it is based on having the client move among discrete spatial anchors, also helps to sort and segregate events so they can be dealt with one at a time (Dilts, 1990).

The walking timeline has several advantages over other anchoring-based change techniques, such as touch anchors (e.g., squeezing someone's arm). For one thing, walking timelines involve using physical movement as an analogue for emotional progression. The instruction to "take this [confidence] and step into that [upcoming family interaction]" is easier to grasp when the client is actually stepping from an external "here" to an external "there" (stepping from one actual floor anchor to another).

A walking timeline also has the advantage being highly procedural, because it is literally a step-by-step procedure (have the person do *this*, and then *that*, and then *this*). It is a uniform process that focuses on addressing specific symptoms. It is easily learned, because the student can always read what the "next step" is in the class manual. Also, it can be demonstrated to hundreds of people simultaneously, in a mass audience venue, because each student can follow along with the procedural instructions. Because of its explicit and reproducible nature, the walking timeline is the functional basis for a large number of relatively quick techniques.

Most mainstream NLP practitioners continue to mainly use the walking timeline, which utilizes floor anchors rather than touch anchors for change work.[2] During the 1980s and continuing to the present, Dilts and his followers developed a plethora of floor anchor techniques and strategies.

In contrast, Rice worked with clients while sitting and talking, in the style of modern (couch less) psychotherapy. He taught a format for interacting with the client for several hours, using multiple change interventions comprised of a number of continuously interweaving elements rather than a quick, one-process technique (J. Rice, personal communication, November 2011).

Because the seated interaction format is conversational and, unlike walking timelines, does not include specific procedures, it provides more opportunity for reframing. Reframing by itself is a profound intervention. For example, in conversation, using NLP tools that are seamlessly interwoven in the exchange, the NLP practitioner can instill in the client the understanding that painful incidents in the past formed the basis for his or her personal growth and current knowledge and skills. Such reframing changes the meaning of the past. Through reframing, there is a shift in the emotions associated with the narrative of what happened. Reframing can involve making direct changes to the representations of images or sounds from the past, but it is more usually accomplished indirectly, through re-description and re-definition of the past, present, and future.

While he rarely used standing interventions such as the walking timeline, during the seated interactions Rice made frequent but subtle use of spatial anchors, mainly through modifying his posture or making certain gestures. He emphasized the use of kinesthetic, visual, and auditory anchoring as a standard part of client work. Rice believed that, compared with using only self-generated floor anchors, this wider range of anchoring modalities allows for greater precision and control. This enables the practitioner to more accurately adjust nuances of the anchoring process to match the needs of the client in the moment (J. Rice, personal communication, November 2011).

EYE-ACCESSING CUES

One of the most significant contributions of Jonathan Rice was his extension and refinement of work with what NLP practitioners call "eye-accessing cues," or observable eye movements that correlate with internal images of emotional experiences. The founders of NLP discovered, formalized, and worked with eye-accessing patterns in the mid-seventies (McClendon, 1989). It had long been common knowledge that humans both generate and store experience through internal representations of the five senses: visual, auditory, kinesthetic, olfactory, and gustatory (sight, hearing, feeling and emotion, smell, and taste). These representations are in both conscious and unconscious awareness. However, Grinder and Bandler were the first to correlate these internal sensory events with externally observable, real-time changes in the physical body (Dilts & Hallbom, 2009).

Eye movements that indicate internal sensory (representational) events were the most notable and easily observable of these early discoveries related to body changes. Grinder and Bandler and their students began using these eye-accessing cues to gain immediate knowledge of the clients' purely internal, and usually unconscious, processes. The founders soon noticed that the patterning of these eye movements was also an excellent source of information about a person's most natural and preferred ways of processing information, and that, as described below, the accesses themselves could be used to support the creation of safety and rapport with the client (Dilts, 2008; McClendon, 1989).

One of the most intriguing aspects of eye-movement patterns was what became known as "the half-second rule." In the 1840s, the German physiologist Hermann Helmholtz had found that nerve impulses are not brought to conscious awareness immediately. Helmholtz and his assistant, Wilhelm Wundt, showed that it takes a fraction of a second for any sensory message to reach the brain, and more time to process what it is. In the 1960s, neuroscientist Benjamin Libet demonstrated in a number of studies that consciousness normally takes a half of a second to process a sensory event. That is to say, it takes about half of a second before people have a conscious experience of a sensation (McCrone, 2006).[3]

What became known as the half-second rule was taught in Cognitive Psychology classes in the 1970s. Robert Dilts took classes in psychobiology at the University of California in Santa Cruz in 1973, where he learned that it takes about a half second for an externally or internally generated stimulus to reach conscious awareness (R. Dilts, personal communication, October 2014). He and the other members of the NLP circle found that when a client was asked, "what stops you from getting what you want?" as part of efforts to elicit conscious information, the client immediately made distinct eye movements. They discovered that such eye movements are always correlated with internal representational events. Asking this question in relation to a desired but blocked outcome would always produce nearly instantaneous, completely unconscious eye movements. The internal pictures, sounds, and feelings associated with the unconscious eye movements that took place within the first half second were always linked to a representation that pointed to the answer to this question (J. Rice, personal communications, November 2011 & August 2014; R. Dilts, personal communication, October 2014). As Dilts describes, "I began applying this law of perception to identifying [preconscious] responses to questions and . . . calibrating limiting thoughts and beliefs from the time I was first involved in NLP [in 1976]." In June 1980 Dilts began writing a book in which he discussed applying the half-second rule to identify limiting beliefs. The half-second rule was also the basis for his biofeedback patent that was filed in 1983 (R. Dilts, personal communication, October 2014).[4]

Most psychotherapists will eventually ask their clients some version of the question, "What stops you from having what you want?" For practitioners who are not trained in NLP, or who are inadequately trained, this question is used to elicit conscious content about the client's experience. Some practitioners also ask clients to describe the pictures or sounds that they are experiencing. However the client is frequently not aware on the conscious level of what was actually being perceived, so the answers are usually about the content of memories stored in the conscious mind. The discovery and use of the half-second rule to get access to the client's unconscious was a major breakthrough.

Robert Dilts and Jonathan Rice both made use of the half-second rule in their practice and trainings, but they used it differently. Dilts refers to it in a paragraph in his book *Beliefs* (Dilts, et al., 1990):

> When I am working with people, I frequently ask the question, "What stops you from achieving your desired outcome?" I then look for an immediate unconscious physiological response that comes before they have a chance to consciously think about it. (This is called the half-second rule.) I'm not as interested in the verbal answer as I am the non-verbal cues that occur in the first half-second that lets me know precisely how the person is getting stuck. (p. 124)

Then, Dilts uses one of the NLP techniques to deal with the representations associated with this event. A preferred method is to resolve internal conflicts by integrating eye movements. "This installs a new pathway for accessing her resources and gives her more choices about her beliefs and behaviors" (p. 125).

Rice found a different way to work with the half-second eye-access cues. He believed that this discovery had monumental significance for psychotherapy, and he made it the center of his practice. As a psychotherapist, he had for years realized that discussions about content are largely useless for gaining new knowledge about the specifics of the client's unconscious internal processes. He realized that "they [therapists in the 1970s and 1980s] had no idea where they were going" (J. Rice, personal communication, January 2015). He observed that any conscious understanding was not likely to lead the NLP practitioner, either, to something newly useful. Hence, Rice was driven to discover a replicable methodology to reliably and precisely access information about early life trauma from the unconscious (J, Rice, personal communication, November 2011).

Rice and the other members of the NLP group had been taught by Grinder and Bandler from the earliest meetings to look for age regression, which the founders had learned from the videos of Fritz Perls. Rice observed that unmistakable physiological signs of age regression always accompanied the eye-access in the first half second after he asked, "What stops you?" He realized that this was a key to accessing imprints of childhood traumas (J. Rice, personal communications, November 2011).

Over time, Rice noticed that the closer he put the questions

"What would you like?" and "What stops you?" together, the stronger was the response that he got from the client. Accordingly, Rice formulated what he called the "Core Sorting Questions" as a way to quickly provoke the client's brain into generating unconscious eye movements that could be correlated with out-of-consciousness internal representations (usually images and sounds) connected with past trauma. Core Sorting involves asking only two or three of the five main questions of the Outcome Frame, which is a set of questions formulated by the founders of NLP originally to gather conscious-content information about the concerns and goals of the client. But unlike classic Outcome Frame questions, Rice's Core Sorting questions are asked not so much to get information about conscious content as to lead up to the question, "What stops you?" The question's purpose is only to elicit eye-accessing cues, which occur automatically in the first one-quarter to one-half second after the client hears those words. While Rice often used the entire Outcome Frame information-gathering format as part of his interaction with clients, observing their eye movements during the entire process, he specifically used the Core Sorting questions as a way to be sure that he was pinpointing original sensory representations connected with childhood trauma that had resulted in self-limiting thoughts, emotions, and behavior. Rice also used Core Sorting questions as a way to demonstrate to students that this method of eliciting eye-accessing cues works reliably, again and again, in answer to the question "What stops you?" (J. Rice, personal communications, June 2011, January 2015, and August 2014).[5]

Rice learned that he could have the client deliberately hold a specific access, thus stabilizing the client's attention on the difficult repressed past content. Using rapport and skillful language, he could then invite the client to bring the heretofore unconscious content revealed by the eye accessing into present, conscious awareness. From this place, it was a relatively straightforward process to recover even more awareness of the content of the past imprinted experiences, including a rapid, conscious understanding of the decisions and beliefs that were originally created during the moments of the imprinted past trauma (J. Rice, personal communication, November 2011).

Now the practitioner could take time to carefully and thoroughly unpack the literal content of the past experiences, (i.e., the specific events involving specific people in a specific time and place.) Thus the therapist could gain access to information about events, decisions, and beliefs that had until now operated unconsciously in the client's unwanted patterning. For example, once he noticed age regression Rice would often ask, "So—what's happening there, what's going on [in that material you have just discovered that you have conscious knowledge of now]?" The client would experience very strong feelings as s/he became consciously aware of the events and emotions associated with the memories that were, until just a few seconds earlier, completely repressed. Rice found that this "unpacking what stops you" process was indefinitely repeatable for each individual, as s/he would always access in the same ways when unconsciously encountering the same imprinted childhood experiences (J. Rice, personal communication, November 2011).

Thus, Jonathan Rice expanded and refined a methodology that assisted clients to *resourcefully* regress to an experience of the childhood trauma during which the person's unconscious system had acquired the imprinting that became stabilized, was generalized, and then produced severe, apparently inexplicable constraints on freedom and well-being. He now had a reliable way to nearly instantly provoke age regression and access original (or representative) unconscious instances of past traumatic learning. Although long ago relegated to the realm of the unconscious, precisely because of its emotionally difficult nature, this past content had continued to affect the beliefs and behavior of the adult in the present. Rice found that by bringing these pictures, sounds, smells, or tastes to the client's conscious awareness—while maintaining rapport and safety here and now—he could assist the client to immediately recover conscious awareness of the original childhood trauma that had generated a pattern of core beliefs that formed the basis of the person's identity. Rice realized that this information from the unconscious was extremely useful as a place from which to begin the process of re-imprinting limiting beliefs (J. Rice, personal communication, November 2011).

Almost without exception, the situations and events revealed in the "What stops you?" eye-accessing process are inaccessible by other means. Material revealed in this rapid, often startling way is of a type and nature that almost never arises in a conventional client/therapist conversation. It is nearly always completely surprising to the client, yet it always accounts for the client's most painful experiences of fear, lack, or limitation in life. A very thorough application of this process is extremely quick, a matter of only a few minutes. Once the original imprints, and the decisions and beliefs associated with them, are unpacked, the practitioner can then choose among a variety of NLP approaches and techniques to begin the process of behavior, belief, and identity revision.

CHANGING LIMITING BELIEFS

In the 1980s, a number of participants in the original Bandler-Grinder group experimented with techniques and patterns to change beliefs that would eventually be assembled under the rubric of "belief-level change." Robert Dilts and Jonathan Rice independently evolved different ways to work with beliefs.

Robert Dilts based his work with beliefs on what he had learned from Grinder and Bandler, including their interpretation of the work of Milton Erickson. Since Dilts had not studied psychology or child development, he did not use the frames of psychotherapy (Dilts & Hallbom, 2009).

In contrast, Jonathan Rice had developed his understanding and work with beliefs within the conceptual framework of psychotherapy and childhood development. Rice's training was in childhood development, and he was accustomed to approaching his work with clients through the lens of beliefs and childhood belief development. He was extremely attuned to the positive intentions (e.g., to survive or gain love) of decisions made by children experiencing threat or loss at various stages of psychological development. Hence, Rice paid more attention than Dilts to the original (almost always unconscious) decisions made by the child, decisions that then continued as the foundation of patterning that would manifest as lifelong pain and limitation. He knew from his clinical experience that if clients could change beliefs and decisions that had originated in childhood, this could influence the entire constellation of their thoughts, emotions, and behavior (J. Rice, personal communication, June 2011).

THE ECOLOGY OF PERSONAL CHANGE

In common NLP parlance, the term "ecology objections" refers to a client's usually unconscious objections to consciously desired change. In the course of change work, an ecology objection usually arises because of unconscious fears about how a supposedly good outcome may affect one's way of life, one's relationships, one's belief system, or even one's core identity (Bostic St. Clair & Grinder, 2001; Dilts et al., 1990).

In the 1987 transcription of the seminars led by John Grinder and Judith DeLozier entitled *Turtles All the Way Down: Prerequisites to Personal Genius*, the two trainers occasionally allude to ecology objections as the client's concern to avoid potential disruption of the stability of his or her model of the world. However, they do not pursue this subject in detail or explain how to work with it in clients (Grinder & DeLozier, 1987).

Robert Dilts paid more attention than the founders to possible ecology issues. He taught his students to do an ecology check to find objections to the desired outcome. He asked clients to respond, on a conscious level, to questions about any problems or difficulties that might result if they had their desired outcome, or whether any part of them has an objection to having the outcome (Dilts, 1990).

Jonathan Rice also maintained that permanent change cannot be accomplished without addressing ecology considerations. However, because of his training in psychology, Rice paid even more attention than Dilts to the issues of ecology that always surround the revision of beliefs. While Dilts usually asked clients to describe their conscious thoughts about possible ecology problems, Rice focused more on understanding and resolving *unconscious* ecology objections to the desired state experience. He used both calibration skills and his extensive understanding of childhood development to reveal deeply hidden patterning and meaning that, unnoticed and unaddressed, would eventually nullify the changes the client wanted (J. Rice, personal communication, June 2011).

Because of his psychotherapeutic training, Rice was able to follow the trail of personal ecology and early belief formation into the intense and usually nebulous territory of imprinted early childhood experience. Rice probed into, and evoked conscious awareness of, the early childhood experiences and needs that were drivers for early decisions and essential behavior patterning that remained to become mysterious—and apparently unshakeable—adult dysfunction. Rice taught his students that through rigorous respect for the larger ecology of the client's experience across time, a practitioner's revisions in the client's old patterning will more naturally align with and support the fulfillment of the client's desired experience in the present and future (J. Rice, personal communication, June 2011).

RE-IMPRINTING

An imprint is a persisting constellation of VAKOG representations that is the consequence of a survived traumatic experience, usually occurring during early childhood. These traumas include life-threatening (or apparently life-threatening) moments of shock, loss, or pain. The memory of the experience and the accompanying emotions are "imprinted" on the nervous system, along with the decision the child made about the cause and meaning of the experience in a desperate attempt to make the traumatic situation understandable and, therefore, more endurable. This decision becomes a belief, usually out of consciousness, that guides the child's actions for the rest of his or her life.

Let us take as an example a child who survives an intensely frightening abandonment, either an all-at-once event or pain and loss a little bit at a time over a long period. The child may conclude, "I am not worth caring about." This decision helps the child to understand why things are the way they are, but it is horribly life limiting.

As discussed earlier, the experiences we learn to survive become the experiences upon which our continued survival will depend. It is precisely because a traumatic situation is experienced to be so life threatening, and then was survived, that for our creature brains it becomes a necessary key to further survival. Therefore, it becomes what I have labeled as "quarantined." "Quarantined patterning" remains untouched by later experience and learning. The neurological imprint of the traumatic experience, and the emotions, beliefs, and patterns of behavior that are associated with it, are fixed and made unavailable for revision; they become *unavailable for further learning,* no matter how many experiences may occur throughout the person's life that later contradict the original decision.

The creature brain does not care whether or not the human brain is happy; it cares only about its survival in physical reality. In the remarkable non-logic of creature-level association, the terrible pain of abandonment (in this example) becomes necessary for continued survival precisely because it could have been fatal, but was survived. Because this terrible pain has been survived, it becomes an experience profoundly associated with survival, and actually becomes *essential* for future survival. Something that is essential for basic survival cannot be permitted to change even a little bit, so the patterning that controls it will be quarantined. Once it becomes quarantined, unless there is an unusually effective intervention, the patterning will never change. Consequently, the core decisions/beliefs generated by this patterning will never really change, no matter what happens later. The person will go through his/her life both resisting and expecting abandonment, hoping and working for love while waiting to be unwanted and left. The quarantined imprint patterning will manifest itself as repeating isomorphic (things having the same shape) experiences, as similar situations occurring again and again in the person's life, and the person will develop a remarkable capacity to consistently make the "wrong choice" about partners, friends, and bosses.

Occasionally, certain life events may break through a person's quarantined patterning and revise outdated beliefs. For example, sometimes a "breakdown" will result in a "breakthrough" after a while. But this progression is rare. Normally, a person with a well-protected belief about his/her worthlessness can win a Nobel Prize, and all this will do is prove to him/her that even worthless people can become Nobel laureates.

There is good news, however: even quarantined imprints can be changed through skillful *re-imprinting.* Re-imprinting is a procedure to reorganize information availability and processing in the human nervous system in order to revise significant imprinted representations that form the basis of a person's identity, beliefs, and behavior. It can change patterns and neuro-linguistic programs no matter how long they have been running and how protected they may be in the human operating system.

Re-imprinting is a basic tool in every version and school of NLP. There are only minor differences between the basic steps of the procedure known as Changing Personal History, which is usually taught as a rudimentary skill, and the more advanced proficiency of re-imprinting. Both of these procedures involve creating and collapsing anchors to move from present-state to desired-state experiences. However, the intention—and therefore the actual progression—of the two procedures is different. The technique of Changing Personal History seeks only to add a resource that will allow the client's painful or unpleasant feelings about a past event to feel better in the present. (The name "Changing Personal History" is tongue-in-cheek, because of course the technique does not change anything historically. It simply provides a change of emotional states *about* the past.) In contrast, re-imprinting does not necessarily seek to make anything feel better or be better immediately (although it often has this effect). Re-imprinting is a much broader endeavor to revise a number of complex belief and identity-level meanings that have stabilized life-long limitations. During the process of re-imprinting, the practitioner seeks to understand and revise the interplay of whole clusters of out-of-date, hyper-stabilized beliefs. Re-imprinting is thus a process of significant internal map revision that is intended to integrate into a person's experience over time. It requires vastly greater rapport, experience, nuanced attention, and depth of inquiry on the part of the practitioner.

The technique of re-imprinting developed organically and independently in the work of both Robert Dilts and Jonathan Rice. Both men had a strong desire to be able to work with issues involving beliefs. Dilts developed the process of re-imprinting as a result of his association with Timothy Leary, the famous 1960s guru of consciousness transformation. In the early 1980s Leary studied NLP with Dilts to improve his abilities in public speaking, and they became friends.

Leary explained to Dilts his theory that much of our internal and external behavior is patterned from imprints. The theory of imprinting in animals comes from the work of Konrad Lorenz, for which he received the Nobel Prize in 1973. In discussions with Leary, Dilts realized that traumatic experiences during childhood frequently cause imprints that significantly affect the development of belief and identity across the span of an entire lifetime. This realization evolved into Dilts's technique of re-imprinting (Dilts, et al., 1990).

In his book *Changing Belief Systems with NLP* (1990), Robert Dilts explains that an imprint is a belief or an identity-forming experience that occurred in early childhood. The imprint is an archetype for how to feel and interact with others. Thus, one's early experiences affect one's present emotions and ability to relate with others. They also create associations between events and feelings—for example, between abuse and pleasure—that are not always appropriate or healthful for the child in the past or the adult in the present. In *Beliefs* Dilts states: "Research validates that often people who have been abused as children unconsciously get into relationships, as adults, that repeat their childhood experience. For example, often women who have been abused as children marry men who abuse them as adults. Males who were beaten as a child may abuse their own children. . . . People abused as children can imprint that this is the typical behavior associated with fathers, mothers, husbands or wives (Dilts, et al., 1990, p. 60).

Dilts writes, "if we can get back to the first belief and shift that one, everything else starts to rearrange itself" (Dilts, 1990, p. 116). Dilts describes Timothy Leary's breakthrough insight:

> Leary contended . . . that under the proper conditions, content that had been imprinted . . . could be accessed and reprogrammed, or 're-imprinted.' Leary considered imprints to be associated with certain biochemical states, and believed that if the state could be re-accessed through drugs (such as LSD) a person could be 're-imprinted' and substitute new experiences for those which had originally been associated during the initial imprinting period . . . . [After discussion with Dilts] Leary became

> interested in NLP and hypnosis as other methods to change imprints that avoided the uncertainties and ecological problems of LSD. (Dilts, 1996b)

Jonathan Rice developed his own methodology for re-imprinting independently of Dilts and Leary. He was not in contact with Dilts after 1978. In 1981 Rice met Shannon Sobel, a body worker who combined polarity therapy and Gestalt therapy, and he was invited to sit in on her client sessions. While observing Sobel's work Rice noticed profound age regression in the clients, and he and Sobel began to pay more attention to this process. They remembered Konrad Lorenz's study of animal imprinting at very early stages of development, and he and Sobel began to tease out elements of belief formation by the clients at the ages to which they had regressed (J. Rice, personal communications, November 2011 & January 2015).

For many years, Sobel had used bodywork to shift her clients into experiences of "age regression." An age-regressed state is a condition in which a person experiences present time through the emotions and belief filters of a much younger version of him/herself. In therapeutic situations, these regressions are typically made to childhood situations in which threat or trauma sparked the creation of beliefs that led to life-long suffering and limitation. As Sobel and Rice worked together, they developed a format that combined her bodywork with NLP techniques. They would use one room to explore their client's unwanted experience. They would then move the client to another room in which they would elicit and stabilize the resource states that, if integrated into the patterning of the unwanted present state, would result in a new integration that would open the way to the client's desired state. Then they would rapidly physically move the client from the second room back into the first one—thus "collapsing" the two different experiences into each other. Sobel referred to this process as a form of re-imprinting (J. Rice, personal communication, November 2011).

Shannon Sobel died in 1984. Rice was left with the question of how to help his clients access original imprinted states without the benefit of the body-based work that Sobel had provided. He found that by using the half-second eye access method, he was able to access original trauma states as reliably, and often more reliably, than when he and Sobel had accomplished this through her body-based interventions. Then, he could re-imprint the client with touch and other anchors while seated in one place (J. Rice, personal communication, November 2011).

There are some striking differences in the way that Rice and Dilts implemented the technique of re-imprinting. As described above, Dilts practiced re-imprinting mainly by using a walking timeline. In contrast, because his work was based on his experience as a psychologist, Rice conducted his re-imprinting processes within a more conventional-appearing, seated, psychotherapeutic interaction, using mostly touch rather than floor (spatial) anchors.

Also, Dilts paid less attention to the client's emotions. The Dilts formats were designed to attenuate the client's experience of unpleasant feelings. Rice, however, often centered his therapy on accessing emotional states as part of modifying the patterning that had made these experiences problematic for the client in the past. In accord with the latest research in psychology at that time, Rice found that the results of the change work could be deeper and longer lasting if the work involved an experience of emotional release that accompanied the cognitive restructuring (J. Rice, personal communication, November 2011).

Another difference in the re-imprinting methods of Dilts and Rice is the extent to which they included a format known as "re-imprinting others" in the system as a routine part of re-imprinting work. This format involves making changes in the client's present experience of others who were significant participants in the client's difficult or traumatic past experience.

Dilts believed that, since limiting beliefs are usually a consequence of the client's past interactions with people in the family or social system, it is useful to help the client to take resources to these significant others (Dilts, 1990). Dilts instructed the client to associate into—that is, to imagine seeing from the point of view of—a significant other in the past experience, and to view the incident from that other person's point of view. He asked the client to discern the positive intent of the other person's behavior in the situation. Dilts then found an appropriate resource and anchored it. The resource was then collapsed into the client's past experience by having the client physically step into the internally imaged other person on the spatial timeline that was already marked out on the floor. Dilts's students are taught to use this procedure—to collapse resource states into internal representations of the client's significant others—as a routine step in re-imprinting (Dilts, 1990).

Rice did not always find it a best practice to include the technique of re-imprinting significant others, so he did not teach it as a standard procedure. While he showed his students some illustrative demonstrations of finding "new" resources for others in the system, he was usually reluctant to rely on this technique to create better experience in the present. His preference was to have the client find a way to utilize the original experience as a basis for change in the present. For example, he believed that in some situations it was more useful for the client to continue to have access to the original memory so s/he could experience that s/he had choice regarding how s/he felt about what happened *despite* the actual facts of how the others behaved. As another example, it may be helpful for a client to understand that things might not have been different even if the others *had* behaved differently. Also, with re-imprinting as with all his methods, Rice's work was never based on a "recipe card" approach (i.e., one way of doing things that is presumed to be appropriate every time with every client) (J. Rice, personal communication, November 2011).

Jonathan Rice used NLP to improve the precision, effectiveness, and depth of his practice of psychotherapy. In the process he created a new paradigm, different from that of Grinder and Bandler or Dilts, that was neither conventional humanistic psychotherapy nor conventional NLP. By folding the new field of NLP into his experience as a psychologist and therapist, and by infusing and revising NLP with this same experience, Rice achieved a vital synthesis that strengthened and enriched both fields. Transformational NLP is largely based on the teachings of Jonathan Rice.

CHAPTER VI
Transformational NLP

The Influence of Jonathan Rice

Jonathan Rice applied many of the innovative discoveries of NLP in his clinical psychotherapy practice. It was the original Santa Cruz group around Bandler and Grinder that first correlated externally visible changes in physiology with reliable understanding, in real time, about how a person was operating internally to generate his or her experience. It was also the original group that discovered "strategies" (working with representational sequences that lead to particular outcomes of experience) and thereby revealed the representational operations within the mind, which the behaviorists had considered to be an unknowable "black box." Yet, after just a few years, much NLP training and practice was minimizing attention to these astounding discoveries and the remarkable behavioral and perceptual tools that were developed because of them. As John Grinder later complained, some of the schools that called themselves NLP ignored the spirit of what the founders had tried to do. The ones that came along later substituted easily-learned formulas in place of creative intervention (Grinder & Pucelik, 2013). Much important material was downplayed or just left behind.

Working on his own after the break-up of the Santa Cruz group, Jonathan Rice continued to use the full scope of original techniques within his psychotherapeutic process. Instead of viewing NLP as a set of stand-alone formulas for treating symptoms, Rice taught his students that mastery of the physiology-based perceptual/behavioral skill set was key to artful and rapid therapeutic success. He said, "When in doubt, follow the physiology!" He emphasized using multiple cues occurring outside of the client's conscious awareness and control, such as eye movements and other physiological indicators, to reveal and connect information about subtle components of the all-important intended positive outcomes that are always aspects of adaptation to early childhood trauma. Rice leaned on research from the field of childhood development to ground and organize the conceptual and emotional spaces within which he worked with ecology concerns and limiting beliefs. Through demonstration and example, Rice taught his students to eschew formulaic procedures in favor of working within the psychological context of each person's life (J. Rice, personal communications, April 1985).

In 1984 Rice was asked to be a trainer at Lynne Conwell's NLP Center for Advanced Studies in Tiburon, California, a training center that Conwell had acquired from its founder, Leslie Cameron Bandler. This is where Rice developed and refined the teaching that had evolved from his decade of experience with integrating NLP with his own worldview and practice of psychotherapy (J. Rice, personal communication, June 2011).

I became a student at the NLP Center for Advanced Studies in 1984, and took a Master Practitioner class taught by Dr. Rice. It was at this time, from Rice, that I learned the sitting-and-talking style that is so different from mainstream NLP.

In 1986 I attended the National Association of NLP Conference in San Francisco, and in the 1990s I attended other NLP conferences in Denver and Salt Lake City. It was my experience that while some of the techniques and clinical tools that were displayed at the conferences were inventive and clever, much of the material was shallow. Most of the presenters seemed to be unaware of the psychological underpinnings of the symptoms with which they were working, and they were apparently unconcerned with the psychological contexts within which they were operating. Additionally, the formulaic NLP they were promoting usually did not include much attention to, and regard for, the emotions related to a particular issue, or for the broader emotional life of the client. I was not attracted to this approach.

I had experienced something radically different at the NLP Center for Advanced Studies. Dr. Rice taught NLP from a position solidly within the context, history, and body of knowledge of the field of psychology, and his perspective was also based on years of direct clinical experience. In Rice's practice, he incorporated deep psychological knowledge and practical know-how into the powerful frameworks of

NLP change work, as well as used NLP to vastly enhance the scope and effectiveness of his clinical work. It appeared to me that Jonathan Rice's integrative and holistic approach was much more powerful than either mainstream NLP or conventional psychotherapy, and that it created deeper, more stable and permanent transformation in the client.

I had learned the usual variety of NLP techniques at the Center for Advanced Studies before studying with Rice. From Jonathan Rice I learned his "Core Sorting" format to access and work with representations from childhood trauma that are usually not in conscious awareness, and I learned his method of re-imprinting. But the most important thing I learned from Dr. Rice was how to do NLP-based change work in a psychological context. Some of his students were practicing psychotherapists or had studied in the field, but what Rice taught could also be learned without previous training in psychology. His lectures and live demonstrations of change work naturally included many of the concepts, frames of reference, vocabulary, and clinical descriptions of the therapeutic processes of a creative and highly experienced psychotherapist. In contrast with the mainstream NLP world at the time, Rice's students learned about child development theory and the primary markers for and consequences of childhood trauma. By watching Dr. Rice, I also learned about the stance of the therapist/client interaction, from which I later developed what I would call "a proper programmer stance." I learned from him how to be a good practitioner and therapist—someone whose scope of inquiry and capacity to respectfully hold the experience of the client are much broader than those of someone who is merely a good operator of NLP "change techniques." This paradigm, combining NLP and psychology, which originated with Dr. Rice and was passed on to me, has been the basis of my own teaching and practitioner work for the past thirty-five years.

Transformational NLP now includes a number of elaborations on and extensions of Rice's model, and although it borrows from and elaborates on both mainstream NLP and conventional psychotherapy, it has evolved to become a unique paradigm. It incorporates material drawn from, or inspired by, the metaphysics of the perennial philosophy such as described by Aldous Huxley (2009), the holographic model of the universe as explained by David Bohm (Friedman, 1997; Peat, 1997), the basic premises of twentieth-century quantum mechanics, my own evolution of Bert Hellinger's trans-generational, systemic constellation work, and many frames and methods—neuro-linguistic and otherwise—that are unique and are the product of my constant curiosity and creativity in the course of working with thousands of clients during my years in private practice.

Transformational NLP compared with Conventional Psychotherapy

There are some apparent similarities between Transformational NLP sessions and psychotherapy. In Transformational NLP, the practitioner and client are seated facing one another, in private, and conversing. Viewed from the perspective of conventional psychotherapy, this looks like the recognizable event called the therapeutic interaction. Yet, there are significant differences between the two approaches.

CONTENT VERSUS STRUCTURE OF EXPERIENCE

In conventional psychotherapy, the therapeutic interaction mainly involves talking about the content of the client's experiences and the emotions that accompany them. This discussion of content, possibly in combination with the therapist's observations, suggestions, or assistance with problem solving, generally constitutes the scope of the therapeutic interaction.

Transformational NLP may include much of this also, with the exception of problem-solving suggestions. However, as psychiatrist Bessel van der Kolk (2014) points out, "the act of telling the story doesn't necessarily alter the autonomic physical and hormonal responses of bodies" or change a person's behavioral patterns (p. 21). Self-defeating behavioral patterns are "not the result of moral failings or signs of lack of willpower or bad character—they are caused by actual changes in the brain" as the result of imprints of trauma (p. 3). Transformational NLP addresses these physiological as well as psychological issues.

During the conversation with a client, the Transformational NLP practitioner is continuously noticing the client's internal representational processes and events. We teach the practitioner to become adept at noticing and working with other-than-conscious accessing cues, the fleeting external markers that indicate how the person's nervous system is operating to sustain his or her unwanted experience. The practitioner uses these observations to reveal hidden patterns. S/he can then draw on this information to directly and indirectly cause changes within the patterning—the instructions that create the experience—so that it becomes possible for the client to have more and more of the experience that s/he desires. There is an intentional, precise, and ongoing revision of map and meaning, of identity, and of relationship with self and others. Thus, Transformational NLP works through attention to both the content and the representational structure of the client's experience.

TRANSFERENCE

Another key difference between Transformational NLP and conventional psychotherapy concerns the psychoanalytic process called transference. The Transformational NLP practitioner/client interaction may at times include some elements related to transference, but generally the practice of NLP-based change work is not based on the dynamics of conventional psychotherapeutic transference and counter-transference, does not involve explicit advice giving or problem solving, and is not critical of other persons in the client's present or past. Rather, the skillful Transformational NLP practitioner models for the client a way of holding and thinking about himself or herself that may be beyond the client's present capacity. The practitioner can do this by demonstrating the actual behavior and attitudes that s/he wishes the client to acquire. For example, the practitioner can regard the client with more respect than the client is able to have for him/herself. This provides the client with a new *external* reference for greater *internal* self-respect and self-appreciation.

The practitioner can also regard and make reference to the significant others in the client's personal history from a different perspective from that of the client. How the practitioner reacts (in the present) to these people (in the client's past) can begin to educate the client about possible alternative ways to think and feel about those individuals.

This is accomplished concurrently with direct and indirect reframing. "Direct reframing" is accomplished by simply redefining the client's experience (which I usually find presumptuous and rarely do), or by offering the client a chance to re-perceive events and behaviors, causes and apparent effects, in a new context or from a new viewpoint. "Indirect reframing" can be almost direct, for example by helping the client to recognize the intended positive outcome of his or her behavior. It can also be very indirect. For example, if the practitioner consistently gestures with one hand when discussing the reality of the client's always having operated from a motivation of "intended positive outcome," later on the practitioner can cause the client to unconsciously consider this possibility by simply gesturing with that same hand while discussing failures and mistakes. All of these tools accompany and support the ongoing activity of making representational revisions in the client's patterns for creating meaning and for generating external and internal behavior.

ATTENTION TO PERSONAL HISTORY AND FAMILY DYNAMICS

As in conventional psychotherapy, in my sessions with clients I am very attentive to the ups and downs of the client's personal history and the family dynamic. (This is unusual, if not unique, in the context of mainstream NLP-based change work.) It is my observation that most unwanted experience is stabilized by ecology concerns that involve both the need for personal survival and an equal, apparently competing need to ensure one's continued belonging within one's family of origin, no matter how painful such belonging may be.

However, there is a crucial difference between my methodology and that of most psychotherapists. Right from the start of any interaction with the client, I begin a continuing process of calibrating (observing and correlating) the person's physiology as it relates to the context of his or her factual family history. Through this calibration process, as well as through words, I seek information about the client's relationship to the family narrative, that is, the story a family tells about itself and about each of its relevant members, both living and dead. My goal is not only to identify and revise the client's out-of-date safety patterning (automatic, ongoing internal representations that were originally created to keep the child safe but are no longer beneficial for the adult), but also to use the tools of NLP to clarify and resolve any obstacles to the client's awareness of irrevocable belonging in the family system.[1]

In the course of doing this, I am also working to assist the client to gradually develop a different narrative, a revised interpretation, of his or her personal past—to show how that particular complex of past experiences, events, imprints, and decisions was a necessary path to recovering freedom and choice in the present, on the way to a greater fulfillment in the future. The goal is not to overcome or negate the past, but rather to incorporate it as part of the path to the future desired state. My objective is to reveal the client's commitment to growth and learning within his or her lifetime thus far, and to show the client that s/he now has the conscious choice to modify the trajectory of his or her life from now on.

COMPLETING THE EXPERIENCE

An important influence of psychotherapy on Transformational NLP is the endeavor to assist the client to complete the experience of the original painful trauma that continues to reverberate in his or her life despite all attempts to avoid or repress it. While the goal of helping the client to complete the experience—so that it can be left in the past and stop affecting the present—is common in psychotherapy, there are significant differences between the approach used by Transformational NLP practitioners and that of mainstream psychotherapists.

One very useful methodology practiced by some psychotherapists is catharsis, that is, encouraging the client to fully feel a past traumatic experience and express the deep emotions often associated with them which had until then been repressed or ignored. Typically, the goal of catharsis is to allow an emotional release, which often causes the memory of the trauma to fade and the affect from it to decrease. The intent of many psychotherapists is also to assist the client to find an increased sense of autonomy or agency, and possibly to have new cognitive understandings about the old experiences as well (Diamond, 2009).

However, working with clients, I have learned that the emotional relief, self-redefinition, and re-direction of thought gained through catharsis are partial and temporary, at best. Through catharsis, one does not generally complete the traumatic experiences to the extent that they can readily be re-patterned. Instead, the past experiences remain available to be repeatedly triggered into present awareness.

Moreover, I have observed the interesting phenomenon that repeated catharsis can condition the client's patterning to recurrently reactivate the unwanted past experiences in order to continue to make them available to be survived. As described in chapter I, our creature-level consciousness, of which we are not actually consciously aware, exists in an eternal "now." For the creature neurology, the experience of the threat and trauma has actually become linked to the experience of surviving the trauma. Old events are kept available to be reactivated, again and again, *right now,* in order to ensure that the organism will continue to survive the trauma, *right now.* While this programming fulfills the imperatives of a-temporal creature-level survival, it is obviously immensely disconcerting for the human being who is struggling to make sense of and attenuate the unpleasant thoughts, emotions, and events that are rising up so strongly in his or her present experience.

One of NLP's brilliant contributions was to uncover the actual structure of repression mechanisms, such as those discovered by Freud. In my practice, I notice both the content and the automatic representational structure of unwanted—but repeating—experiences, with the objective of making the internal, out-of consciousness events that generate these unwanted experiences available for changing. This allows me to communicate with the client's creature self, past self, and present self, so that the client's entire system can thoroughly register that the past traumatic experience was in fact survived. Through use of dissociation and anchors I can then recode the misperception of a retroactive threat of death, hence eliminating the illusory survival value of continued present reactivation of the past trauma.

Thus, the Transformational NLP practitioner can assist the client in completing the experience of heretofore resisted or blocked past traumas so that s/he can finally be released from their grip. Now the client can come into more and more rapport with himself or herself about the past events, and as a result s/he can move more easily toward more creative and constructive future experience. (When the relevant past traumatic events have occurred in previous generations of the family, I accomplish much the same thing through the intervention called family constellations, which will be discussed in a later section.)

In sum, Transformational NLP sessions are conducted in a context *resembling* psychotherapy, in that the practitioner and client sit together privately and talk about the client's issues. However, this is a superficial resemblance. During the Transformational NLP sessions, unlike in mainstream psychotherapy, there is a continuous revision of behavior, capability, belief, and identity through both verbal and representational means.

Transformational NLP Compared with Mainstream NLP

Transformational NLP incorporates all of the presuppositions and many of the techniques of mainstream NLP. Yet, there are substantial differences between Transformational NLP and the mainstream NLP approach.

TECHNIQUES VERSUS TRANSFORMATIONAL CONVERSATION

For most mainstream NLP practitioners, NLP is a collection of change techniques, an often quite extensive menu of procedures from which the practitioner can select any number of discrete, standardized interventions. The practitioner discovers the desired state, identifies the problem state, and then "runs a technique" that will change the client. In conventional NLP, in general, talking with the client is what one does to find out what technique to use to "fix" something.

Viewed through the lens of conventional NLP, a Transformational NLP session would often appear to involve little explicit "NLP." This is mainly because the skilled Transformational NLP practitioner does not rely solely on overt, standard procedures to revise the client's map of reality and change his or her relationship with self and life. I believe that it is critical for the wellbeing of the client that the practitioner take into account the broad scope of the psychological and emotional context of the client's experience rather than just jump in with powerful change techniques that may produce potential unwanted side effects.

Since a person's sense of identity and belief system provide his/her orientation in the world, it is best to change only what is necessary in order to dissolve resistance and progress toward the desired outcome. Also, a change in belief or identity is often followed by experiences of uncertainty, disorientation, and—sometimes—fear. It takes some time for the individual to adapt to the experience of not encountering accustomed limitations or of having significantly different presuppositions about life. It is therefore important for the practitioner to pay attention to the maintenance of homeostasis even while simultaneously operating to destabilize unwanted patterning.

The less the quantity of revision, the easier it will be for the client's system to hold the change, and the less difficulty there will be with maintaining a stable, yet updated, personal ecology. Therefore, when modifying internal and external behavioral patterns, my goal is to provide the least amount of revision that is sufficient to cause and stabilize desired changes. I pay close attention to how much change work can be done without destabilizing identity coherence more than is useful in the moment. This is best accomplished by using subtle approaches most of the time and explicit change techniques only sparingly. When they are used in Transformational NLP, standardized procedures serve mainly to stabilize and secure revisions that have already been introduced into the client's cognitive and emotional processing through a continual flow and inter-mixing of more subtle methods.

My work with clients involves an ongoing interplay of information gathering and reframing about past events. If there is great rapport between the practitioner and the client, reframing can be accomplished almost as a background activity that only occasionally moves to the foreground of the interaction with the client. In addition to nearly non-stop reframing (which is essentially non-stop revision of past, present and future), I employ subtle—and sometimes more overt—"change techniques" as they are needed and appropriate.

In the course of the session's conversation, the Transformational NLP practitioner pays close attention to the structure as well as the content of the client's experience. Throughout the session, the practitioner is continually reorganizing the client's internal representational processes. There is a continual, in-the-moment revision of habitual or imprinted representational processing that has locked the client in past pain and complicated, or prevented, movement toward his or her desired future experience. The client's patterns of perception, thinking, emotion, and behavior are thus modified even without recourse to overt techniques. When techniques do come into play, they are as much as possible seamlessly embedded in the context of the conversational interaction.

INTENDED POSITIVE OUTCOMES

Like both Jonathan Rice and Robert Dilts, Transformational NLP teaches that an important part of the practitioner's work is to ensure that the truly benign, protective intentions beneath past limitations are respected and incorporated into new perceptions and decisions. By promoting a respectful and appreciative understanding of what I call the intended positive outcomes of problem states and experiences, the Transformational NLP practitioner supports clients to be more in rapport with themselves regarding their previously automatic reactions to fear and pain, over which they had no choice at the time. When people no longer impelled to disrespect or attack their past and present experience, they feel less and less at odds with themselves, and this in turn greatly eases the healing movement toward the desired state. My experience is that it is much easier to imagine and stabilize future success and well-being if one is relieved of perceptions of past failure. Also, by encouraging—and even requiring—that the client hold his or her previous choices and experience with proper respect, the practitioner opens the way for the client's unconscious to release lingering objections to the changes that come with the fulfillment of the desired state.

In conventional NLP, the concept of original positive intention often includes an operational orientation toward destroying old meanings and limits. In my work with clients, in contrast, I point to the validity and purposefulness of all experience, however negative, painful, or limiting it was or is experienced to be. My intention is to cause the client to reevaluate past experiences and situations that have always been labeled as examples of the client's most severe weakness, shortcoming, or failure, and by doing so to notice that the past events and patterns were, without exception, the best possible solutions to crises of survival and personal validity. At no point is there an intention to wipe out the previous descriptions of self and the world, or to simply obliterate old patterning for creature-level survival or soul-level devotion to all that has come before. Instead, as discussed above, a primary objective of this change work is to bring the client into an experience of deep and respectful rapport with the previous versions of themselves, so that there is nothing about them that needs to be abandoned or destroyed.

This concept of intended positive outcome (IPO) takes the notion of original positive intention somewhat further than the teachings of either Dilts or Rice. Transformational NLP underscores the principle that *all* experience, and *all* behavior, *without exception*, are sourced from a positive intention that made total sense at the time.

WORKING WITH ECOLOGY

Transformational NLP also offers additional perspectives on the questions of ecology and so-called ecology objections to change. Commonly, NLP practitioners view ecology objections as conscious and unconscious systemic concerns about the possible negative future consequences of present positive change. This perspective is important in my practice as well. However, in my work there is an added element. Although I am asking the client about the future, I am also seeking to provide the client with yet another way to more positively reassess his or her *past.*[2] While conventional attention to ecology focuses on avoiding or minimizing future loss, my approach includes attention to future opportunities as a means of re-affirming the necessity and wisdom of past choices, no matter how painful and costly those old choices have been revealed to be. The goal is to show how the past—whatever it contains—leads directly to the desired future. Thus, I use inquiry about future concerns to even more deeply reconfirm the intended positives within all of the client's past limitations. This approach does not replace more conventional, future-oriented ecology checking, but works in parallel with it.

In addition, I have observed that, in actuality, ecology concerns are frequently a continuing but retroactive attempt on the part of the client's system to *forestall negative developments in the past* (developments that may or may not have actually occurred). The client has been confusing future, present, and past, although not consciously, and doing so in ways that are detrimental to what s/he truly wants.

Similarly, regarding desired life outcomes that have remained blocked or unfulfilled for any significant time, it is almost impossible for a human being to think about the desired positive experience without immediately—instantly—loading up some of the pictures and soundtracks that are associated with past frustration and failure. This is not a faulty operation—it is merely evidence of old safety patterning at work, and it is this very safety patterning that has been blocking the client's movement and fulfillment in this area of his or her life.

Transformational NLP change work subtly assists the client to adjust this amalgamation of past, present, and future representations (which are producing the client's thoughts and feelings *now*) so that they become more aligned with the client's desired outcome. The adept Transformational NLP practitioner will notice and re-sort the unconscious internal pictures and sounds that produce the conscious negative feelings. The past can be put in the past—visually, verbally and spatially—and the future can be opened to resourceful imagination and exploration. These changes can be made obvious to the client, or they can be left just outside of conscious attention, as parts of what has seemed to be just a straightforward conversation about present desires and difficulties. Because it works with both unconscious structure and conscious content simultaneously, Transformational NLP can seem like magic.

RE-IMPRINTING

I agree with Jonathan Rice that although re-imprinting the parent or significant other person can sometimes be a useful intervention, it is not always the best way to resolve the present experience of past pain. For me, even more than for Rice, re-imprinting others is an intervention to be used only as a last resort. Improperly handled, the technique of re-imprinting others can mislead the client into thinking that the continuing bad effects of past negative experiences are immutable unless the other person(s) *will have been different* in the past.

While Transformational NLP, like conventional NLP, changes the client's experience of and meanings about what happened in the past, I usually do so without recourse to methodology that would appear to revise the facts of the experience of the client's younger self. Like Rice, I generally avoid asking the client to imagine others behaving differently in the past. I will lament that they did not, and wonder aloud what it might have taken for them to do better, but I will not ask the client to cancel anything out. I prefer to let the original version of events stand, and to assist the client to make new and more useful meaning in the present *despite* the way the others acted in the past. This distinction between revision of past events and revision of present meaning about past events is crucial. While for Dilts the goal of re-imprinting significant others seems to be a way to make the past be better in the client's mind now, my goal is rather to support the client's *present-tense choice to create a better experience now, even though the past happened the way it did.* My primary objective is to help the client realize that s/he has more choice now.

Another reason that I hesitate to re-imprint significant others is to preserve identity coherence. It seems that one reason that people (unconsciously) maintain their limitations is to sustain evidence of past injustice and injury. An intended positive outcome of someone's maintaining hurt in the present is actually his or her profound reaching for, and even insistence on, acquiring change—*in the past.* I believe that it is important to respect the positive intention behind this continuing assertion of past damage, and therefore of being aggrieved, because from the time that the adaptations occurred, the aggrieved status has functioned as a central part of the foundation of the client's sense of self. Human beings frequently turn their lives into living memorials of past loss and trauma.

The technique of re-imprinting the parent is a form of personal identity revision, often radically so. Because *identity* is about who and what we unconsciously declare ourselves to be the same as and not the same as, revising one's internal representations of one's past bad parent effectively revises some of the internal representations (e.g., remembered visuals) that have functioned as a source of "I am *not* like that" identity stability. To ensure that the client maintains identity coherence, we should be careful to use re-imprinting of parents, or any other direct (i.e., explicitly anchored) re-imprinting of authorities or perpetrators involved in past neglect or abuse, only very prudently. Even then, I believe that we should only take resources to the client's representations of the parent when that parent was himself or herself a child—being careful to then imagine the parent-as-child growing up again, to quickly become the parent-as-revised-parent—so the client can sense the positive possibilities that might have unfolded for everyone involved.

While I do not seek to substitute revised facts (in the client's mind) for the actual historical data, I do want to induce a feeling of a positive developmental path whenever possible. We can facilitate the revision of the client's map so that the system acquires access to new experiences or meanings. The facts remain while the feelings and meanings are opened to change now. We can then transfer these resource feelings back to the younger self. Doing this does not change the client's actual history, but it does change the client's experience of that history.

When the client is able to achieve this crucial re-perception of past events, I know that there is also a newly available "dis-integration" or "de-coherence" of the old automatic patterns, mechanisms, and instructions for creating meaning. It is not simply that the client's conscious self has discovered a new or reframed interpretation of the past—it is also that the unconscious meaning-making machinery is momentarily disorganized at a deep level. It is in these moments that the methodology of Neuro-Linguistic Programming, in contrast to simple talk psychotherapy, becomes indispensable. This momentary de-coherence, or breakdown, of the mechanisms for meaning very often opens the way to revise the patterning (via reframing, re-imprinting, etc.) that has been generating negative experience. It affords us an opportunity for revisions in meaning and emotions that can be stabilized in service of the client's desired future.

METAPHORICAL TIMELINE

Parallel to the "walking timeline" developed by Robert Dilts, I developed the "metaphorical timeline" for seated interactions with clients. This is an invisible, imaginary line of time that is explicitly marked out in actual, physical space, and as a result of which all of the past and future are within range of an easy glance to the left and right.

When people externalize and visually objectify a representation of themselves having their own experience, they naturally acquire perspective and distance about past events that went into creating the painful previous experiences. This is especially important when the practitioner is in the process of assisting a client's unconscious to disclose information about important aspects of past events that have been generalized into safety programming that manifests as self-limiting patterns that continuously repeat themselves in his or her life.

People often unconsciously generate pictures of what happened in the past in the same external physical space they use to represent experiences in the present. This keeps the emotions of past trauma alive in the present. The practitioner can change the location of the representations to mark out that the past events are actually in the past instead of the present. Even a slight gesture toward the client's left side—which is where the brain usually codes that it happened in the past—while mentioning past events, has a strong meaning that conveys to the unconscious that the events under discussion are *not* located in the here and now.

By using casual-appearing hand gestures and subtle changes in voice tempo and tone while discussing the past and imagining the future, the practitioner is able to directly point out the location to the left of the client where past events occurred and the location to the right of the client that holds representations of the future. This lets the unconscious know, to the client's immense relief, that the past is not now and it is different from the future. It generates a number of nearly spontaneous revisions in the client's felt sense of the presence of the past. The result is that past events are now perceived as being in the past rather than the present, with the client now poised to turn a milestone corner in the present. The client is now on the way to a better future experience that only requires the passage of some time to have unfolded positively and correctly. In this way, a skilled practitioner is able to gradually re-sort and re-narrate a client's lifetime of experience.

This is usually the first time clients have been specifically instructed to create a dissociated picture of themselves. Most people have never been asked to make, let alone to move, an internal visual representation of their present self. It is a startling discovery for the clients that they have a choice about the mechanics and representational characteristics of these internal visual events. Although they may have had the experience of picturing *content* intentionally in a "guided visualization" activity, almost certainly nobody had ever instructed them to make a *structural* (location and distance) change in their internal visual experience. Discovering the possibility of making such representational maneuvers has profound consequences and implications for a person's capacity to be at choice about his or her experience. (See Appendix D for an example of how Carl uses a metaphorical timeline.)

CHAPTER VII

Unique Perspectives of Transformational NLP

While Transformational NLP builds upon methodologies offered by NLP and psychotherapy, it also incorporates perspectives that are unique. Within the Transformational NLP paradigm, the practitioner's interaction with the client is enhanced by a variety of specific behavioral and perceptual skills that are not part of or based on either the conventional NLP or the conventional psychotherapeutic models.

Rapport

A main differentiator between Transformational NLP and conventional change work, both NLP and psychotherapeutic, is over-arching attention to—and unique perspectives on—multiple aspects of rapport. The under-pinning and main goal of TNLP teachings can be summed up in the phrase: "To increase the experience of Rapport with Self, Rapport with Other-Selves, and Rapport with Life Itself."

The founders and leaders of mainstream NLP recognized the importance of rapport between the practitioner and the client, and it became basic to the practice of good NLP. Rapport skills cover a broad range of perceptual and behavioral abilities that enable deep connection with those with whom we are interacting, on the unconscious as well as the conscious levels. This is accomplished by use of subtle behavioral (visual, auditory and spatial) signals—which are based on finely tuned perceptual skills—by the practitioner to the client's unconscious through such techniques as mirroring, matching, and pacing (Dilts, 1980; Lewis & Pucelik, 1982; McClendon, 1989).

In Transformational NLP, we emphasize that "rapport" is more basic than simply liking someone, or being likeable oneself, or being agreeable or pleasant, or showing empathy and caring, or making adjustments in the content of conversation. Creating and maintaining good rapport necessitates communicating to another person's creature neurology, on an other-than-conscious level, that it is in a safe environment in which the flow of experience will continue to be aligned with its well-being. Creature-level rapport is based on an absence of threat. It is generated by providing someone's creature brain with the experience of being in the presence of a rough approximation of itself. The creature brain has no ego and no voice, but if it did it would continually ask itself, when in proximity to another creature, "Am I with like kind?" If the answer is affirmative, then creature fear and threat are naturally reduced, allowing the human to feel more trusting and open with the other person. When the "creature self" is less wary and on alert about "what" s/he is in proximity to and interacting with, then the "human self" has an easier time relating to others.

In Transformational NLP we also take the understanding and application of rapport to another level. We do everything we can to encourage our students and clients to experience what we call "rapport with self." The experience of "rapport with self" is more complex than the creature-level rapport described above. It is a distinctly human, fourth-brain experience. Being in good rapport with oneself is not the same thing as liking or loving oneself. We can describe rapport with self as the awareness that one has the right to exist, that one has value and a meaningful purpose in life and the world, that one has the capability to connect with, respect, and appreciate the different (possibly conflicting) aspects of oneself, and that one has the capacity to experience connection with others.

An important component of what we call "rapport with self" concerns finding and holding a stance of appreciation and respect for oneself in the past and present, notwithstanding the self-limiting thought and behavior patterning that one would like to change. The Transformational NLP practitioner supports clients to be more understanding of and compassionate with themselves regarding their previously automatic reactions to fear and pain, over which they had no choice at the time, and which has engendered patterning that they would now like to modify. This sense of rapport with oneself, when a person is no longer impelled to disrespect or attack his or her past and present experience, allows clients to be less and less at odds with themselves, and this in turn greatly eases the healing movement toward the desired state.

Conventional NLP is very effective in assisting the client to achieve a desired state. It contains many powerful tools for "annihilating blocks" and "overcoming limitations" of the present state. In the process of using these tools, however, mainstream NLP can convey the message to clients that their main shortcoming has been a lack of desire and ability to defeat some aspect of themselves and their natural inclinations. While the desired outcomes might be important and useful for the person within a narrow range of current life necessity, the process itself can be disrespectful and even damaging to the larger scope of a person's life and relationship with him/herself over time.

It is not entirely beneficial for a person's wellbeing and self-image to revise limiting patterning without also respecting and appreciating the previous versions of themselves. Rapport with ourselves is based on including (in other words, "consenting to the facts of") *all* of our experience in the past and present, including those aspects that are disappointing or painful, despite our instinct to resist or deny negative and painful experiences. When we are at odds with our experience, we are unavoidably at odds with ourselves. To be in rapport with ourselves and with our experience, it is helpful to acknowledge that we are the creator of our experience—and to respect and appreciate all the brilliance that went into our creation of who we were in the past and who we now are in the present. This understanding can empower us to change in the way we want, enjoyably and gracefully, without having to go to war with parts of ourselves. In my classes and therapy sessions, I assist my students and clients to come into more rapport with, and appreciate, all versions of themselves: who they are in the present, and also who they were in the past and who they are becoming in the future.

In Transformational NLP, "Rapport with Other-Selves" includes the conventional NLP rapport skills, but it goes far beyond that skill-set. I teach my students that rapport with clients is based on the practitioner including and consenting to and respecting *all* of the client's experiences, no matter how negative and painful. For change work to be permanent and for it to become seamlessly integrated into the client's psyche, it is necessary for both the practitioner and the client to acknowledge and respect the original positive intention of the unwanted behavior. It is important for the practitioner and the client to understand that people always do the best they can with the alternatives they have available on their map of life. Therefore, they should acknowledge and value the efforts of the past versions of themselves that had done the work of acquiring and perfecting the best possible programming under the circumstances. The adept Transformational NLP practitioner has rapport with—and teaches the client to have rapport with—everything that falls within the range of the client's experience, past and present, as well as that which they both desire for the client's future.

To experience "Rapport with Life Itself" is to have a state of mind in which one is not at odds with the processes, events, or apparent outcomes of life. This state of mind must persist even if—and especially when—one is working diligently to radically change these events. There is little to be gained by attacking the mirror that reflects our choices and intentions back to us. We presuppose that the processes of life have no faults, and that the mechanisms of feedback about our state of affairs, individually and collectively, are reliable although and because they "lack compassion." There is an adage in the Human Potential movement: "If gravity were compassionate, no one would ever be able to trust walking." Every human must learn to respect gravity as an entirely reliable teacher and irreplaceable aid to learning about a foundational aspect of the human skill set—walking upright. Similarly, having "Rapport with Life Itself" is having an awareness that we are always supported in all of our learning in this world. Without this understanding, life is a struggle that is cruel and unfair. With this stance, life is a precious opportunity to acquire more and more wisdom and alignment with Natural Law (however hard won and heart-breaking the learning may be) as a beloved child of the Universe.

In order to be able to encourage clients to learn to experience rapport with self, others, and life in general, practitioners must first be able to experience such multi-level rapport within themselves. At NLP Marin the classes are focused on the personal transformation of our students, whether they are proceeding along a "practitioner track" or not. We teach an array of innovative personal and professional skills in the course of supporting the fulfillment of each student's human and spiritual potential. This is accomplished without asking people to accept any dogma or discipline, or suggesting that individuals can improve their lives and circumstances by turning against themselves or others. The main channel through which this transformation occurs is the experience of increasing rapport with oneself, with other selves, and with Life itself. [See Appendix E for a description of how Transformational NLP promotes personal transformation.]

Practitioner Stance

In the model of Transformational NLP, much of the client's change is facilitated through what we describe as the therapist's "practitioner stance." The practitioner stance is a self-defined body of values and presuppositions about oneself and one's relationship with life. This constellation of beliefs, values, and commitments goes considerably beyond conventional prescriptions such as having good rapport or unconditional positive regard.

As an example, one's practitioner stance can include attention to making sure that one is working with one's "proper weight." This concept is inspired by the teaching of Bert Hellinger. It refers to a person's expression of energetic presence and influence, which are a function of the self-respecting assessment of his or her life experience. For Hellinger, these qualities and capabilities develop as a consequence of certain kinds and intensities of life experience. In Hellinger's construct, a semi-literate person who worked in a factory for thirty years to support his or her family would likely have more weight than a college student who pursues a deep study of something but has little life experience or a highly educated and accomplished professional who has never participated directly in the raising and support of children. Other factors that add to one's weight are one's age, history of service, training, and general experience of participation in the ups and downs of life.[1]

In Transformational NLP, to work with one's proper weight refers to the ability and responsibility of practitioners to ensure that they do not assert either more or less of this weighted life authority, or "phenomenological gravity," than they actually have. A practitioner who asserts more weight than is properly his or hers is generally specious and unbearable, while one who asserts less is usually not sufficiently useful to the ones whom s/he seeks to serve. For example, it has been my experience that although s/he has not lived long enough to acquire much weight, a twenty-three-year-old practitioner with a good sense of proper weight can do very effective and respectful work with a client forty or more years his or her senior. Without correctly calibrating and occupying the proper weight, the young practitioner would likely slide into a stance of lightweight uselessness or insulting pseudo-authoritative unpleasantness.

Other aspects of practitioner stance include conscientious attention to participating with the client from a place—a stance—that recognizes that the client is a soul who is equally wise, creative, and free. Although the client may not recognize these attributes in him/herself, the practitioner must always maintain this perspective as part of assisting the client to acknowledge and more deeply incorporate an awareness of his or her own validity. Moreover, the Transformational NLP practitioner has a conscious commitment to always hold the client and the client's experience with more respect and appreciation than the client may be able to generate for him/herself at the moment.

A proper practitioner stance also includes the presupposition that there will be a positive sum relationship between the practitioner and the client. This is a foundational stance that the practitioner assumes in relation to life, others, and oneself. In this paradigm, the practitioner's intention to benefit from the interaction is the very foundation of a respectful relationship. The benefit for the practitioner includes, for example, learning and growing, feeling fulfillment in achieving agreed-on goals, and the unfolding of a deep connection with another person. In practical terms, the nature of the positive sum interaction eliminates the need for the practitioner to guard against assuming either a victimized or a perpetrating stance in relation to the client. The deep respect for all human experience that is required in a "proper practitioner stance" enables the practitioner to forgo the seduction of self-importance in relation to the client.

At NLP Marin, we do not offer a formula or procedure through which students are instructed to find this place of valuing and respecting all of human experience. Instead, I try to provide a continuing modeling of this life stance, both explicitly and implicitly, in everything I teach. In the presence of a properly expressed practitioner stance, the client's resistance to his or her previous experience—as well as inappropriate attachment to well-intended but unproductive attempts to "overcome" the past—gradually dissolves. This is because, in Transformational NLP all attention paid to past experience actually operates not to focus on old wrongs, but rather to resolve old resistance to present and future solutions.

Practitioner Desired Outcomes

Other shifts in the views of the Transformational NLP practitioner (in order to appropriately assist the client) involve what I call programmer outcomes or goals. One of the main practitioner objectives is to directly and indirectly educate the client about who s/he really is in relation to the life issues that are at hand. Our foundational presupposition is that the individual is a spiritual being and the creative source of his or her full experience. With this view, one learns to expand one's ability to love oneself and to experience others as a mirror and even an aspect of that self. This presupposition is rarely presented explicitly, yet it underlies all discussion and interaction. During a session, the skilled practitioner continually weaves together multiple representational and linguistic interventions that accomplish this goal.

Another key programmer outcome concerns the practitioner's perception of different meaning associated with the client's past and present, and how it is that this path leads to the client's desired future. The Transformational NLP practitioner is taught to always presuppose that the client's unwanted present experience—no matter how great its pain or long its duration—is always better (more bearable, more survivable, somehow more favorable) than what it replaced in the past. We presuppose that all unwanted present state realities are the legacy of fulfilled choices regarding a previous desired state. The present problems are merely brilliant solutions that have over-stayed their welcome.

By presupposing this out-of-date intended positivity, the practitioner can add new information into the client's system without the practitioner having to set himself or herself at odds with anything in the client's previous learning and patterning. These additions and adjustments may be accomplished both overtly and covertly. Overtly, the practitioner discusses with the client what s/he would like and interacts with the client to help conceive the desired future. However, even when the future is not explicitly the topic of discussion, and even without the client's conscious awareness, the skilled practitioner maintains an internal, steady intention about and imaging of that future for the client. The practitioner makes his or her own internal representations (VAKOG) of the client's desired state.

As discussed in the next chapter, in terms of a world view that is more quantum than Newtonian, there is no distinction between objective and subjective reality; there is no "in here" versus "out there." Although most people are still governed by mainly Newtonian reality expectations, my observations over the course of my many years in practice confirm the view of many quantum scientists and philosophers that the thoughts of one person can influence the thoughts and behavior of another. Within the focused and profoundly benign field of a session of change work, the practitioner has an extraordinary opportunity to help co-imagine, and therefore to help co-create, the client's desired state. While externally the client and practitioner may be discussing the client's past, and may be paying explicit attention to what has not been working in the client's life, a portion of the masterful Transformational NLP practitioner's inner attention is always directed toward finding the images, sounds, and feelings that can best be used to encourage the client's system to realign itself with the fulfillment of his or her desired future experience.

When I am working with a client, my internal representations of the client's past and future experiences are not necessarily specific, but they are sufficiently clear that, in their presence, the client's system is encouraged to release objections and resistance to appropriate re-solution toward what the client is consciously choosing. In the course of doing this, I also assist the client to experience emotionally what life will be like in the desired future state, and to change his or her heart and mind about the past and present by viewing them as the path to that desired future. The practitioner can use his or her own perceptions and responses to the client's past pain to create a template, or foundation, upon which the client will begin to spontaneously generate new meanings about his or her personal history. Although I accomplish much of the process described above purely internally—that is, within my own awareness as the practitioner—I am careful to continually calibrate and confirm the accompanying changes in the client's external physiology and behavior.

Respecting All Experience

Our students are taught that as practitioners, they must respect all of the client's experiences, even those experiences that are extremely negative and painful. The word "respect" is most often used to indicate approval and high regard. However, this is far from my use of the word in this case. There is only one usage of the word "respect" that directly conveys how I mean it to be used in the context of transformation change work. It conveys the meaning of "recognize and acknowledge the significance" of the experience or person. An analogy is, "They say that an old sailor has learned to respect the sea." In this sentence, it does not at all matter whether the old sailor approves of the sea, or if he admires it or holds it in high regard. These are not relevant states or meanings for sailors as they accomplish their work. The sea will not be affected by the sailor's attitude about it. However, the sea definitely affects the sailor's wellbeing and progress on it. The sea is very big; the sailor is small compared to it.

In like fashion, the proficient Transformational NLP practitioner must respect the experience of the client. Without this respect, progress is questionable and the client's life becomes just an obstacle that impedes the practitioner's success. If the practitioner happens to admire the client and the client's experience through life, then so much the better, but this is not a necessary condition. When proper respect is present, admiration or the lack of it is almost a moot issue. The important factor is that practitioner occupies a properly respectful stance in relation to the client's life experience, including all its facets and including everyone who has participated in it with the client. For example, if the client has or had a tremendously cruel and abusive parent, it is essential that the practitioner be able to respect this parent—not condone or approve, but simply *respect*, as it is meant in this distinctive and incredibly important way.

Perception of the Nature and Meaning of the Past

Most people in Western culture, including most NLP practitioners, regard the past as a *fait accompli*, a fixed reality that has caused the present. However, what "actually happened" in the past is malleable, shaped by a person's selective memory. There are billions of facts in one's immediate environment that occur every second of one's life. Cellular biologist Bruce Lipton writes that the subconscious mind processes some 20,000,000 environmental stimuli per second, but only forty of them are interpreted by the conscious mind in the same second (Lipton, 2005). Humans must select a set of very few facts to perceive and provide the narrative and meaning that they give to the past.

Nevertheless, to maintain identity coherence, people must experience their identity—who they are—as the product and natural progression of a story of what occurred in their past. Psychologist Stanley B. Klein (2001) points out that the self is not only a concept or an image, but also one's memory about oneself and one's life. "Our sense of self is very much tied up with the 'story' of what we have experienced and what we have done." This view goes back to John Locke, who in the seventeenth century wrote that the self consists entirely in the continuity of memory. David Hume in the eighteenth century argued that "our self-narrative also includes events that we know *must* have happened, given what we *do* remember—whether they actually happened or not" (Kihlstrom, Beer, & Klein, 2001). Sigmund Freud in the twentieth century added that the important memories are stored in the unconscious and are not always consciously accessible. Carl Rogers was probably the first to study the self as a memory structure empirically, and his work has been replicated and continues to be expanded upon through the present time (Kihlstrom, Beer, & Klein, 2001). As Harvard professor emeritus of English, Paul John Eakin, points out, memory of the narrative of our lives is "not only literally essential to the continuation of identity, but also crucial in the sense that it is constantly revising and editing the remembered past to square with the needs and requirements of the self we have become in any present" (Eakin, 2000, pp. 293–94).

Transformational NLP assists the client to change the meaning of the past so that this meaning becomes congruent with a future in which his or her desired positive changes are fulfilled. Obviously, the changed meaning of the past and revised content of the future are created and exist in the "right now" of the client's interaction with the practitioner. The Transformational NLP approach allows the client to perceive that a different and better future experience is automatically unfolding because of, rather than despite, past events.

As described above, in my practice I assist the client to transform objections about the past experience into an understanding that they were previous solutions that are now outdated. I teach the client to respect and appreciate the past as a previously fulfilled desired state. Current problems, along with all the limiting behaviors and thoughts that go with them, are merely obsolete and fossilized past solutions. When we "re-solve" the fossilized past, we are actually revising the meaning-making machinery that was itself the source of the unwanted previous experience. Inappropriate or destructive past behavior and events are revealed to be our best previous attempts to move toward our present choices and new possibilities for congruently achieving our true desired state. Through reframing, and by re-representation of past situations and events, clients are supported to now perceive the past as part of a path to an inevitable positive future. I want my clients to recognize—and actually experience—that they have created a past that has operated flawlessly to catalyze certain new choices that will inevitably open into an experience of future fulfillment.

As discussed previously, one of the main practitioner goals in Transformational NLP change work is to achieve the most identity revision possible so as to be in alignment with desires and intentions for the future, while simultaneously assuring that the client can maintain the essential elements of his or her identity coherence. We can accomplish identity revision through the processes of "reweighting" the brain neurons that store the representations that coalesce to become our narrative of the past. Neuroscientist Sebastian Seung in his landmark work *Connectome* (2012) uses the term "reweighting" to refer to the selective strengthening or weakening (or even the creation or elimination) of connections among brain nerve synapses. As neuroscientist Jeffrey Satinover explains in his work *The Quantum Brain* (2001), "Depending on their weights, the connections either enhance the signal they are transmitting or diminish it" (p. 20). It is experience that modifies the neural weights and connections. The Transformational NLP practitioner provides this experience through the techniques of reframing and re-imprinting as well as other anchor-based methodologies. This process can change the feeling and meaning of what happened, as it is experienced in the present. It changes the clients' relationships both with actual past events and with themselves in the past.

When we revise the apparent meaning of past events, we also revise the meaning of the results that they have caused to manifest in the present. While on one level past facts cannot be changed, the present meanings about the facts can be changed. The present meaning of the past facts is the same as the present result. If we change the meaning of past facts, we can change the present result. Hence, we can actually revise the results of past facts, as for example when a client no longer identifies himself or herself as being a victim or even a survivor, but rather as the creative consciousness at the source of his or her experience.

This process comes to the edge of replacing the official facts with different facts. When we put our attention on other facts or aspects of the past, not only does the meaning of the facts change, but we can view the facts in a context that modifies the perception of the actual facts themselves. Through reframing and re-imprinting, the present thus changes the past. The different present state necessitates a revised perception of the past, and this new perception actually brings the client to the border of a different narrative of the past. Thus, the Transformational NLP practitioner helps the client to radically transform his or her relationship with that internal vortex of memories and emotions that is usually labeled "the past." The goal is to empower the client to view the past not as a fixed source of immutable loss, but rather as a dynamic wellspring of creative decision-making and learning.

This approach to the past is supported by the views of Nobel Laureate Daniel Kahneman, the founder of behavioral economics. Kahneman explains that there is a profound difference between the experience of being happy and remembering the experience of being happy. The experiencing self lives in the present, but the remembering self is a storyteller. They are two different selves. Our memory tells us stories. A crucial part of the remembered story is how it ends. A story is defined by changes, significant moments, and endings. Most of our life experiences are lost to memory. We consider ourselves happy if we remember a good story rather than remember the experiences themselves (Kahneman, 2010).

Since the past exists only in the client's mind *now*, while we cannot change the facts of what happened in the past, we can reweight and revise the very representations that generate the meaning of those events in the present. What really happened is not as important as what "what happened" means to us *now*. With change work such as reframing, re-imprinting, and representational reweighting, we can revise the feeling and meaning of the past, which amounts to changing the narrative without deleting or denying the facts. If we consider the present moment to be how the story ends, as Kahneman maintains, a happier ending in itself changes the story of the past.

Hope for a Better Past

One of the most curious features of human beings is their unconscious but persistent hope that the past (or some parts of it) will have been different than it was. In NLP, it is common knowledge that when people who want to change pain-sustaining thought and behavior patterns have great difficulty changing, there may be an "ecology problem," or concern about the possible unwanted consequences of otherwise good changes. In conventional NLP, the locus of attention for all ecology-related losses is concern about the future: What is it that we value that might be compromised or lost in the future as a consequence of new choices and changes that are made in the present? Very often the answers to this and related ecology concerns have to do with loss of relationship, loss of financial stability, loss of opportunity or freedom, and so on. This inquiry makes complete common sense, but my experience has taught me that something else is involved, something that limits present change even more than caution (both conscious and other-than-conscious) regarding possible future loss. That something else is the entirely out-of-consciousness concern about *loss of hope for a better past.* My experience is that whenever changes that are done properly and respectfully will not go in, or when they will not stick, this concern about *past loss* is a large part of the reason.

Maintaining hope for a better past is never a conscious endeavor. It makes no sense in reason. Instead, all hope for a better past is mediated through our emotions. Although the emotions themselves are detectable, the mechanisms that give rise to them are not noticeable in conscious awareness. Yet the feelings created by the mechanisms are strong enough to sadly contaminate our ability to make choices and follow through with these choices about important things in our lives.

One of the drivers for holding onto or otherwise avoiding the resolution of present pain, in order to prevent the loss of hope that things will have been better in the past, is what I call "Suffering Obligations of Love" (SOL). "Suffering" has a unique definition here: it can be described as "the terrible things we do to ourselves in an unworkable effort to say 'I love you' to someone else."[2] It seems that people tend to suffer for some part of the experience of their ancestors. As far as we know, humans are the only creatures who use suffering to communicate love, and the only creatures who compromise their present and future well-being in an effort to improve the experience of their forbears! If our pain diminishes, we have the bad feeling that we are abandoning the ones we love (abandoning them in their present and our past!), so we unconsciously find ways to maintain our pain by arranging things so that our own lives will not improve until theirs do in their present (which of course is impossible, since it is our past!). Or, on those occasions when we cannot avoid some improvement in our own experience, we can still accomplish most of the same outcome by arranging to feel just as bad as we always have, no matter how much better things get. Of course, when the disparity between how bad our lives feel and how good they actually are gets to be too inexplicable, we start to feel quite crazy. When this crazy feeling gets to be too much, a simple general collapse of most of the good things in our lives will always serve to realign our actual reality with our unpleasant feelings about our reality.

On a deeply other-than-conscious level, all present pain that has come from past trauma is coded as an indication that the trauma is not over. When the trauma is not over, because we continue to feel its negative and awful effects in our present, then the game is not over. As long as the game is not over, there is some hope that the outcome can change. As long as the outcome can still change, there is a possibility that we, and the people we care about, can still win—whatever that might mean—and this gives us hope. A real and lasting resolution of our pain would end our hope to have had a better past, and this ending or loss of hope can feel unbearable.

One way that an SOL maintains past pain and violation in the present in service of a better past is by fixing things up so that, again and again, we fail to change. When someone or something in life presents us with a positive, workable re-solution for our pain, a re-solution for which we have no doubt longed and toward which we have often worked diligently and admirably, perhaps for years or decades, the desire for that better future might be incredibly strong, but one way or another we do not really allow ourselves the revisions and healing. This is because, on an unconscious level, we hold onto a forlorn hope that things that were terrible and heartbreaking can still get better in the past, so that they won't really have happened the way they did.

In another example, hope for a better past can be hope for justice. The words that describe how this works are these: "Attention perpetrators from my past! What you did to me (or my ancestors) was so, so cruel, and so, so wrong, and my humiliation and defeat at your hands was so, so complete, that I will never let the results of all that change. If I allow myself a decently abundant and joyful life now, I am just saying that what you did to me was okay, and I will never give you that. My life of misery will be my personal 'holocaust memorial', a perpetual indictment that will point at your guilt for all to see." We tend to use the felt experience of our present loss and pain as *evidence* that we were treated unjustly and that we are now continuing to work—retroactively but very conscientiously —to achieve better outcomes *in the past.*

Obviously, to assist people to wean themselves from these entirely unworkable and destructive hope structures requires us to have immense rapport with them, as well as limitless respect for their experience, all combined with a cheerfully edgy annoyance that they are continuing to harm themselves in service of the past. This is all adjustable, and we can end the suffering, but we cannot change things until both the clients and we can appreciate and respect the loving intentions behind their every continuing hurt and loss. Then magic can happen.

The method of assisting people to lose hope for a better past in service of their better present and future entails a quantum perspective. In Newtonian ("classical") physics, causes precede effects and effects are consequent to causes on the unidirectional "arrow of time." Past events on the time arrow are not available for revision. But in a quantum frame, time moves both ways on its arrow—past-to-future and future-to-past. When we re-imprint past traumas and the belief structures that come from them, we are working in *both* the classical Newtonian and the quantum approaches. Classically, we are causing some of our local neurons to make new connections with new potentials for new responses and new meanings *about* the past. But quantumly, we are in a way *revising* the past itself—actually organizing something different to have happened on our personal time arrow. When we re-imprint a trauma, we are in a sense arranging for things in the past to have had the potential to have unfolded differently in our lives. We are not violating Newtonian causality when we do this, because we are not *replacing* one personal history with another. We are merely using our human faculties to create and stabilize a relevant parallel probability in our conscious and unconscious mind. The availability of this parallel probability generates relief, not amnesia. Relief from life-long suffering always makes further growth (different experience) more available. A better past makes the reality of a better future more probable.

Consenting to the Past

As part of preparing my clients to accept and benefit from change in the past (which is, of course, only in our minds right now), I educate and empower them to first "consent" to having had this past. A resisted experience is very hard to change, and all painful experience is instinctively resisted. A painful past experience must be "completed" before we try to revise it, because all unwanted experience continues until it is completed. Completion of an old experience begins with consenting to the fact of our having had the experience, just as it was, no matter how painful and traumatic things were.

This "consenting to the past just as it was" is not the same as condoning what happened. Consenting is also not the same as accepting what happened or surrendering--acceptance and surrender are both more passive than consent. In Transformational NLP, the act of consenting is a confirmation that the experience happened the way it did. When we consent to a tragic and painful past we are *not* saying, "It's okay," because it is decidedly *not* okay—but we *are* saying, "Okay, it happened." This consent is the first step in making it easier to change the unwanted present consequences of past experience. Consent to what happened helps to dissolve the resistance to the past that has operated to keep old patterning alive in the present.

As humans, in order to resist something, we must create representations of whatever it is that we are resisting. That is, in order to put our attention on what we do not want to experience, we have to be thinking about this experience. Since the internal representations that allow us to resist an experience are almost identical to the representations of the experience itself, the resistance against unwanted experience actually brings little comfort. Instead, it creates even more vivid representations and a stronger impression of that which we do not want. Hence, resistance *now* to what was experienced *then* only operates to make *then* continue *now*, which is precisely the opposite outcome from what is truly wanted.

However, when we learn to consent to the past rather than resist it, the representations that create the impression of the unwanted feelings and meanings are actually revised, and it is this revision that opens the way for a rapid resolution to past blocks and impairments. When we consent, the past comes to rest; it loses momentum. It is complete and completed. We can acknowledge the trauma and permit the emotion, and this allows the client to move on. Now we are far more available to ask ourselves, ". . . and, what would I like now?"

Ordinarily, the Transformational NLP practitioner supports the client to consent to past events exactly as they are perceived to have actually occurred. However, sometimes these events were so horrific or heartbreaking that the client is simply not able to even imagine consenting to them. For the person presently bound up in past trauma, "consenting" seems to be the same as approving or condoning what happened. In these situations it is necessary to be clear that although we do not condone what happened, we nevertheless need to stop resisting the fact that it happened.

In such circumstances, the practitioner can sometimes assist the client to consent by helping him or her to view the past figures and events from a different perspective. Sometimes this "different perspective" is literal—it involves having the client change a visual sub-modality of distance, angle, or height. More often, the perspective change is figurative. For example, I help the client perceive how a person who hurt the client could have behaved if s/he had been more informed, more aware, less afraid regarding his or her own safety or belonging in the family, and so on. The key question that I pose to the client is, "If [that person] could have done it differently, would s/he have? (S/he couldn't, so s/he didn't, and s/he never will,have done it differently, but if s/he could, would s/he have?)" The understanding that I am seeking to evoke in the client is, "Yes, of course." If the answer "yes" is not available in the client's thinking or feeling, then this question is premature—I will not pose the question until I can be sure that the client has the wherewithal to come to this new perspective. This momentary re-perception of the significant other(s) can go far toward helping the client to consent to what happened in the past, and to thereby find in himself or herself a stronger sense of the authority to have choice about the future that is appropriate for who s/he really is now.

For deep and lasting change, the practitioner as well as the client must actively consent to the operation and effects of the client's past creations. I gradually invite clients to both experience and consent to the past so that they can begin to consent to the inevitability of their better future.

The Client is the Source of the Experience

Transformational NLP teaches students to presuppose that the outcome of any situation, interaction, or event reflects the true—and usually non-conscious—intention beneath that experience. The Transformational NLP practitioner points out to the client that, behind the creation and unfolding of all of his or her past experience, something of the client's own consciousness has been at work. Repressing or feeling victimized by the memories and unpleasant emotions associated with the past inevitably leads to a diminishment of mental and physical integrity, culminating in suffering and disease. Instead, the practitioner reframes the meaning of past events so that the client recognizes the wisdom of his or her past and present creations.

The power in this stronger formulation comes not just from its assertion of something positive having been at work in previous times, but also from the recognition that there has been something active within the client's own consciousness—some kind of agency, a force of intelligent and personal intention—behind the creation and unfolding of all of one's past experience. Working in this expansive inclusion frame preserves our dignity as conscious beings by fully respecting, and even learning to appreciate, the legacy of our choices over time. This not only facilitates the healing of the past, but empowers the client to more consciously exercise personal choice for the present and future.[3]

The Transformational NLP practitioner shows the client—both explicitly and through conversational implication—that the client is him/herself the source of all past and present experiences. The client can, therefore, change the feeling and meaning of the past and present. For example, in a Transformational NLP session I might explain to the client, "Your system is generating and sustaining some pictures and sound tracks *right now* that are producing these really bad feelings, and through those feelings a lot of unpleasant, limiting, and not useful meanings. While your system has been hijacking you into bad feelings and limiting behavior, it has always been operating in the service of your safety and wellbeing. However, these bad feelings and limiting behavior patterns are no longer appropriate for your life and what you want now. You've had a problem with this processing for some time and you've been wanting a different experience. We just want to revise the patterning so it is an up-to-date and respectful expression of who you are now."

CHAPTER VIII

Alignment with Quantum Physics

There is another fundamental difference between Transformational NLP and conventional schools of NLP. As a generalization, we may say that most NLP practitioners, as well as mainstream psychotherapists, continue to work within the conceptual framework of Newtonian physics. My approach is more aligned with the discoveries of quantum physics. This alignment informs all of the philosophy and methods that I teach at NLP Marin.

The Nature of Reality and Consciousness

The classical or Newtonian view is that all reality is a vast machine of matter and energy obeying universal and eternal laws. Although scientists have disputed whether light itself exists as particles or waves since at least the seventeenth century, this wave-particle dichotomy did not interfere with the classical conceptual framework that all phenomena in the universe, including humans, follow laws that are fixed, deterministic, and predictable (Rosenblum & Kuttner, 2006). Thus, in the past two centuries science was generally equated with materialism and determinism.

The field of psychology also followed this scientific model. Even today, despite the growth of the field of humanistic psychology, mainstream views concerning psychology and biology as well as physics are still largely informed by the view that humans are determined by their genes, their environment, and the accidents of their personal history. What this means to most therapists is that the best possibility to alleviate the client's problems is to work backward from the person's present pain to the physical or emotional causes that created it. If we can discover why the problem occurred, we can understand and address the symptoms in the present.

The revolution in scientific thinking at the beginning of the twentieth century forced scientists to open their minds to new possibilities about the nature of space and time. In 1900, Max Planck showed that light energy is not continuous, but rather manifests in discrete quanta (later named photons) (Rosenblum & Kuttner, 2006). In 1905, Albert Einstein's Theory of Special Relativity, with the equation $e = mc^2$, showed that matter and energy are really the same thing in different forms, and that one form can be converted into the other (Friedman, 1997). Einstein echoed the philosopher Immanuel Kant when he declared, "Time and space are modes by which we think and not conditions in which we live" (Friedman, 1997, p. 60).

In the 1920s quantum scientists confirmed, through rigorous experimentation, the theory postulated by physicist Louis de Broglie that atoms can behave either as a wave (energy) or as particles (matter), depending on the arrangement of the experiment. In 1925 Ervin Schroedinger formulated the equation that described the wave function of atoms and molecules, as well as everything made of atoms and molecules in the entire universe (Rosenblum & Kuttner, 2006). Richard Feynman, the quantum physicist who won the Nobel Prize in 1965 for his contributions to the development of quantum electrodynamics, explained that all atomic objects, whether electrons, protons, neutrons, photons, or quarks, sometimes behave like waves and sometimes like particles. In their unmanifest aspect, atomic objects are only waves spread out over space. These waves become manifest by collapsing into particles (Feynman, 1965; Nave, 2012; Wolfe, 1985).

The question that has been consuming the attention of quantum physicists for the past several decades is: What causes the wave to become a particle? In the 1920s, quantum scientists made the astounding discovery that the crucial factor that makes a wave become a particle is the act of observation. An unmeasured electron is always a wave of potential, but as soon as it is measured (observed with an instrument), it collapses into a particle (Friedman, 1997; Rosenblum & Kuttner, 2006). "That is, until we 'look,' there is no objective reality, but rather an underlying state of potential. . . . this potential is really a superposition of all possible states" (Friedman, 1997, pp. 61–62). As Deepak Chopra explains, "The world is a reflection of the sensory apparatus that registers it. . . . All that is really 'out there' is raw, unformed data waiting to be interpreted by . . . the perceiver" through the senses and consciousness (Chopra, 1993, p. 11). Quantum objects are actually non-local waves that become particles only when consciousness focuses them so that they can be observed in one place (Goswami, 1993; Friedman, 1997). Thus, the observer actually creates a particle from the quantum wave. It is the consciousness of the observer that participates in bringing possibilities into actualities.

Yet another astonishing discovery was that every element in the universe is connected with and influences every other element regardless of space or time (Friedman, 1997; Rosenblum & Kuttner, 2006). Physicist John Stewart Bell's theorem of quantum entanglement demonstrates that particles influence one another instantaneously no matter how separated they are by long distances. This is because we live in an interconnected universe in which everything affects everything else (Friedman, 1997). Quantum scientists such as Amit Goswami and John Hagelin explain that all matter in the universe, including atoms, is made of consciousness and is contained in a unified field of consciousness. This field of consciousness, and therefore all elements in it, is non-local, and therefore all of it influences everything else (Goswami, 1993; Hagelin, 2006).

This all seems very counter-intuitive. How do these principles relate to our everyday experience, which seems to function according to Newtonian principles? One scientist who attempted to bridge the gap between quantum science and everyday experience was the renowned quantum physicist David Bohm.

David Bohm explains that "matter and mind are two aspects of one overall reality . . . matter is the form that consciousness takes when introduced or projected into our everyday world" (Friedman, 1997, p. 124). More precisely, "matter is the form taken by consciousness when a probability selected from the hidden domain is projected into the level of space-time" (Friedman, 1997, p. 136).

According to Bohm, there are three aspects, or levels, of the one overall reality. There is an aspect of reality that is unmanifest as well as that which is manifest. The unmanifest reality, which he calls the implicate order, is a vast ocean of energy and unlimited potential. Our everyday world is the manifest, explicate order, which contains matter, space, and time. A third aspect of existence is what Bohm calls the superimplicate order, and is a field of information. Bohm says that information is what determines space and time (Friedman, 1997; Peat, 1997).

Thus, matter and mind are different aspects of one reality. The objects in our three-dimensional world of individuation and matter are merely small waves in a vast ocean of energy which has limitless implicate possibility. This infinite potential can be described as wave functions that, through the operation of an observer's consciousness, can be manifested in the world of our sensory experience as particles of matter. In between observations, the particles do not pass through space-time, but rather jump in and out of the field of a sea of infinite possibilities (Friedman, 1997).

David Bohm explains that instead of having a linear causality between two distinct events, causation is non-local—any part of the whole affects all other parts (Sheldrake, 1995a; Peat, 1997). The "implicate order" underlies both physical reality and thought, so "it transcends the usual materialist-idealist dichotomy." This implicate order is "a wholeness which embraces parts and sets up relationships between them. They're linked together within a new whole, which didn't exist before." Hence, there is an "implicit intelligence in matter as it evolves," and "it's actually not moving causally in a sequence but is constantly created and replicated" by being continuously being projected out of and reabsorbed back into the implicate order (Sheldrake, 1995a, p. 244).

Bohm turns science upside down when he explains that one projection in the manifest world does not directly cause another. Instead, all causation occurs in the implicate order, and therefore is non-local. The implicate order *projects* forms into the explicate (manifest) order, which then *injects* these forms back into the implicate order, where they are *re-projected* outward. It is an infinite feedback system. All of the influencing of forms occurs in the implicate field of all possibilities, and is influenced by many factors other than the immediate external cause.

The explicate forms include thoughts as well as material objects. While in the explicate order consciousness is separate from matter, in the implicate order they are not separate. Thus, in Bohm's concept the manifest world can influence the implicate field of all possibilities which then projects a new manifestation (Friedman, 1997). It is an eternally evolving universe, with the potential and the manifestations influencing one another in an infinite non-local interconnection.

The implications of this scientific theory are huge. This means that there is no deterministic path for experiences from cause to effect. Although, statistically, electrons as a group operate according to predictable probabilities—which are the basis of all calculations in such fields of physics as electrical engineering—each individual electron appears to be free to choose its own path in the universe. While such individualistic choices are not probable manifestations in reality, they are nevertheless possible. As Amit Goswami (1993) declares, "Quantum physics . . . challenges old concepts, such as deterministic trajectories of motion and causal continuity. If initial conditions do not forever determine an object's motion, if instead, every time we observe, there is a new beginning, then the world is creative at the base level" (p. 42). In other words, at every juncture we can choose anew.

Quantum physicist Fred Alan Wolfe, in his article "Quantum Consciousness" (1985), maintains that the wave-particle duality of quantum physics is also true of the brain. He explains how the physical brain itself, with all its neuronal networks, can be changed by observation, or self-reflection:

> What we call the brain is the particle-like behavior of our observations. What we call the mind is the wavelike behavior of atomic objects, invisible and unobserved. Mind is then an outgrowth of the basic laws of quantum physics together with the actions of the observer, which . . . [are] acts of consciousness.
>
> For example, one act of consciousness could cause a change in quantum surface waves acting along the thin membranes

> covering our neurons. These waves are associated with the movements of the protein-gate molecules embedded in the neurons' walls. A "particle" observation would momentarily "freeze" the molecules' positions, resulting in the appearance of thought. Another complementary "wave" observation where the proteins remained unobserved would *produce* changes in the energy of these waves, resulting in the arousal of feelings. (Wolfe, 1985)

My practice of Transformational NLP corresponds with the conceptual framework of David Bohm, Amit Goswami, and Fred Alan Wolfe. I too believe that people are not determined by their past. While information about people's backgrounds has predictive value statistically, it does not predict in an absolute sense the path of growth of an individual. Instead, the conscious observations and intentions of the client and the practitioner, as well as specific NLP techniques, can influence the client's experience of freedom and choice in the future.

The Future Influences the Past

Quantum physics also informs the Transformational NLP view of the relationship of the past and present to the future. The renowned scientist and philosopher Terence McKenna maintains that the future attracts the present to itself. Biochemist Rupert Sheldrake explains that evolution in psychology as well as in nature seems to entail "a pulling from in front rather than a pushing from behind" (Sheldrake, McKenna, & Abraham, 1992, pp. 7–8, 31). It all exists already, and only needs to be manifested.

I too believe that, in a very real sense, instead of the past determining the present and future, the future can actually influence the past. My work is based on the premise that people yearn toward fulfillment of their human potential. We operate as if there is a future version of the client that is calling him or her into alignment with itself.

This view is substantiated by the findings of quantum physics. For several decades after the electron was discovered in the late nineteenth century, physicists explored how electrons produce an electric field (American Institute of Physics, 1997; Pais et al., 1997). By the 1930s, physicists noticed that electrons not only generate their electric fields, they also interact with and are affected by the fields they generate! In his lecture when he accepted the Nobel Prize in December 1933, quantum physicist Paul Dirac explained the process by which the field of electromagnetic radiation created by electrons in turn actually creates other electrons (Dirac, 1933; Feynman, 1965; Hestenes, 1983). In 1945, quantum physicists John Wheeler and Richard Feynman developed the absorber theory of electromagnetic radiation. This theory uses mathematical equations to explain the integration of magnetic and electric fields over time. Wheeler and Feynman shocked the world by their experiment during which not only did an atom emit light, which was absorbed by a second atom sometime in the future, but the second atom sent a wave back in time to the original emitting atom. In other words, the future literally influenced the past and merged with it to create the present (Feynman, 1965; Friedman, 1997).

Wheeler writes that humans, through consciousness, create their own reality. Reality consists of the interpretations that humans make about what they observe through the senses and instruments of measurement. There are numerous experiments showing that the past has no existence except as it is recorded in the present. These experiments show that one's observation not only creates a present reality but also creates a past appropriate to that reality. In other words, how we observe something in the present can influence what actually happened in the past (Friedman, 1997; Rosenblum & Kuttner, 2006).

Wheeler and Goswami pursue this line of reasoning even further down the temporal rabbit hole. They explain that our choice of how we interpret our observations in the present moment creates not only a probable past that goes with it, but also a corresponding probable future. Likewise, what we choose for the future can determine the present as well as the past (Friedman, 1997; Goswami, 1993).

At NLP Marin, I teach that the future creates the present against a backdrop of the past. This means that through our awareness and choices, both conscious and unconscious, we are always selecting which probable future we would like the present to be the past of. The unconscious choices are what we call beliefs.

In my practice of change work, I act on the premise that the field of potential thoughts, emotions, and actions functions as the master source of possibilities for what each person thinks and does. In turn, people's actions as they evolve also affect the field of potential. Thought (desire) activates (conveys the client into a relationship with) a probable future in which the goal is fulfilled. This future is one of many probabilities. In that future, the present becomes the past (of the future goal). This creates coherence between the future and the present.

The future creates the present in the sense that, in the illusion of linear time, the present is always what precedes and therefore leads to the future. The present is the point of power, that is, where the choices are made. It is in and from the present that we make our selections of which alternative futures and pasts we would like to be the past and future of. In the present the client chooses a future for which he wants the present to be the past. That picture of the future creates its past, which is the present. This present thus leads inevitably to the future. The present is the future's past, and is therefore what has already occurred on the way to a (now) pre-existing future fulfillment.

Therefore, once we select a future, and then consent to the present becoming, and to always having been, that future's past, then we create the potential of an apparent linear chain of events that has already unfolded from past to future. It is the future that is doing the creating of a past congruent with itself and it is the present that chooses itself to be congruently the past of a particular future. The present does the choosing about the future, but it is the future that does all the creating of the past.

Accordingly, in the framework of Transformational NLP, causation works from future to past, as well as from past to future, moving in both directions simultaneously and continually. This perspective allows the Transformational NLP practitioner to encourage the positive inevitable. We work to shift the viewpoint of the client from past and future to different presents. As psychologist Philip Zimbardo writes in *The Time Paradox* (2008), and philosopher Eckhart Tolle explains in *The Power of Now* (1999), there is only the present. What the client chooses to observe affects both the past and the future, since they both actually exist in the present in the person's mind.

The client facilitates this alignment when s/he becomes coherent about the inevitability of the path that leads to the desired future, and makes him/herself available to it. In my work, I presuppose this possibility and process and use language that supports this presupposition. I assist the client to create an experience and story of how the future has been accomplished through what is happening in the present based on a revised version of what happened in the past. As I explain to my clients and students, "The past has operated flawlessly to catalyze certain new choices and learning in the present, so that these new choices will have inevitably opened into future fulfillment" (Buchheit, 2011, p. 145).

CHAPTER IX
The Family System

In Transformational NLP there is a strong emphasis on both the local and non-local workings of family systems, and especially on patterns of unconscious trans-generational loyalty. Humans appear to replicate family pain and dysfunction generation after generation, with an instinctive precision that is both horrifying and unconscious. Each family, and each individual within the family, demonstrates the workings and effects of what I call the structure of devotional patterning. Robert Dilts explains that "in order to be loyal, in order to keep their allegiance, their affiliation with their family, they have to follow the family pattern. It is kind of like: 'Who am I to be any better than those people who are my models, my mentors?' Furthermore, if they transcended the family pattern they have no role models; they are on their own" (Dilts, 1990, pp. 129–130).

In my work, I pay even more attention than Dilts to what I call Suffering Obligations of Love. I am inspired by the works of Anne Schutzenberger, Rupert Sheldrake, Ervin Laszlo, and Bert Hellinger, which provide the context for my efforts to access the energetic imprints of the family system across generations so that dysfunctional devotional patterning can be resolved in the service of the client.

Influences on Transformational NLP

ANNE ANCELIN SCHUTZENBERGER

Anne Ancelin Schutzenberger is a renowned French psychotherapist who found that, as she describes in the preface to her book *The Ancestor Syndrome* (1998), "We continue the chain of generations and, knowingly or not, willingly or unwillingly, we pay debts of the past: as long as we have not cleared the slate, an 'invisible loyalty' impels us to repeat and repeat a moment of incredible joy or unbearable sorrow, an injustice or a tragic death. Or its echo" (p. xii).

The Ancestor Syndrome provides case studies (which Schutzenberger calls genosociograms) of recurring patterns of occurrences that continue in families from generation to generation. Schutzenberger finds that all humans have inherited, negative feelings and imprints of patterns of behavior. Important events and traumas experienced by our ancestors have been imprinted on our genetic structures and reveal themselves generations later. We seem therefore impelled to unwittingly re-enact the life events of previous generations, as if there were a sort of invisible loyalty. For example, Schutzenberger relates how the date of a tragedy in the past, even 500 or more years ago, can be stored in unconscious memory and acted out by following generations. Such acting out may include not only coincidences in dates or behaviors, but also in health problems and accidents that seem to repeat generation after generation, and without plausible explanation.

In *The Ancestor Syndrome*, Schutzenberger illustrates how she has been able to assist her clients to overcome seemingly irrational fears and other psychological and even physical health problems by discovering and understanding the parallels between their own lives and the lives of their forebears. She writes, "fidelity to ancestors, which has become unconscious and invisible (invisible loyalty), governs us. It is important to make it visible, to become aware of it, to understand what impels us and possibly see if we may not have to reframe this loyalty in order to become free again to live our own lives" (Schutzenberger, 1998, p. 43). She argues that we must remember the past with all its pain in order to end the suffering and move on with our lives:

> The therapist's role is to accompany clients by helping them to rediscover their "history" through speaking it, to be able to represent it to themselves in a coherent manner, to be able to see the thread and the meaning. And . . . helping clients finally leave the chaos, the unthinkable, the unspeakable, the unspoken—and the repetition—and fully accept and shoulder their family history and their past. (Schutzenberger, 1998, p. 139)

She explains that:

> We can reframe an event: a curse could become a blessing . . . when we see, when we understand . . . a context is transformed . . . and things change. The subject can breathe, gets rid of the weight of the past, often his body changes, his life changes. He becomes another person . . . and (sometimes) in addition is cured of serious or even life-threatening illness. (Schutzenberger, 1998, pp. 128–129)

RUPERT SHELDRAKE

The work of Rupert Sheldrake, an English biochemist and plant physiologist, is also a key influence in my work. Sheldrake explains that there are organizing fields, which he calls morphogenetic fields, which determine the development of plants and animals. Sheldrake believes that morphogenetic fields work by imposing patterns on otherwise random activity. These morphogenetic fields are not fixed, but evolve and are transmitted from past to future members of a species through a "morphic resonance" (Sheldrake, 1995a, p. 13).

Sheldrake explains that formative causation acts in a non-local fashion, that is, it operates instantaneously across space and time (Sheldrake, 1995b). Once a particular form has been learned by a system, it will be more easily learned by a similar system anywhere else in the world. For example, "If an animal, say a rat, learns to carry out a new pattern of behaviour, there will be a tendency for any subsequent similar rat (of the same breed, reared under similar conditions, etc.) to learn more quickly to carry out the same pattern of behaviour" (Sheldrake, 1995a, p. 14).

All members of a species influence the field, and this influence is cumulative. The form and behavior of each individual is influenced, in addition to environment and genes, by the form and behavior of the entire species both in the past and present, and in turn exerts an influence on it. Like Lamarck and Darwin, Sheldrake believes that acquired characteristics are inherited (Sheldrake, 1995b).

In *A New Science of Life: Morphic Resonance* (1995a) Sheldrake poses the question:

> If morphogenetic fields are responsible for the organization and form of material systems . . . where do these field-structures come from?" [He answers that] "they are derived from the morphogenetic fields associated with previous similar systems: the morphogenetic fields of all past systems become *present* to any subsequent similar system; the structures of past systems affect subsequent similar systems by a cumulative influence which acts across both space *and time*." (p. 13)

In other words, what we have called the laws of nature are actually more like habits (Sheldrake, 2005).

Sheldrake does not speculate on how the fields of new organisms came into existence in the first place. Instead, he reaches the startling conclusion that "the invisible organizing principles of nature, rather than being eternally fixed, evolve along with the systems they organize. . . . The fields themselves evolve. Their expression is affected by the conditions and habits of life, as well as by genetic mutations" (Sheldrake, 1995b, pp. 114, 225, 313).

Sheldrake's theory of morphic resonance extends from the realm of plant and animal development and behavior to human behavior, memory, and cognition in general. In *The Presence of the Past* (1995b) Sheldrake explains that morphic fields are the organizing principle not only of animal and human behavior, but also of social and cultural systems, and of mental activity, all of which "contain an inherent memory" which influences other systems around the world (p. 113). "In the human realm, there are many examples of parallel social and cultural patterns that seem to have originated independently in different parts of the world" (p. 289).

Sheldrake proposes that each individual is influenced by the morphic field of the collective memory of its species, as well as by the memory of the individual's personal past. These memories are not stored in the brain. He writes that there are no material traces of memories in the brain. The brain remembers by tuning into the morphic field. The memories are stored in the morphic field, and become accessible through resonance from ourselves in the past. This self-resonance is the basis for individual memories and habits as well as learning. Humans are influenced by morphic resonance not only to ourselves in the past, but also to others in our family and social groups in both the present and the past (Sheldrake, 1995b).

DAVID BOHM

Quantum physicist David Bohm, in an interview with Sheldrake, maintains that his own ideas are consistent with those of Sheldrake. Bohm too believes that there is a collective consciousness that springs from the interconnectivity of everything in the universe. The two scientists agree that there is a sort of cosmic memory, akin to the Hindu concept of the Akashic records (Sheldrake, 1995a).

ERVIN LASZLO

The brilliant scholar Ervin Laszlo in his landmark work *Science and the Akashic Field* (2004) took this theme even further in his study of the scientific applicability of the ancient wisdom of the Akashic records. He claims that what is called the quantum vacuum is not really a void, but instead a unified field of consciousness that carries and stores information and energy. Laszlo argues that the universe and evolution are not merely a combination of random events. The information field links the entire universe and nature as well as consciousness in a holographic manner. The interconnectedness that quantum physicists discovered on the level of atoms and subatomic particles is characteristic of all matter and life.

Laszlo thus shows the connectedness between consciousness and the phenomenal world. He explains that this field of information "links all things in the universe, atoms as well as galaxies, organisms the same as minds" (Laszlo, 2004, p. 3). Like Bohm, Laszlo maintains that *in-formation* is a process that actually forms the phenomena in the world (Laszlo, 2004). The Akashic Field is a reservoir of information that stores all information—about all past, present, and future events and potential for events—holographically in wave patterns. All the possible permutations and combinations that exist as potential—as wave patterns—in the Akashic Field may or may not get materialized (i.e., made observable). If they become manifest, their exact details are recorded in the Akashic Field (Laszlo, 2004).

Laszlo (2004) clarifies that this information, which is stored forever in the Akashic Field, can be accessed across any distance or time period. He speculates that telepathic communication, for example, is transferred faster than the speed of light. Every person's conscious experience, including that of the ancestors in the past, is stored and available to be accessed. Laszlo writes that:

> Normally the most direct and evident resonance occurs between our brain and the hologram we ourselves have created. This is the basis of long-term memory. . . . [w]e do not address the memory stores in our brains: we "recall" the information from the hologram that records our experiences. Such recall could involve more than just our own experiences. Our brain is not limited to resonating with our hologram alone; it can also resonate in the harmonic mode with the holograms of other people, especially with those with whom we have (or had) a physical or emotional bond. (p. 116)

Thus, Laszlo makes the case that our brain can become tuned to the holographic record of another person. The Akashic Field connects everything with everything else, including the present with the past and even with the future.

BERT HELLINGER

Bert Hellinger independently found a way to work with a similar concept of cosmic memory in his unique system of psychotherapy that he calls family constellations. While he was not directly influenced by the scientific theories of Sheldrake, Bohm, or Laszlo, or even by Schutzenberger, he found in their works a confirmation of what he had discovered in his own work with clients.

In a panel discussion in 1999, entitled "ReViewing Assumptions," Sheldrake, Schutzenberger, and Hellinger shared their ideas with the public and confirmed that they had independently discovered, through different venues, a force that connects all humans through space and time. Sheldrake exclaims that Hellinger's constellations are an example of morphic fields in action. Schutzenberger agrees with

Hellinger that people seem to be punished for the sins of their ancestors. She points out that when a person begs pardon for what was perpetrated by his or her ancestors in past generations, very often the "curse" is resolved and the individual's current symptoms disappear (Hellinger, Schutzenberger, & Sheldrake, 1999). While these original thinkers share many ideas, Hellinger provides a methodology for resolving family entanglements that is unique.

Hellinger explains that there are rigid laws for what he calls the family soul, according to which certain events are repeated again and again over many generations in an attempt to achieve balance between opposites such as guilt and innocence, perpetration and victimization, and so on. There is an unconscious common conscience in the family soul that works to preserve the integrity of the group. Hence, a child may (unconsciously) take on the fate of an ancestor or balance out in some way an action that is not life supporting by manifesting a symptom that is at the opposite extreme. Unconsciously, children's loyalty and innocent love blindly perpetuate the harm done to or by earlier members of their family (Hellinger, Schutzenberger, & Sheldrake, 1999).

According to Hellinger, the force that binds the family together over space and generations is love. There is a natural flow of love in the family, which is very often hidden and distorted. When there is a psychological or even a physiological problem, the basis usually can be found in an interference or distortion in the flow of love. Hellinger's goal is to discover the hidden patterns of the flow of love in families, so that the proper flow can be restored and the family relationships healed (Hellinger, 1998).

While the dynamics that operate in relationship systems are normally hidden, Hellinger found a way to make them visible through the methodology of the family constellation. The constellations reveal the forces operating in the family system that cause great suffering. Events such as an abortion, the exclusion of a family member, a trauma of an ancestor, a murder, or some other family secret can lead to entanglements which cause psychological despair or physiological malfunction in the client, seemingly without valid cause in the present. Very often, the entanglement is in the form of the unconscious longing of the adult child to take on the fate of the ancestor in an attempt to somehow balance the system. This is the child's attempt to love and belong to the family members, both living and dead, by loyally living out the consequences of another's life (Hellinger, 1998; 1999).

Hellinger explains that, "In systemic family therapy, we're interested in discovering people's entanglements in the fates of previous members of their families. This is something that comes to light in a family constellation. When it's out in the open, they can find a resolution of the entanglement more easily" (Hellinger, 1999, p. 1). He continues, "A person is entangled when he or she unconsciously takes over the fate of an earlier member of the family and lives it out" (Hellinger, 1999, p. 3). The resolution is to bring the family members (living or dead) and the original issue into the system by bringing them into the constellation, and accepting and honoring them. In a family constellation, "The dead are brought back into the picture so they can be reintegrated. Many illnesses and disturbances are attributable to the exclusion of rightful members of a system, and these are often the dead members. When they are brought back in, the others are free" (Hellinger, 1999, p. 58).

Hellinger clarifies that this does not mean that we justify the action that brought us pain. It only means that we accept that it happened rather than repress it or reject the family member who caused the pain. When we reject someone, we become just like him or her. When we accept and acknowledge that it happened as it did, we can accept and acknowledge ourselves as we are. We weep for the action, without judging, accusing, or attacking the perpetrator. Likewise, when the representative of the client discovers that suffering on behalf of the ancestors does not help the ancestors, s/he is encouraged to acknowledge and consent to what happened in the past and leave it with them. Such acceptance leads to reconciliation and a transformation in the person's psychology, and very often a disappearance of the disturbing symptoms (Hellinger, 1999).

In a constellation that is either facilitated by Hellinger or conducted in his style, a client presents the issue that has brought him or her to the therapist. The observers sit in a wide circle facing the center.

When the facilitator initiates the constellation, the space inside the circle somehow becomes a field that provides information that is beyond the boundaries of local time and space. (See Appendix F for more information about the way that the facilitator of a Hellinger family constellation sets up the field.) How is this possible? Hellinger (1998) says, "I'm unable to explain this phenomenon, but I see that it's so, and I use it" (p. xii).

Hellinger views his work as being phenomenological. He is an empiricist, observing and acknowledging what he sees in the constellation rather than deciding what needs to be done in advance. He is interested in what really is going on, rather than how it should be. Hellinger is adamant that he and those who try to do this type of work must relinquish theory in favor of observation (Hellinger, 1998; 1999). "Standing in a constellation as a representative gives convincing experiential evidence suggesting we are all connected to one another in unexpected ways. It's not a matter of belief, but of taking seriously the representatives' felt experience" (Hellinger & Beaumont, 1999, p. 9).

Once the unconscious connections with the fates of family ancestors are brought to light, the therapist—without being judgmental and abstaining from providing theories about the family—offers:

> Healing words and ritual movements that "re-member" forgotten and excluded family members, that dissolve hidden identifications and that transform destructive loyalties. Therapists move the representatives within the constellation, allowing them to compare the effect of different positions, and offer them experimental sentences. Careful observation of the effect of the sentences and movements is essential. Accurately formulated sentences name the hidden dynamics that cause terrible suffering . . . and they also point the way to healing . . . [w]hen love and spontaneous connection between estranged persons occur, we know we are moving in the right direction. (Hellinger & Beaumont, 1999, pp. 9–10)

In a constellation, when the representative of the dead perpetrator and the representative of the dead victim reconcile with each other, this heals the symptoms of the living on both sides (Hellinger, Schutzenberger, & Sheldrake, 1999).

Hellinger originally viewed family constellations as a form of psychotherapy. In an interview in 2004 he explains that, "we let the client choose and place representatives, then intervened according to our ideas, and according to our understandings of the orders of relationships, and looked for good solutions. First we looked at the problem, and then for the solution" (Schenk, 2004b).

In later years, however, Hellinger has evolved in a new direction. He no longer intervenes as a facilitator. Instead, he encourages silent constellations, in which the representatives move on their own accord. Hellinger calls these organically unfolding events "movements of the Spirit Mind" in spiritual family constellations. Hellinger explains that it had become apparent to him that the representatives were in immediate contact with a larger field than the family soul. He believes that there are forces of the Greater Spirit that have effects beyond the represented family system and which cannot be influenced by them. He sees that the representatives are suddenly brought into contact "with forces of fate, in the face of which we are powerless" (Schenk, 2004b).

Hellinger points out that the movements of the participants are often in contradiction to our own concepts of what they should be. He says that when we disrupt such movements, we cannot effect real change. Only when we refrain from acting can the real help begin.

> A new power has taken the leading place. I submit to this power, and suddenly I know whether I have to do something and what I have to do. . . . Beyond family constellations and movements of the soul I now move with spirit . . . spirit takes over now and exerts completely different ways of acting than the movements of the soul. (Schenk, 2004b)

Since everything is guided by spirit, there are no good or bad people or actions, so we must refrain from judging. Instead, we look for reconciliation.

Since, according to Hellinger, the soul will move toward resolution without need for interference, the facilitator must help in a way that is different from what was done in the previous type of family constellation. S/he must remain aloof and not vested in any particular outcome. In the movements without words the unhealed situations reveal themselves, and with further movements, the healing occurs through reconciliation. Hence, the helping is no longer intentional acting, but rather allowing it to happen. Much of the current Hellinger constellation is done in silence, so for one or two hours the participants just move around as they feel inclined without receiving instructions or talking (Hellinger, 2006; Schenk, 2004a; 2004b).

As Hellinger explains during the constellation he did in Washington, D.C. in July 2006:

> The movements of the Mind, or of the Spirit . . . are very . . . very slow, and they take a long time to develop. . . . Many people cannot stand that. . . . They want to do something. If you do something, you spoil it! But . . . I go with the movement of that Spirit, of that Mind. I am in tune with that. How do I get in tune with that? I am in a connection of well-wishing with everybody—whatever happened, with everybody—because once you enter into connection with these movements, you let go of the distinction of good or bad. Although it may appear here that there were some victims . . . and somebody was [injuring] them, they are all on the same level—no difference. Once you enter into these movements, you give them a place in your heart, equally, and then you are in a position to understand where the movements go, and whom you have to choose to add. . . . And sometimes you have to intervene when you see someone is escaping the issue, and you know the issue, because you feel that too. . . .
>
> Now, if you compare that to the family constellations you are used to, you see, it is quite different, quite different. The facilitator does not do anything. Doesn't talk anything, doesn't ask anything, doesn't want to know what anybody is feeling. . . . [t]he main interference in the movement of the Mind is your curiosity, because what you get when you are curious . . . is . . . a fraction of the truth, just a fraction, and the unimportant fraction, and you lose your connection with that movement. (Hellinger, 2006)

Hellinger asks participants to bear and even fully agree to the conflict as the first step toward reconciliation, thus resolving the usual distinctions between good and evil. The therapist must release all moral judgment, and agree to what is. S/he accompanies the client rather than practices therapy on or to him/her. Hellinger declares that:

> A great force is at work, something good that took . . . [us] into its service . . . [t]hat which we do, is not dependent on what we think. This movement takes us along with it, irresistible. . . . If we observe things as they are, it becomes quite clear: The Divine, the primal power, the power which moves the world, wills the conflict. (Schenk, 2004b)

Our task, then, is to come to a position of love of everything and everyone as they are, with the movements toward reconciliation within families, ethnic groups, nations, and so on being the means of healing and growing.

Recently, Hellinger has modified his methodology even more. Now, he is not so interested in the emotional or psychological dynamics of the family. In fact these days, since the mid-2000s, he usually does not work with the family system at all. Increasingly, the only participants are the subject and a representative for the future, or the subject and a representative for the dysfunction. Hellinger believes that the resolution of the dysfunction comes through the movement of the Spirit Mind, or the Great Soul, without interference from the facilitator (Hellinger, 2004a). Nevertheless, he still does occasionally intervene if he feels guided to do so.

Family and systemic constellations at NLP Marin

I have been tremendously educated and inspired by Bert Hellinger's extraordinary work in systemic constellations. When I saw Hellinger working with clients, in person, during his first training workshop in the United States, I was awestruck by his ability to quickly and straightforwardly explicate the usually baffling operation of trans-generational entanglement and suffering. I observed the remarkable capacities of Hellinger's method to reveal the elusive mechanisms whereby—through the workings of an entirely positive drive toward healing—the experience of love actually becomes distorted and destructive in families and relationships. I was amazed to discover an even deeper significance in the classic NLP presupposition that all experience is sourced out of some kind of intended positive outcome. Hellinger's explication of the rules of love's working in families, what he calls Orders of Love, showed me that devotionally distorted efforts to fulfill intended positive outcomes can reach much further than the usual child/parent/grandparent generational scope of conventional family healing work. Indeed, the imperatives of these intended positives can sometimes reach entire centuries into the family's past.

Today, numerous students of Hellinger's work are doing systemic constellations all over the world. Many of these practitioners are several learning generations removed from Hellinger himself. Some systemic constellation work that was inspired by Hellinger has taken new directions and evolutions, as one would expect from a body of ideas and methods as fertile and important as his. I am pleased and honored to be a part of this extension and unfolding of Hellinger's work, and I am gratified to be able to contribute some important differences in purpose, methodology, and the general tenor of the work.

One significant difference between Hellinger's newer formats and my constellations is that I continue to work with family dynamics that have been at play in family systems across generations. As in Hellinger's original constellations, I sometimes work with representatives of specific members of the family: the classic representations of Father, Mother, Sibling(s), Grandparents, and so on. However, I have also entered new territory, representing the forces and factors that have compelled the family into certain kinds of disordered and dysfunctional behavior across generations. Frequently, the only person being represented in the constellation is the client, with the other representations being a Force, or a Flow, or some other kind of dynamic element that has been affecting the family's well-being. Such representations might be labeled, for example, "That Which Impels the Family Toward Cruelty" or "Whatever It Is That Has Been

Distorting the Family Toward Illness." These constellations continue to be about family dynamics, even though they are about the architecture of the dynamics rather than directly about family members themselves.

Another key difference between my approach and Hellinger's (both classic Hellinger and the more silent and sublime Spirit Mind work of current Hellinger) is that I am comfortable working with a focused intention on finding a solution (or resolution, which I hear as "re-solution") for the client, rather than only a movement toward it. Instead of just letting the movement unfold without interference, I believe that the constellation process often benefits from some gentle guidance toward resolution of the problem. Hence I, as the facilitator, frequently intervene, although I always stay within the boundaries of where the constellation goes. Sometimes this gentle guidance may take the form of my being clear that I do not know what the resolution is. This acknowledgement inevitably invites an additional clarity or precision of perception on the part of the representatives that then allows the constellation to unfold in a productive way.

Another dissimilarity concerns Hellinger's insistence on silence during the constellation. I agree with Hellinger that showing the client the patterns of entanglement is in itself a therapy. I believe, however, that total silence during the constellation is dismissive of human experience. It deletes the narrative of the client's experience. Through the narrative, we can connect the dots about what the hidden dynamics are. Chaos is revealed to really be an orderly evolution toward resolution. I rarely ask the representatives to speak to one another within their roles, but I am constantly inquiring about what their experience in their roles is. This sharing informs me and engages the attention of the observers sitting around the circle. This attention seems to contribute to the energy of the field, and provides a more dynamic movement among the participants. The dynamic seems to be as authentic as in a silent constellation, and as much a manifestation of Spirit, but the movement is faster and the resolution quicker.

In the constellations I facilitate, very serious work is often accomplished with humor and laughter. I often provoke shared laughter about the client's specific family predicaments as well as about the more universally experienced dilemmas and common tragedies of human beings. I find that occasionally being very light about that which is usually heavy and dark often has good effects. Humor provokes a momentary change of perspective, providing an opportunity for some dissociation from the serious or tragic events and meanings that are unfolding within a few feet of everyone in the physical space in which the constellation is happening. When a moment of laughter is over, I observe that the various elements in the system—informational, emotional, and energetic—can be quickly brought back together with noticeably more clarity and power than were available previously. A moment of silliness can often reframe the information and events that are revealed in the constellation. This releases tension, affords the facilitator better access to information, and allows the entire system to work more readily and productively with the serious issues of the client's life.

In addition, it is my impression that I am even more focused than Hellinger on showing adult children that they willingly, albeit unconsciously, suffer in order to assert the blamelessness of their parents and ancestors. Very often, while people consciously make bitter accusations against parents and family about neglect, abuse, and cruelty, they simultaneously—*and entirely unconsciously*—create or allow relationships, situations, and experiences that recapitulate the original abuse. In constellations, I have found that this phenomenon can often be represented by these words: "Dear Mother/Father, if this [terrible situation] is the best you can offer me, your loving child, then in your honor, and to protect you from all accusation and blame, I will make sure that no one treats me better, sees me better, or does a better job with me than you have—I promise. I will live my life in a way that shows everyone that you were right to do what you did." As mentioned previously, I coined the term Suffering Obligations of Love (SOL) to describe this devotion-driven urge to replicate and extend the agonies and perpetrations of previous generations.

Another fascinating phenomenon is the proclivity of people to imitate exactly those traits that they deride in their parents and that hurt them so much. This experience can be captured in the phrase,

"To honor you, and to ease your suffering, and to amend the bad experiences and conditions of your life, I will be like you, I promise!" These unconscious loving sentiments, and the destructive decisions and actions to which they give rise, are always directed toward past events and toward family members who may have already died. Thus, such suffering devotion is always completely pointless. It is compassion without any good effect. It is a severely distorted expression of love.

More than Hellinger, I am intent to reveal the dynamics of the client's SOL structures and behaviors, making explicit the unconscious processes and actions through which ancestral tragedy and loss are replicated in the present generation—although usually with some conversion to other forms of expression. For example, one of my clients had an inexplicable, severe, and occasionally life-threatening gastro-intestinal medical condition. His constellation revealed that this manifestation of illness was linked to, and was attempting to replicate, some experiences of events from the Armenian genocide during which nearly everyone in the client's family had perished a century earlier. The client partially replicated the experience of death by bayonet in the abdomen, which was how members of his family had been killed, by presenting symptoms of severe gastro-intestinal illness and pain.

Of course, the client has no conscious awareness of an SOL entanglement. Indeed, the idea that one would deliberately compromise one's own well-being on behalf of people caught in a nightmare from a century ago would seem absurd. Yet, in the constellation such entanglements are revealed as an unconscious but irresistible desire to try to do something to help those who came before.

The main task of constellation facilitators is to help clients reveal—to and for themselves—both the existence and the operational nature of trans-generational devotional entanglements. Properly done, constellations explicate what has been occurring in the family, and also open the way for clients to re-choose about the means they would like to use, henceforward, to demonstrate love and respect. The social setting within which constellations are usually conducted provides the client with a safe, interactive space within which to gather new information that can lead to new choices. The field effect of the constellation, the mysterious presence of windows into the past and future of the client and the family, somehow empowers the client to make new choices that are not merely new insights or ideas, but the actual basis of a new template the family can use—across generations—to find less distorted means to say "I love you." In the format of the constellation, we are actually able to resolve the devotional entanglements that have distorted the flow of love and the movement toward wellbeing across generations.

Time—or, more to the point, the absence of the usual effects and experience of time—is a fundamental aspect of the quantum, non-local nature of nearly all work within the constellation field. Within the field of the constellation all time is *right now*. For example, if there are five generations interacting within the field, each generation is fully present in its own *now*, although they are obviously in past and future states relative to one another. Amazingly, trans-generational family interventions accomplished within the constellation field "now" appear to affect both the past and the future of the client and his or her family.

I am more aligned with Hellinger's newer, more explicitly spiritual perspective than may be immediately apparent. We both believe that there is a force beyond the family soul that moves us all toward reconciliation. We both believe that the therapist cannot use his or her mind alone to figure out the solution. Hellinger opens his mind to the movement of Spirit (which he refers to as the Conscious Field), and allows it to guide both him and the representatives toward movements that will re-solve the discordance in the system. As the facilitator, I too intend to be an instrument of the Conscious Field, and am as much a part of the movement of the Field as each of the other participants in the constellation. My intention and practice is to facilitate from within the Conscious Field rather than as an outside observer or authority. This approach seems to allow most constellations to move to a more transcendent level.

Unlike Hellinger, however, I work almost exclusively in what I term a veiled format with respect to the sharing of information with representatives and observers. This is done to ensure that the information and work of the constellation are sourced solely from within the Field (or, as Hellinger would say, guided by Spirit) and not by himself or the participants. In Hellinger's constellations, at least when he was still working with representatives for specific family members, usually everyone knew from the beginning what the family story or dysfunction was, and what issue the client wanted to resolve. As a consequence of doing open interviews, the observers as well as the representatives were provided with explicit knowledge about who was representing which living or dead member of the system, or which nation or nationality, or which disease or body organ, etc.

In contrast, in the veiled format, no one knows who represents whom or what. The client's interview with me is done in private. I write the roles to be represented on individual cards, which are folded so that the writing is hidden from view. The client or I choose the representatives. The cards are randomly presented to the representatives without anyone—not the client, nor the representatives, nor the observers—knowing who has received which card. Even I do not know whom the representatives are representing, until I need to know in order to understand what to do next. Without fail, the roles specified on the unviewed index cards proceed to unerringly unfold themselves within and through the experience of the representatives.

Veiled constellations are clear demonstrations of the availability of non-local, or quantum, information. None of the information and experience that is revealed by representatives (before I, as the facilitator, unveil the issues and roles) can be accounted for in traditional Newtonian terms. As an example, at the very beginning of one constellation, within moments of the roles' arrival into the awareness of the representatives, one of them screamed, grabbed his head, and fell to the floor in an experience of agonizing pain. Upon asking to see the card that this representative had been given—which had been folded over twice and given to the representative randomly, without the representative ever looking at it—I found the words: "Great Uncle/severely disabled/head wound/WWII/ignored by family."

The information that allows something like this to occur is obviously non-local in nature. Sometimes participants and observers are not told anything at all about who or what is being represented until the very end of the constellation, or, if the client wants anonymity, perhaps nothing will be revealed even then. Amazingly, there is almost always resolution and reconciliation that changes not only the patterns and experience within the constellation, but also the patterns and experience within the actual lives of the clients and their families (and very often the representatives and observers as well).

In constellations, I am always focused on one main question: "Out of devotion to whom or what is the client suffering because of an SOL?" In addition to Hellinger's Orders of Love, I use other concepts from different sources. I am greatly moved by the statement of a wise soul:

> My observation is . . . that every time I am confronted with the experience of moving forward, I am inclined to resist and avoid becoming more of what I already am . . . [because] every time I am confronted with moving forward, I am also confronted with allowing someone else to stay where they are. . . . My experience is that the source of suffering is in the ways we suffer for other people in an unworkable attempt to say I love you. (Kaskafayet channeled through E. O'Hara, personal communication, July 1977)

This frame of suffering, which is from the teaching of a master named Kaskafayet, antedates Hellinger's constellation work by more than fifteen years. (See Appendix G for a description of my encounter with Kaskafayet, and how Kaskafayet's teachings influenced my work.) I use the term "devotional suffering" to capture and synthesize the essence of the views of both Kaskafayet and Hellinger.

I also teach and practice an integration of constellation-like work—investigating clients' Orders of Love and Suffering Obligations of Love—in one-on-one private sessions. In my work with individual clients I occasionally set up (either through visualization in the client's mind or by using index cards representing family members) a constellation-like format for gathering trans-generational family information. In addition I created a simple, yet remarkably powerful visual format called The Family Bleachers, in which many generations of the family sit or stand in the bleachers of a gymnasium or football stadium. Through such methods, with proper guidance, it is usually possible for a client to gain access to the origins of their personal devotional suffering.

In my private sessions with clients, I continue to pose the question succinctly articulated by Jonathan Rice: "What are the Vs (pictures) and As (sounds) that are making the negative Ks (feelings)?" (J. Rice, personal communication, April 1985). In addition to working with the negative feelings related to the drive to survive, I also investigate how feelings of devotion to the ancestors create limits and damage in the client's life. What are the other-than-unconscious Vs and As that drive people to do those things that cause them suffering, both on the level of survival and the level of devotion to our family members and ancestors?

The unique conceptual framework of Transformational NLP is reflected in a phrase I use concerning the two main unconscious drives in people's lives: survival patterning and devotional patterning. I teach a model of what I call (tongue-in-cheek) The Oreo of Eternal Doom, in which the pain of human beings is like the sugary filling in the middle of an Oreo cookie. Humans find themselves sandwiched between the mandates of safety and survival and the compulsion to compromise or destroy their own well-being out of devotion to their ancestors. The former is programming that at one time may have been necessary or useful to survive, but is outdated and causes tremendous suffering in the present. The latter is a massively distorted and entirely unconscious attempt to remedy the losses and tragedies of preceding generations. Through Transformational NLP's combination of NLP procedures in a format resembling psychotherapy and our evolution of the family constellation, we can revise both the survival and the devotional patterning that create obstacles to living with free choice in the present.

CHAPTER X
Manifesting Alternative Realities

Perhaps the most fascinating work I have done is based on my interest in potential alternative realities. John Grinder and Richard Bandler had studied Carlos Castaneda's books about his experiences with the Native American sorcerer, don Juan Matus, to understand how to assist people in changing their reality.[1] Castaneda's description of don Juan's sorcery strongly influenced the founders and therefore the development of NLP (McClendon, 1989; Dilts & Hallbom, 2009). Transformational NLP takes this work even further.

Influence of Carlos Castaneda's Don Juan

Don Juan's basic premise is that the world of everyday life is not real, or "out there," as we believe it is. Instead, the world we all know is only a description of the world that has been instilled in each child by his or her culture from the moment s/he is born. The perceptual interpretations that make up the world run uninterruptedly in our minds and are rarely questioned (Castaneda, 1972; Keen, 1972).

The teacher explains that personal power depends on how clearly a person can "see." For don Juan, "seeing" means to experience the world directly, without the preconceptions we have been taught since infancy and outside of the descriptions we have learned to call reality. When we can "see" clearly, then we can begin to develop the freedom to perceive and describe the world as we wish. In other words, we will be able to rewrite our personal stories (Keen, 1972).

Don Juan elaborates that in order for a person to really "see," s/he first has to "stop the world" (Castaneda, 1972, p. 14). In an interview with Sam Keen for the magazine *Psychology Today*, Carlos Castaneda clarifies that "when we stop the world, the world we stop is the one we usually maintain by our continual inner dialogue. Once you can stop the internal babble you stop maintaining your old world. The descriptions collapse. That is when personality change begins" (Keen, 1972).

Castaneda learned from don Juan a number of different techniques to stop the world. Sometimes psychotropic plants were used to stop the flow of ordinary interpretations. Another technique was to disrupt one's routines. A third way was to learn to observe and manipulate one's dreams. Yet another method was to focus on the noises in the outside world until the mind got tired and dropped into the gap (Keen, 1972).

Thus, don Juan was helping Castaneda to experience the space between thoughts so that he could begin to see the possibility that his thoughts and perceptions could be changed at will. Like mystics in all cultures throughout the ages, the Native American shaman demonstrated that experiencing the gap or source of thought was the first step to recognizing that one had created the thoughts and could just as well have other thoughts. However, accessing the source of thought is not by itself sufficient for the person to be able to create a new reality. To choose a new reality, one needs an alternative possible description of the world, that is, new information (Castaneda, 1972). It is necessary to provide the subconscious with new information so that one can choose different thoughts about oneself and the outside world.

Castaneda elucidates that, "One of the earliest things don Juan taught me was that I must erase my personal history" (Keen, 1972). To do this, and to support learning to change realities at will, one has to avoid being known and categorized by others. He clarifies, "The more you are known and identified, the more your freedom is curtailed. When people have definite ideas about who you are and how you will act, then you can't move. . . . If little by little you create a fog around yourself then you will not be taken for granted and you will have more room for change" (Keen, 1972). Thus, even the information that others have about you can impact your own consciousness.

In this way, don Juan taught Castaneda that he could change his personal history by going to the source of thought and changing the information from that level. Bandler and Grinder believed that they could do this with hypnosis, anchoring, and reframing (McClendon, 1989; Dilts & Hallbom, 2009). Later, Dilts and Rice added re-imprinting.

Like Bandler and Grinder, I was deeply affected by the teachings of don Juan and read all of the books by Carlos Castaneda. I was also influenced by Castaneda's public teaching programs, held in the 1990s. These events were primarily focused on teaching shamanic magical passes, formalized physical movements that had been passed down by the sorcerers in don Juan's lineage for thousands of years, in a modernized form that Castaneda called Tensegrity. (See Appendix H for my experience of Carlos Castaneda's Tensegrity training.) The magical passes consist of a complex series of physical movements, the performance of which (according to Castaneda) would redistribute a person's energy in order to open up the ability to perceive energy fields and their flow in human beings as well as in the universe. Once a person became conscious of the energy fields, s/he could utilize and manipulate them (Castaneda, 1995). This was a first step to freeing oneself from the confines of inherited, rigid descriptions of reality, including one's personal beliefs and identity.

Change of Life Version as well as Life Vision

In Transformational NLP I also offer additional maneuvers of consciousness. Like don Juan, I strongly emphasize the direct and indirect re-telling of one's story by creating a change of *vision*, which is an essentially linear, Newtonian endeavor in the tradition of Jonathan Rice. This is a change of perception that leads to a re-interpretation of the causes, effects, motivations, and meanings of one's life experience, all based on the remembered, established "facts" of one's history.

However Transformational NLP, like don Juan's teachings, can also involve creating a change of life *version*, not just of vision. This involves more than just new discovery and interpretation. I facilitate the creation of a new version of ourselves and our world by selectively calling forth the influence and effects of what did not occur. This endeavor to manifest an alternative reality is aligned with some of the implications of quantum mechanics.

Quantum physicist David Bohm elucidates that:

> Before a quantum measurement is registered, there are vast possibilities for alternative outcomes, each of which is present within the field of information associated with the quantum potential—each of them is potentially "active." But after the measurement has been registered, only one of the possibilities becomes an actuality. Information about alternative possibilities is still present within the quantum field, but it has ceased to be in an "active form" and cannot affect the future of the quantum system. (Peat, 1997, p. 297)

Transformational NLP, however, sometimes taps into these alternative possibilities in such a way that they actually can influence the future. For example, the practitioner may ask the client to imagine a story about his/her life that s/he wishes were true instead of what actually happened. This can have a very beneficial effect on a client who is unwilling to stop being negatively affected in the present by his or her particularly abusive actual past. It is a human instinct to base one's identity on resistance to past horror, but this resistance cannot lead to full healing and future freedom—one remains a living memorial to the past nightmare realities. Therefore, asking such clients to imagine having had a more loving parent, along with all the feelings that come with having been nurtured by that parent, can create a positive opening that would not have developed in any other way.

As neuropsychologist Rick Hanson (2013) describes, "imagined experiences build neural structures through mechanisms similar to those that actual, live experiences use" (p. 105). David Bohm explains that our thoughts and words cause objective chemical changes in the brain: He writes, "Words . . . unfold in the brain, producing changes in its chemistry that permeate the whole body. . . . [These] somatic reactions . . . in turn modify our thinking. Words, thoughts, feelings, and intentions have their objective correlate as chemical processes within the brain; likewise, objective chemical processes have their subjective correlates in movements of thought" (Peat, 1997, pp. 278–279).

While the facts of a person's history remain the same, the effects of a potential alternative reality can be manifested in the person's nervous system and other-than-conscious processes for making meaning. Psychiatrist Bessel van der Kolk (2014) explains that reworking the past to create new, alternative, virtual memories that live side by side with the painful realities of the past can provide antidotes to memories of hurt and betrayal. The client still knows what the facts of the past were and are, but s/he suffers from them less.

It is important to note that we are not endeavoring to change the memory of the actual facts of what happened in the past. Instead, the objective is to change the meaning of what those actual past experiences mean now. An experience of a potential alternative reality both takes away much of the negative charge associated with the memory of the actual past and enables the client to conceive of having more choice in the present.

However, while offering an imagined better past can often support having new and healing choices now, the imagination should never be used to remove the need for making new choices about the present and future. Similarly, the activity of "re-imprinting significant others" can be used to ease present pain and extend present comprehension of what actually happened, but should not remove the opportunity and necessity to make new choices.

Our challenge and task is to choose a better way for ourselves despite the struggles of the past—not to obviate the need for loving, healing re-choosing by arranging for there to have been no fear or struggle to begin with. Again, we want to find a way to change our feelings about what happened in the past, not the facts themselves, since our feelings determine what the meaning of what happened. Enabling the nervous system to experience a potential alternative reality can facilitate a change in the meaning of what actually occurred.

Another example of working to manifest an alternative reality is the systemic family constellation. In the previous chapter I discussed the format of the family constellations I facilitate, their potential in terms of changing consciousness, and the similarities to and differences from those of Bert Hellinger. In this section, I will discuss family constellations as a way to manifest changes in external reality as well as in internal consciousness.

I teach my students that it is the work of the practitioner to complete no-longer-useful threads of cause and effect within the client's life and world, and replace them with revisions in what we may call the "topology of family karma." Topology is the mathematical study of shapes that preserve the essential properties of the space they occupy, despite any stretching, bending, or twisting that may be applied. Topologically transformed shapes can appear to the eye to be entirely different things, although they remain identical at the level of the core mathematics that describes them. Likewise, in the trans-generational workings of family systems, the perceivable "shape" of outer family events may or may not be recognizably similar to what happened in previous generations, but the forces underlying these events are identical. I teach that it is the task of the constellation facilitator to recognize these important trans-generational core symmetries even though they may appear as radically different shapes from one generation to another. In constellation-format family dynamics, the goal is to reveal and modify—outside of space and time, because that is where the changes in constellations occur—the information that has given rise to the shape of the way things have been, so that events can unfold in new ways in the client's and the family's future.

As discussed previously, changes in the family's past by means of corrective movements in constellations are always accomplished in the "now" moments in which the constellation is taking place. For example, if now during the constellation the representative of a parent who abandoned the family—in (the constellation's revelations about) events that occurred a hundred years past—is supported to reconnect with and remain properly supportive of children and grandchildren, the family consciousness, which transcends generational limits, immediately gains access to a different "past" geometry that governs the flow and expression of love in the family. Although past facts remain unaltered, the events and experiences that become possible for the family in the present and future can change as if the past facts had been different.

This process has different effects from those of re-imprinting the client or significant others. Re-imprinting changes a person's internal patterning without requiring a related shift in family consciousness across time. Constellations change systemic realities, which can support corresponding changes in one's personal thoughts, feelings, and outer behavior. If we were to describe this phenomenon in David Bohm's terms, we would say that the movements of intention and consciousness that occur in a constellation allow a different set of explicate events to unfold from the infinite field of implicate past potentials.

For example, in a family in which a tragic loss was denied or ignored in an earlier generation, it is likely that a least some descendants of the ones who experienced the loss will experience similar losses, albeit in a manner or in ways that have an entirely different-appearing shape. Events that occurred in a village that was wiped out by invaders can give rise, generations later, to contemporary lives in which people are wiped out by very different-appearing forces, such as political or financial devastation. In the context of the consciousness called the family soul, one of the main laws (what Bert Hellinger calls Orders of Love) that govern wellbeing is, "No one may be forgotten, denied, or cast out for any reason." Beginning from the presently available facts of the client's unwanted experience (tragic financial loss, in this example), it is the facilitator's task to discover what persons, events or situations were forgotten, denied, or excluded, or were simply allowed to go unacknowledged, during the progression of generations. When the relevant deleterious symmetry is perceived, the revision of the underlying structure is accomplished by having (the representatives for) the ones who originally turned away from the victims turn toward them now, in the constellation, and perhaps say the words, "Now we see you. We could not bear to see you before, but now we see you." In some mysterious way, this reconciliation now during the constellation often changes the relevant geometries of the family's past in service of its future. Illnesses mysteriously disappear, "accidents" stop happening, family members change their attitudes, and so on.

A similar topological adjustment in the client's family history can occur in the course of a session of one-on-one change work. It is accomplished through the practitioner's attention to possible symmetries across generations. In this situation, the practitioner's task is to imagine a new shape that can serve to organize the unfolding of future personal experience and family events. This can also be described as finding a new attractor, a new idea around which future life events can be imagined. This is accomplished as a maneuver of consciousness, a momentary adjustment in the practitioner's attention and intention. It can be as simple as imagining new options for the client's map of reality. It may or may not be in the client's best interests for the practitioner to present these new options explicitly to the client. Either way, this maneuver expands the field of available probabilities within which the practitioner and client are working together toward a more positive future. Even when unspoken, it may somehow even affect the client's psyche more directly, in some mysterious way. This intention of the practitioner for a better future for the client provides a guideline for the very process and path to accomplish this goal.

I believe, in the language of biologist Rupert Sheldrake, that such changes can also be manifested in the larger morphogenetic field, and thereby influence the evolution of humanity at large. Any individual organism both informs and is informed by the experience of every being of that type, both now and through time (Sheldrake, 1995a, 1995b). Hence, the experience of all humans affects every human. Every person who imagines a more positive past, present, and future for him/herself is contributing to the wellbeing of everyone, everywhere.

However, humans tend to value the whole track of our experience and learning, not just the results of our progress in the present. Hence, all of this re-versioning of heretofore fixed past events needs to be accomplished within a framework of continued awareness of and respect for the client's personal ecology. I teach my students to support the movements and changes in both *life vision* and *life version* while remaining within the context of our personal history.

All schools of NLP are based on Korzybski's insight that the map is not the territory. As NLP evolved, so did the ways that practitioners viewed the relationship between the map and the territory. As discussed above, Grinder and Bandler began their NLP journey by developing the Meta Model. The Meta Model works with the conscious mind to create a fuller and less distorted map by challenging the out-of-consciousness violations of generalization, deletion, and distortion that limit the client's representational flexibility and, consequently, his or her access to a wider range of life choices (Grinder & Pucelik, 2013). This approach can be summed up by saying: "the map is not the territory, but let's get them more correlated."

Then the founders discovered the work of Milton Erickson, and they subsequently distilled from it what they termed the Milton model. The inverse of the Meta Model, the Milton model allows easier access to the unconscious mind by utilizing, rather than challenging, the effects of Meta Model violations. Rather than asking the client for specificity, the Milton Model language patterns work through hypnotic generalization and artful vagueness. The goal is to loosen or even dissolve the client's habitual patterns of representing and making meaning of experiences, so s/he can more flexibly and creatively navigate in the world without a fixed map (Grinder & Pucelik, 2013). This approach can be summed up by saying: "the map is not the territory, so let's dissolve the map so we can act without fixed preconceptions about the contents and rules of the territory."

Transformational NLP adds a new perspective on the relationship between the map and the territory. My work with clients and my teachings are based on this premise: the map actually *creates* the territory. As quantum physicists observe, the events that unfold in our lives appear to mirror our personal consciousness, that is, our beliefs and emotions. The consciousness of the individual participates in bringing one of many alternative probabilities into actual manifestation (Friedman, 1997; Rosenblum & Kuttner, 2006). I base much of my work with clients on this foundational assertion of quantum science. Transformational NLP describes, analyzes, and works with what Grinder and Bandler called "the structure of magic"—not only in the frame of the Metal Model and the Milton model, but also of the more mystical ways that human beings choose and manifest their experience. Perhaps Carlos Castaneda and don Juan would consider such maneuvers of consciousness to be a form of sorcery.

CHAPTER XI

Can People Reprogram Themselves?

This history of the profound contributions and innovations in the field of Neuro-Linguistic Programming up through the present time may lead some readers to inquire: Why bother with all this change work? There is a trend in contemporary society in which many people believe that humans can change their programming and their reality by their own intention alone. A plethora of publications such as *The Secret* and the Abraham-Hicks writings maintain that the Law of Attraction guarantees that reality will conform to our desires if we focus clearly on them.

Even modern science increasingly supports this worldview. Quantum physicists tell us that there is no objective, external reality other than the one we create in our own minds (Friedman, 1997; Rosenblum, 2006). In his acclaimed work *Mindful Universe: Quantum Mechanics and the Participating Observer* (2010), the eminent quantum physicist Henry Stapp maintains that the world "is constituted not of matter, as classically conceived, but rather of an informational structure that causally links . . . the psychologically described contents of our streams of conscious experience with the mathematically described objective tendencies that tie out chosen actions to experience" (p. 38). Stapp argues that human consciousness influences the objective world in the process of observing it. "The subject's conscious effort is *actually* causing what his conscious understanding *believes*, on the basis of life-long experience, that effort to be causing" (p. 48). According to Stapp, what we perceive as the objective, physical world actually consists of clouds of probabilities. The quantum wave functions contain many alternative quantum possibilities, and collapse into one "reality" only when conscious minds select it. "The acquisition of knowledge does not simply reveal what is physically fixed and settled; it is part of the process that creates the reality that we know" (p. 160). Hence, a person's conscious intention and choices can influence physical reality. Similarly, Deepak Chopra writes that:

> All that is really "out there" is raw, unformed data waiting to be interpreted by you, the perceiver. You take "a radically ambiguous, flowing quantum soup," as physicists call it, and use your senses to congeal the soup into the solid three-dimensional world . . . there is no color in the natural world, and no sound . . . no textures . . . no scent . . . in short, none of the objective facts upon which we usually base our reality . . . [hence] you can change your world . . . simply by changing your perception. (Chopra, 1993, pp. 11–12)

Chopra (1993) further elucidates that:

> A reaction anywhere in space-time, including past, present, and future, causes a shift in the entire quantum field . . . . every intention is a trigger for transformation. As soon as you decide that you want something, your nervous system responds to reach your desired goal. . . . This means that when you have a desire, you are actually sending a message into the entire field—your slightest intention is rippling across the universe at the quantum level . . . [and] the field has the organizing power to automatically bring fulfillment to any intention. (pp. 85, 103, 106)

It seems that the views of contemporary quantum scientists have much in common with those of mystics. The great mystics from all cultures and time periods tell us that it is consciousness that creates our universe and perceptions of reality, and that, indeed, matter, energy, and consciousness are only different aspects of one Whole (Friedman, 1997; Peat, 1997; Goswami, 1993; Maharishi Mahesh Yogi, 1990); Hagelin, 2006).

Recent discoveries in science seem to support this perspective. Quantum physicist John Hagelin (2006) wrote: "In the last decade we had the superstring revolution—the discovery of a single, universal, unified field of intelligence that underlies and pervades us all, a unified fountainhead of all the diverse laws of nature that uphold the universe at every level" (p. 11).

It would seem that our awareness of the Universal Consciousness, and the understanding that we are manifestations of it, and have the same properties as it, should itself be sufficient to propel us into the realm of freedom from past programming. However, we have all had the experience of not having our desires fulfilled, and finding that our old limiting beliefs are still determining our present reality. Scientists and mystics alike have tried to understand why we are so bound by our past.

Quantum physicist David Bohm was preoccupied with the question of how people can change their reality through intention, and provided a transcript of his discussion about it with the Indian sage Krishnamurti. In this discussion, Bohm points out that thought is conditioned by heredity, tradition, culture, and environment to falsify and distort our perception of reality. The brain wants to reduce all perceptions and actions to habit. Bohm observes, "Tradition goes back to that feeling of belonging to the family and to the community, of being approved of because you are not only doing what they say, what you're supposed to do, but believing what you are supposed to believe, and believing in what [you are told to believe] is real. This tradition includes the belief that we have a correct consensus as to what is real, a belief that we don't create our reality" (Krishnamurti & Bohm, 1999, p. 92).

Likewise, cellular biologist Bruce Lipton (2005) tells us that our programming is much stronger than our conscious awareness and will. He explains that our conscious thoughts have an effect on behavior only when they are in harmony with subconscious programming. He elaborates, "The fundamental behaviors, beliefs and attitudes we observe in our parents become 'hard-wired' as synaptic pathways in our subconscious minds. Once programmed into the subconscious mind, they control our biology for the rest of our lives . . . unless we can figure out a way to reprogram them" (p. 164). He emphasizes that positive affirmations are not enough: "No amount of yelling or cajoling by the conscious mind can ever change the behavioral 'tapes' programmed into the subconscious mind" (p. 170).

Lipton (2005) maintains that there is, however, a way to change human programming. He writes that the evolution of the prefrontal cortex allows humans to observe their own behavior and emotions. Because of this ability to be self-reflective, humans have the ability to edit and reprogram their subconscious. Nevertheless, Lipton admits that it is extremely difficult to change the programming of the powerful subconscious mind.

In contrast, Krishnamurti maintains that the solution to programming is developing the ability to love unconditionally. He maintains that only unconditional love can break down perceptions of limitation and separation among people and create a new brain that sees the reality of Oneness (Krishnamurti & Bohm, 1999). However, he does not explain how we can learn to love unconditionally if we are not first de-programmed from long-standing patterning that creates fear and the experience of separation.

Deepak Chopra (1993) clarifies why so few people have been able to re-program their own minds: "[When you have an intention] the result you get back from the field is the highest fulfillment that can be delivered to your particular nervous system" (pp. 106–107). In other words, we have to be in a self-realized state in order to be able to fulfill our intentions. Only when we are in such a de-programmed state can we immediately manifest our desires because the Creational Source will mirror their fulfilled forms back to us. As Chopra (1993) explains, we must lift our awareness beyond the immediate confines of space and time, and from that level we can create our own reality in the manifest world. Only when a person attains the self-realized consciousness of identity with the Unified Field can his/her every conscious intention be fulfilled virtually automatically.

The question remains: How can we produce a nervous system that supports and fulfills our intentions so that we can be independent agents, free from the past? Chopra and many other scholars, scientists, and researchers as well as mystics claim that there are techniques, such as meditation, that can bring us to this awareness of and identification with the Universal Consciousness (Chopra,

1933; Hagelin, 2006; Wheeler, 2009). However, our experience in the West as well as in the East is that most people who have practiced meditation and other techniques for many years have not become enlightened. While they seem to have benefited from these practices, the great majority have not attained the degree of self-realization that Chopra has. Despite achieving better health and greater happiness, their patterns of thought and behavior continue to be bound to a great degree by past conditioning.

Even those who become self-realized do not necessarily become entirely free from past programming. A person reaches enlightenment when s/he realizes his or her identification with the Pure Consciousness of the Unified Field. Enlightened people have the ability to access the Source of infinite potential and energy, and may even have the ability to affect the processes of energetic and material manifestation. While they continue to seek experience in life and the world, they no longer identify with their personal experiences, or personality, or behavior, or even with their own beliefs and thoughts. Hence, although they are unique individuals with distinctive personality traits, they no longer suffer from separation (Chopra, 1933; Hagelin, 2006).

Yet, while a person in an enlightened state of consciousness lives in the "eternal now" and does not act from stress from the past, s/he is not infallible. S/he can still have faulty logic. S/he can also have personality characteristics that come from past conditioning. Long-term meditators and other seekers have learned from experience that it is a mistake to assume that enlightenment automatically brings with it freedom from past personality or behavior traits. In Vedic philosophy, such ingrained habits of personality and thought are called *laisha vidya*, or leftovers from the past. Even those who attain the highest states of enlightenment may demonstrate some traits of personality, such as anger or jealousy, which do not seem to be aligned with their high state of consciousness.[1]

This distinction between enlightenment and freedom from past conditioning has been understood by mystics for thousands of years. In the Bhagavad Gita we read: "Creatures everywhere follow their own nature. Even the enlightened follow their own nature . . . what can restraint accomplish?" (Maharishi Mahesh Yogi, 1990, p. 229). The scripture explains that, "Even if you were the most sinful of all sinners, you would cross over all evil by the raft of knowledge alone" (p. 308). "Knowledge" here refers to knowledge of the nature of Reality, and the ability to attain permanent transcendental consciousness. The last verses of the Bhagavad Gita reiterate that even an evil-doer can attain self-realization (Beck, 2001).

Thus, even the most spiritually developed people do not seem to have the capability to substantially revise their own neural programming without assistance. Although they may have more ability to witness rather than identify with the personality, and their nervous systems are more flexible (and therefore it is easier for them to change), it seems that even they cannot reliably succeed in achieving the change they may want in their programming by themselves. It seems to require some outside influence to assist a person to change personal beliefs and identity as well as thought and behavior patterns that are programmed into the nervous system. While meditation and other spiritual practices can make us much happier because we identify less with our personalities and histories, if we want to have more choice we have to be able to not only transcend our conditioned programming, but actually change it.

How can we change our programming? To answer this question, we can look at the findings of modern science. Quantum physicists Paul Dirac, John Wheeler, and Richard Feynman made the amazing observation that electrons not only generate their own electric fields, but they actually interact with their fields, and are in turn affected by the very fields they generate (Dirac, 1933; Feynman, 1965; Hestenes, 1983; Nave, 2012). David Bohm elaborated that the implicate order (the quantum field) unfolds to an explicate order (manifest reality), which re-enfolds to affect and change the potential in the implicate, which is already unfolding as a potentially different explicate, and so on in a continuous feedback loop (Friedman, 1997, p. 105).

Considering that the Field contains infinite possibilities, what determines which path an electron will take? Why does one possibility become manifest rather than another? The answer, as the scholar Ervin Laszlo explains, is information (Laszlo, 2004). The Field of all potential is a reservoir of both energy and information. This field contains information about everything that ever happened and the potential for anything that could happen in the future. All the different possibilities exist as potential (wave patterns) in the field. Any of these possibilities may or may not get materialized. The element that decides whether one potential event—rather than another out of an infinite number of potential events—will become manifest, is information. Information is the process that actually forms manifest phenomena out of the field of energy.

Similarly, each human consciousness creates a unique field. As Sheldrake describes, humans interact with and are affected by their own consciousness fields. People generate a field that affects the creation of what they experience (Sheldrake, 1995a; 1995b). The process of manifestation of each individual's consciousness and experience is determined by information.

In order to change the trajectory of a person's life, just like changing the path of an electron, it is critical to provide appropriate new information. It seems that to accomplish such change it is necessary first to access the deepest level of a person's subconscious and from that level change the information from which it generates new manifestations in the world. In Deepak Chopra's words, "To change the printout of the body, you must learn to rewrite the software of the mind" (Chopra, 1991, p. 12). John Grinder and Richard Bandler embarked on just such a search for ways to access the subconscious mind in order to change the information in people's psyches that give rise to self-limiting thoughts and behavior.

Conclusion

Throughout history people have considered mental as well as physical suffering to be an inevitable part of life. The evolution of Homo sapiens several hundred thousand years ago included the development of the brain's cerebral cortex, which is responsible for perceiving, thinking, and understanding language. There are four main sections, or lobes, in the cerebral cortex. Two of them, the parietal lobe and the occipital lobe, are involved in receiving and processing sensory information and vision. The other two lobes, the frontal and temporal lobes, allow us to think abstractly. The frontal and temporal lobes are the ones that make us distinctly human—and also neurotic (LeDoux, 1998).

The frontal lobe, specifically the prefrontal cortex, enables humans to represent information not currently in the environment. This allows us to guide our thoughts, emotions, and behavior to achieve a goal. It provides the ability to control our impulses, anticipate and plan for the future, make decisions, and solve problems. However, by giving us the faculty to imagine that which is not actually present, these wonderful human capabilities also enable us to worry about the future. We are continuously besieged by concerns—and the emotions that drive them and give them such significance for us—about our finances, relationships, health, goals, apparent failures, and the inevitability of death and what might, or might not, lie beyond it (LeDoux, 1998). Our fears about suffering in the future cause us to suffer in the present.

The temporal lobe is involved with memory, emotion, and language. Located in the temporal lobe is the hippocampus, which is involved in forming memories. Also found in the temporal lobe are the amygdala and the limbic system, which govern such primary emotions as fear, rage, and pain. Just as we have the capacity to imagine futures, we also have the ability to maintain past memories and emotions in the present. This allows us the capability to learn from past experience, but it also makes the past difficult to forget. We routinely run the film of past grievances, and their emotional impact, over and over again in our minds (LeDoux, 1998; MacLean, 1990).

Neuropsychologist Rick Hanson (2013) explains that human memory has a negative bias. Negative emotions affect us much more strongly and for a much longer time than positive ones. The brain has evolved to be constantly scanning for threats. This negativity bias in our memory is a remnant of the Stone Age brain that still lives in humans in the twenty-first century. "The negativity bias is tilted toward immediate survival, but against quality of life. . . . This is the default setting of the Stone Age brain" (pp. 29–30). Hanson elucidates that positive and negative emotions use different memory systems in the brain. Negative emotions are fast-tracked into long-term memory storage, while positive emotions usually do not readily get converted into neural structure that is transferred into long-term memory. "Your brain is like Velcro for negative experience but Teflon for positive ones" (p. 27).

Thus, the evolution of humans has provided for the development of the frontal lobes, which cause us to worry about the future, and the temporal lobes, which cause us to be deeply wounded, again and again, by our experience of the past. Unlike all other species, with rare exceptions, humans are not able to automatically live in the present moment. Our evolution and ability to think abstractly have come at the price of great suffering as a natural part of being human.

Throughout history, people in all cultures have located the source of their suffering in forces beyond their control. Many religions have taught that suffering is part of the human heritage of sin as a result of defying God or gods, whether at the beginning of creation or in our everyday lives. With the advent of the Enlightenment, there was a widespread assumption that the scourges of hunger, war, and disease were the main causes of suffering, and that if these could be ameliorated, people could finally live in peace and happiness. However, this theory has proved to be incorrect. In the contemporary world many millions of people have an abundance of food and other necessities and live in countries with peaceful circumstances, with medical advances that have eradicated the worst diseases and promise a longer and healthier life than ever before. Yet, there seems to be no end to the suffering, even among those who possess the most material wealth.

In the twentieth century, different schools of psychology have attempted to scientifically investigate what makes people the way they are and to discover modern methods to alleviate suffering. Behaviorism was the dominant paradigm of psychology in America in the first half of the twentieth century. Founded by John Watson in 1913, behaviorist psychology was an attempt to scientifically determine not *why* people feel and act the way they do, but rather *how* their behavior can be systematically modified by external influences.

The behaviorists believed that psychology should only be concerned with what can be seen and measured (i.e., observable behavior). They were not interested in the mind's subjective, inner experiences because they are not objectively measurable. They maintained that any discussion that hypothesized why people are the way they are, that was curious about internal events and internal behavior, was more properly the domain of humanism and philosophy rather than psychology. Behaviorists argued that the physical brain, like the mind, is a "black box"—nothing can be known about what goes on inside it. However, knowing what is inside the black box is not necessary for determining how behavior is affected by stimuli from the environment (Miller, 2003).

Following the lead of Watson, psychologist B. F. Skinner popularized behaviorism. Skinner maintained that people are essentially a compound of conditioned reflexes determined by their genes and external environmental influences. He argued that behavior, including thoughts and emotions, can be explained as a product of environmental factors and can be modified by manipulating conditions and events within the environment. Influenced by the classical conditioning theory of Ivan Pavlov, the behaviorists believed that there was no difference between animals and humans regarding behavior, as both could be conditioned in similar ways. Behaviorist psychologists measured and quantified conditioned responses to stimuli with the goal of being able to predict and control human behavior (Miller, 2003).

However, in the early 1960s the models of Cognitive Psychology challenged and generally supplanted the behaviorist paradigm. In 1960 George Miller, Eugene Galanter, and Karl Pribram wrote *Plans and the Structure of Behavior,* in which they claimed to be able to explain what happens in the "black box" of the human mind. They presented their T.O.T.E model—Test, Operate, Test, Exit (often restated as Trigger, Operate, Test, Exit)—to explicate black box events. Extrapolating from the operation of control programs created for digital computers, these authors reasoned that human beings must have internal signaling that provides cues for when to begin cognitive operations, how to know when these operations are in process, and how to know when they are complete so that the next operation can commence. Of course, all of this signaling occurs so quickly, and is often so far from conscious awareness, that it is generally not part of our actual experience (Miller, Galanter, & Pribram, 1960).

In 1980 John Grinder and Richard Bandler, in collaboration with their students Robert Dilts, Leslie Bandler, and Judith Delozier, explained how they used this work as the basis for what, in their novel Neuro-Linguistic Programming terminology, they called "strategies." In the language of NLP, a "strategy" is a sequence of internal and external sensory representations that leads to a particular outcome. The outcome might be a bit of external behavior or any moment of internal experience. A proper strategy elicitation can reveal the unconscious representational events that produce the experience of making a decision, or perhaps the experience of continuing indecision, or a moment of strong motivation, or one of entire lack of motivation, or of anything else that humans are able to experience (Dilts, Grinder, Bandler, et al., 1980).

The T.O.T.E. strategy elicitation procedure provides information that is much more helpful than simply guessing about black box events based on one's own assumptions about what makes people the way they are. Using T.O.T.E.s to help organize external perceptions about the events of inner experience is a great improvement over having to rely on and interpret vague statements from the client, such as "Something is really bothering me." (See Appendix I on T.O.T.E. strategies.)

Nevertheless, by itself the T.O.T.E. model is still too imprecise to be really useful in change work. Its imprecision lies mainly in its unavoidable reliance on the subject's conscious reporting about very nearly unconscious internal events, and this obviously presents the practitioner with severe limitations. Thus, while the T.O.T.E. model diminishes the mystery of internal processes somewhat, it still does not provide sufficient specific information about these invisible inner events, and it does not provide any information at all that has not already been mediated through the filters of conscious attention.

The objective of knowing about specific black box events is to make these operations available for specific revision (re-programming). However, we cannot actually revise how experience is being created until we can reliably notice and track the specific internal representations that are relevant to this experience. To be truly useful as tools for understanding the actual, immediate, operational structure and events of the client's experience, T.O.T.E. events had to be made externally confirmable. Whereas the developers of the T.O.T.E. knew that *something* was happening internally, they had no way to know specifically *what* the events occurring outside of the client's conscious awareness actually were.

In the mid-1970s, the founders of NLP discovered the crucial missing observational tools. What they described as representational accessing cues (eye movements, pupil dilation, breathing shifts, skin color changes, and so on), are other-than-conscious behavioral events that are externally observable and confirmable. However, the actual content of these other-than-conscious events remained nebulous. Although the practitioner now knew, reliably, that the client was making internal pictures, it was often unclear what these pictures were actually about.

In the late 1970s, some members of the NLP group discovered that they could reliably use the client's unconscious eye-accessing movements, especially those occurring in the first fraction of a second after being asked certain specific questions, to gain access to immensely relevant events and decision points in the individual's personal history. Jonathan Rice realized that the information so derived, which was often from long-forgotten events and decisions stored in the deep unconscious, was of a nature that made it extremely unlikely that it would ever have arisen through therapeutic conversation. He was excited to find that he could gain this access immediately and at will in the therapeutic moment, and that the information obtained thereby was confirmable and the methodology was replicable (J. Rice, personal communication, November, 2011). This discovery transformed the T.O.T.E. ideas from vague concepts into a practical, immediately useful tool for assisting in the process of profound change work.

Using the half-second eye access, a sufficiently skillful practitioner can notice the fleeting external evidence of crucial, unconscious internal events and, when the time is right, can cause these events to repeat in ways that allow them to then be brought into the client's conscious attention without guesswork or interpretation. Thus, the black box can be opened to external observation—and thereby both the operational programming and the experience created by this programming can be made consciously, almost miraculously, accessible to both the client and the therapist. The unwanted experience and the patterning that generates it are now available to be specifically noticed and intentionally and precisely revised so that the client can have the experience s/he desires. This was an extremely significant turning point in the evolution of NLP and psychology.

Within the intellectual atmosphere of the Human Potential movement and the Cognitive Revolution, John Grinder and Richard Bandler had based their explorations of how the mind works on the brilliant discoveries of Alfred Korzybski and Noam Chomsky and modeled the psychotherapeutic approaches of Fritz Perls and Virginia Satir. They also learned Milton Erikson's permissive hypnotherapy so they could access the unconscious mind through trance induction and other hypnotic processes. Grinder and Bandler were moreover strongly influenced by Carlos Castaneda's description of don Juan's sorcery and metaphors in the service of changing personal history (McClendon, 1989; Dilts & Hallbom, 2009). Additionally, they experimented with such psychic phenomena as mind reading and induced hallucinations (McClendon, 1989). These led to the development of techniques—such as those for age regression, deep trance identification, and trans-derivational search—to gain rapid access to past experiences, primarily for use in change patterns.

Later, Robert Dilts collaborated with Timothy Leary, the legendary proponent of LSD, in developing re-imprinting, while Jonathan Rice simultaneously worked out his own method of re-imprinting through his observation of body-based energy work therapies. Rice also used the discovery of the half-second eye access to evolve a reliable methodology in his clinical practice for both observing representational structure and precisely eliciting its associated unconscious content, eliminating much of the projection and guesswork that had plagued therapists and healing practitioners until then.

Subsequently, my own work has taken these innovations even further. It includes several forms of systemic and trans-generational interventions, originally inspired by Bert Hellinger, to accelerate the resolution and redirection of forces that distort the expression of love. I have also developed other map-altering methodologies that help to create and allow the desired alternative realities in students' and clients' personal lives.

These innovations in reality-altering change work notwithstanding, the school of Transformational NLP that I founded remains firmly grounded in Bandler's and Grinder's original discoveries about the external calibration of internal representational events. In humans as in animals, the creature brain does not acquire or process information in the form of concepts or high-level human language. Creature experience is programmed in and generated through sensory processes, through a programming language of pictures, sounds, smells, tastes, and feelings (VAKOG). The human can decide what s/he would like to believe and experience, but the actual capacity to change one's beliefs and experience is accomplished through modification of the creature-level neural programming. With NLP, the desired outcome of destabilizing and deconstructing obsolete patterning can be achieved by *directly* revising the sights, sounds, and feelings that form what we experience as our thought and behavior patterns, our outdated beliefs, and even our identity. As we revise out-of-date survival patterning, we make room for the new perceptions, behaviors, and beliefs—as well as the self-defined, more up-to-date identity—that we *choose* to have in our present and future experience. These desired behavior, thought, and belief patterns can then be installed by the practitioner, and permanently acquired by the client, through skillful and deliberate Neuro-Linguistic Programming.

Krishnamurti pointed out that all limitations are the same in that they restrict free choice, and all of them are based on the illusory perception that we cannot create our own reality. Alfred Korzybski started an intellectual revolution with his quest for methods by which people can change their reality by changing their neural programming. When we have the choice to become and to experience our true selves despite past conditioning, we will know experientially that reality is our own invention within an ongoing process of creation. We will no longer be trapped in a hyper-stabilized reality that we have inherited and learned in the past that is incongruent with who we are learning and growing to be now. We will have much more free choice to create the reality that includes what we truly desire.

Building on the foundation laid by Korzybski, John Grinder and Richard Bandler developed brilliant techniques to reprogram the nervous system. These techniques were refined and popularized still further by Robert Dilts and his students. However, increasingly the techniques became isolated from the context and dynamic of the person's underlying consciousness. Working independently, Jonathan Rice also expanded and refined the toolbox of NLP techniques, but he integrated them into his practice of psychotherapy. Using hypnotic patterning he learned from Milton Erickson as well as other subtle methods, Rice guided people through both the content and the representational structure of their subconscious, and from that level empowered them to actually create the reality they desired.

My own work has followed in the footsteps of Jonathan Rice. I frequently use mainstream NLP tools and skills to elicit information about the content of the client's experience, paying continuous attention to subtle representational accessing as a means for staying in real-time awareness of the person's internal sensory events. I gather information about both life content and representational structure regarding the client's desired state as well as the present state experiences. I use this information to revise the client's patterning—utilizing conventional NLP as well as Rice's approach and my own methodologies—so that the client can have the experience s/he desires.

Like Jonathan Rice, I do change work not as a series of stand-alone interventions, but rather within a context that notices and respects the trajectory and purposes of the client's entire life, including paying attention to the client's past. The change work that I practice and teach is based on deep appreciation of and respect for every aspect of human experience—past and present, positive and not positive. In addition, I have incorporated a conceptual framework drawn from the quantum world view as well as from ancient and contemporary spiritual wisdom, and added numerous novel methodologies that I have developed in the course of my experience with clients. I believe that this new synthesis of psychology, NLP, and practical spirituality fulfills more of the promise of each field, and creates a new paradigm for supporting personal transformation and happiness and the fulfillment of human potential.

Appendix A

Research on NLP

In the middle 1980s a number of articles in *The Journal of Counseling Psychology* and by the National Research Council, in addition to papers presented at other psychological conferences, concluded that there is no firm empirical evidence supporting certain NLP claims. For example, these researchers found no evidence that primary representational systems (VAKOG) can be identified by sensory predicates in a person's language and eye movement patterns, or that predicate matching has benefits in counseling. In a paper presented to the Fourth European Congress of Hypnosis in Psychotherapy and Psychosomatic Medicine in 1987 in Oxford, England, M. Heap (1988) writes that the current state of the research reveals no evidential support for the claims of NLP. This conclusion was reiterated in the articles by C. F. Sharpley (1984; 1987) and B. Beyerstein (1995). A research committee working for the U.S. National Research Council in 1988 also found no scientific support for NLP claims (Druckman & Swets, 1988).

However, these negative conclusions have been contested on the grounds that the researchers involved in the studies had inadequate training or competence in NLP. For example, P. Tosey and J. Mathison (2007) declared:

> There has been virtually no published investigation into how NLP is used in practice. The empirical research consists largely of laboratory-based studies from the 1980s and 1990s, which investigated two particular notions from within NLP, the `eye movement' model, and the notion of the `primary representational system', according to which individuals have a preferred sensory mode of internal imagery indicated by their linguistic predicates. (Grinder & Bandler, 1976;Tosey & Anderson, p. 9)

According to the authors, this is not sufficient information on which to base relevant conclusions.

A more recent discussion of the scholarship on NLP emphasizes that:

> The preponderance of the published literature largely comes down on the side arguing against NLP but for entirely the wrong reasons; they never tested NLP, only their own maps of what they thought it was. . . . The most cited of these studies were flawed by consistent errors of fact and interpretation. The first of the errors is an assumption about the basic tenets of NLP. Most of the studies were based upon the idea NLP stands or falls on the validity of the PRS [preferred representational system]—which is assumed to be a foundational construct of the field—and its assessment by EACS [eye-access cues] and conversational predicates. These interpretations were wrong at the time of the research and remain wrong today. These publications have resulted in the accumulation of false findings regarding the theoretical validity of NLP. The second error appears to be an over reliance on the historical research with the assumption that that research tested the actual claims of NLP. Many of the studies either did not investigate NLP in sufficient depth to understand what was and was not central to it while others simply relied on the conclusions of previous researchers. (Gray, Liotta, & Cheal, 2012)

There are more positive claims for NLP in articles by C. E. Beck and E. A. Beck (1984) as well as E. L. Einspruch and B. D. Forman (1985). Additionally, the European Association for Neuro-Linguistic Psychotherapy, which promotes the training and practice of NLP as a form of psychotherapy, collected an impressive amount of scientific research done in the 1980s and 1990s to show the benefits of using NLP techniques in psychotherapy (Association for NLP, n.d.). In 2001, Neuro-Linguistic Psychotherapy (NLPt) was recognized by the United Kingdom Council for Psychotherapy as an experimental form of psychotherapy (Mcdonald, 2001), and in 2002 the Neuro-Linguistic

Psychotherapy and Counseling Association was formed (Neuro-Linguistic Psychotherapy and Counseling Association, 2014).

Yet, to this day NLP is derided as a pseudoscience; it is still not taken seriously by the academic, psychiatric, or medical professions (Devilly, 2005; Lilienfeld, et al., 2003). This dismissive attitude is probably exacerbated by the hyperbolic claims of some over-enthusiastic advocates of NLP who are not restricted by the constraints of academic discipline. For example, the claim by NLP practitioners that eye movements correlate with the internal representational process is sometimes misinterpreted as "eye-accessing cues tell us what someone is thinking." This is, of course, over-simplified and distorted information. In fact, credible schools of NLP are careful to make the distinction that eye-accessing cues reveal nothing about *what* someone is thinking, only about *how* s/he is doing it.

Another point of denunciation is that not enough research has been done to verify the scientific validity of the claims of NLP. However, as of November 15, 2016, in the NLP Research Data Base there are 363 articles on NLP research that date from December 15, 1997 (Kammer, 2016). It seems that there are enough studies supporting various claims of NLP to at least warrant further research. Although the costs in money and time for large-scale research are prohibitive, efforts in this direction are currently under way by such dedicated groups as the NLP Research and Recognition Project (Bourke, 2015).

Appendix B

Survival Equivalence

In my practice, I have again and again observed the conflict between the primal survival imperatives of our creature neurology and the happiness and values of the human mind and heart. The curious phenomenon at the basis of this conflict is what I call "survival equivalence."

The primary criterion of creature neurology is physical survival—heartbeat, blood pressure, respiration, and so on. This neurology is patterned to value and move toward any experience that enhances the possibility of survival. Creature neurology does not think, speak, or analyze, but if it did, the one question it would use to evaluate its performance would be, "Are we dead yet?" If the answer is "no," then—for this creature neurology and its associated patterns of perception and behavior—what it is doing is one hundred percent effective.

The creature neurology is also programmed to notice significant threats to survival. If it finds itself in a situation in which its continuance—its survival—is profoundly threatened, it notices the situations, events, sense perceptions, and emotional states that are part of this *in extremis* experience. If it does not perish, the creature neurology is programmed to regard these *in extremis* events and sensations as having great survival value.

Once the survival value of a near-fatal event establishes itself at or above a certain threshold, the experience of that event becomes an important means of ensuring survival. That is, the creature neurology will seek out replays of near-fatal past trauma because this near-fatal past trauma has never once resulted in death. Events and experiences that have been assigned a high survival value become a means of not perishing. The creature neurology therefore tends to seek out and/or invoke these experiences as part of ensuring its well-being.

For the creature self, the traumatic events are equivalent to—that is, identical with—continued physical survival. Thus, we have a survival equivalence.

Obviously, this is very confusing and difficult for the human being whose life is being routinely compromised by the creature self's ongoing endeavor to ensure physical survival by putting itself into replays of terrible situations from which it did not perish. The last thing the human self wants more of—for example, the experience of being "shamed to death" in a relationship—is exactly the thing that the creature self continually locates and promotes more of. The implications of the workings of this survival equivalence patterning as part of our human process for selecting mates and business partners are staggering.

Appendix C

Alfred Korzybski

In the preface to the third edition of *Science and Sanity* (1994), Alfred Korzybski explained the basis of the notion that human nature is fixed. Because humans are able to use language to summarize and generalize their experiences and pass them on to others, this saves others from having to reinvent what had already been discovered and from making the same mistakes. Each generation can begin where the former left off. However, this can lead to stagnation. The reason that some primitive tribes have not progressed for thousands of years is because they have refused to depart from time-honored habits and prejudices.

Korzybski sought to change this mentality through his transformational grammar and his innovative approach to individual therapy. He explained that the therapist must tell the patient to "remember that your words occur on the verbal levels [showing him with a gesture of the hands the hanging labels], and that they *are not* the objective level" (1994, p. 421). Korzybski instructs the therapist to:

> Wave the hand, indicating the verbal levels; then point the finger to the objective level, and, with the other hand, close your own lips, to show that on the objective level one can only be silent. When performed repeatedly, this pantomime has a most beneficial, semantic, pacifying effect upon the "over-emotionalized" identification-conditions. (1994, pp. 421–422)

According to Korzybski, there are great psycho-physiological benefits from practicing this technique to achieve the consciousness of abstracting. He explains that the neurological mechanisms of the two ways of thinking are themselves different. If we orient ourselves by verbal definitions, our orientations depend mostly on the cortical regions of the brain. If we orient ourselves by the facts, this involves thalamic factors and cortically delayed reactions, which necessitate a process orientation in life. This brings about an integration of the cortical and thalamic functions. This physiological change, according to Korzybski, can itself do much to heal the psychological imbalance of many people in modern society.

While Korzybski's method of disciplining the mind was extremely laborious and difficult, it was a pioneering effort that was a landmark in our cultural history. It laid the foundation for development of the far more simple and effective methods of NLP and subsequently of Transformational NLP.

Appendix D

A Metaphorical Timeline: Temporal/Spatial Sorting

An example of how I use a metaphorical timeline is a technique I developed called temporal/spatial sorting. The client is asked to "please make a picture, in your mind, of you from yesterday." Assuming that the client is sitting opposite me, I ask him/her to move the picture so that it is behind me and slightly to the left of his/her visual centerline. The client is then asked to imagine a "timeline" extending from the "self yesterday" to the "self now." Practitioner and client can then extend this imaginary line of time from "now" into an indefinite future. This is accomplished by having the client, while the head is facing forward, look up and to the right and extending the timeline out. Depending on topics and outcomes, the client might imagine this future timeline to be one year in the future, or five, or ten, or whatever seems most supportive for the material that is being worked with. The next step is to ask the client to look up and to the left (with head straight and only eyes moving), and to imagine an approximately four-year-old version of him/herself. The client then visually draws a timeline from the four-year-old self over to the self from yesterday, thus completing what I call a "lifetime-at-a-glance." In this format, the client discovers that the far past no longer connects directly to the present. The present is connected only with yesterday and the future.

The "lifetime-at-a-glance" aspects of the temporal/spatial sorting format provide several important benefits. Within moments, the client is actually looking "back" into the past and looking "toward" the future, separating them in his/her mind temporally as well as spatially. Moreover, when the flow of the interaction calls for the client to "step into" his/her past or future experiences, s/he actually has a spatial change away from the "space in time" called the present. The client can move to another "place in time," past or future, near or very far in either direction, without leaving his/her seat, and then have the experience of returning again to a present that is—figuratively and literally, in the space of the consulting room—not contaminated with the past or unproductively intimidated by the future. Even more importantly, the past and future are not directly connected, except through the experience of physical location and conscious choices that can only occur "now." The necessity to make two imaginary 90-degree turns—one as the client moves from the past to the now, and the other as the client moves from now out toward the future ("connect in right here, and turn the corner now")—prevents the past from flooding over into the future. This is invaluable in even the most basic change work with human beings. Of course, anything desirable can be intentionally carried from the past into the future, or vice versa, in whatever ways serve the unfolding of the client's desired state experience. In most of my client sessions, I use the temporal/ spatial sorting method more or less continually for the entire session.

Appendix E

How Transformational NLP Promotes Personal Transformation

At NLP Marin, the class format is a combination of lecture, demonstration, and practice. During the lecture students learn the theory and background of each approach and the changework that implements it. Students are encouraged to speak up with their own personal stories that are related to the issues being discussed. When students talk about the traumas and challenges in their personal histories, they discover that they are not unique and that the other students have similar issues. When they describe the personality and behavior patterning they have that they do not want, they are more and more able to dis-identify with them. Students learn that who they are is not their personality or behavior patterning, or even their beliefs, and that any of this can be changed. This dis-identification is reinforced as the students practice the change work they are learning.

When the trainer does a change work demonstration with a student as the subject who has volunteered to work in front of the class, everyone in the room benefits. In addition to having a chance to observe theory being put directly into practice, many students spontaneously identify with the experience of the demonstration subject to the extent that the change work integrates into them as well. Because we do not discuss problems without also describing and implementing solutions, the very pain and confusion that are such a large part of being human become catalysts that open the way to better, more fulfilling experiences in the future.

The students are asked to apply new ideas and tools almost immediately after they are first offered. They spend much of each class day sitting in small groups, trying out every new method that is presented. A teaching assistant facilitates each practice group, answering questions and assisting in any way that may be helpful. Each student takes turns programming another student, being programmed, and observing one student program another. Each of these positions provides an opportunity to practice rapport with the others in the group and, most importantly, to practice keeping rapport with oneself. When students practice with one another, the so-called subject, programmer, and observer all experience healing and change that brings them closer to their personal goal. Thus, we have created a new paradigm for personal transformation.

Appendix F

The Hellinger Family Constellation

In preparation for a Hellinger family constellation, the therapist/facilitator interviews the client to acquire information about the family. The information about family history that is deemed useful for Hellinger constellation work is quite different from what is usually valued in conventional family therapy interactions. The therapist seeks to gather information only about some specific facts and historical events in the family's experience. S/he is not interested in the client's descriptions of the psychological or emotional reality of the family, such as, "My mother was distant and cold." Instead, s/he is interested in statements of family fact. For example, the facilitator might ask, "How many children were in the family?" "Did anyone die young, or lose a child?" "Who was lost or cast out?" "Who was in a war, especially in combat?" "Who has a particularly difficult fate?"

This information gathering allows the therapist to select which family members will be represented as the constellation opens. The client or facilitator then chooses participants (from among the group that is present to participate in the constellation) to represent these people. One by one, the client walks the selected representatives to a place somewhere within the space defined by the circle of seated participants, so that, in terms of their placement, the directions the representatives are facing, etc., the resulting constellation is similar in feel to the client's intuitive impression of the actual family system. The client then sits down next to the therapist, and the constellation is considered to have begun.

Almost immediately, the various representatives begin to have some impression of the thoughts, emotions, body sensations, or other awareness of the people they are representing. It is important to note that the representatives receive no external or local information from the therapist or client. Unlike some other approaches, such as family system psychodrama, there is no coaching, no molding of representatives into gestural complexes or body postures, and no indication of the client's experience of anyone involved in the system. Indeed, it is possible that some of the family members being represented will have lived and died generations before the client was born. This is truly quantum therapy.

Appendix G

The Influence of Kaskafayet on Transformational NLP

In July 1977 I was invited to a meeting led by a person named Edward O'Hara, during which O'Hara channeled a teacher named Kaskafayet. Another participant at those meetings wrote, as dictated by the teacher, "The purpose of the Kaskafayet trainings is to illuminate your relationship with your Ultimate Self, and to discover the compassionate intention behind your every action, thereby releasing your ability to manifest your true intentions in the world" (Medicine Eagle, 1991, p. 222).

I was struck by the teacher's explanation that having desires is not a bad thing. "Desire is the grease in the wheels of your spiritual machinery" (Kaskafayet as channeled by E. O'Hara, personal communication, July 1977). This was a key concept in my later understanding of NLP.

At one of the sessions with Kaskafayet, I heard the words that profoundly affected my thinking and provided the foundation for much of my work in NLP Marin:

> My observation is and has been that every time I am confronted with the experience of moving forward, I am inclined to resist and avoid becoming more of what I already am. My experience has demonstrated to me that every time I am confronted with moving forward, I am also confronted with allowing someone else to stay where they are.
>
> It has been in discovering more and more workable ways to reconcile the illusion of conflict in this dilemma that has contributed the most to my own conscious evolution. To be more direct, my experience is that the source of suffering is in the ways we suffer for other people in an unworkable attempt to

> say I love you. (Kaskafayet as channeled by E. O'Hara, personal communication, July 1977)

The question that filled my consciousness for two decades was how to resolve (or, as I like to put it, to re-solve) what I came to call our Suffering Obligations of Love. Twenty years later, in 1997, I observed a systemic constellation facilitated by Bert Hellinger. I watched Hellinger put into practice an elegant and subtle, although direct and flexible, format for explicating and resolving the universal dilemmas inherent in these Suffering Obligations. As discussed in the text, I took the principles of Hellinger's work, which Hellinger terms Orders of Love, and evolved them as the basis for my own constellation formats. This work continues today as an integral part of NLP Marin's curriculum and public offerings. I have also developed a number of more explicitly NLP-like formats that assist my clients to re-solve the dilemmas involved in what I call their devotional patterning.

Appendix H

The Teaching Programs of Carlos Castaneda

The teaching programs offered by Carlos Castaneda in the 1990s were presented in huge event spaces such as the Convention Center in Anaheim, California, and were attended by thousands of people. These public performances marked a radical departure from the hidden, deeply esoteric character of the teaching and learning formats that were at the heart of the 10,000-year-old lineage of don Juan and Carlos Castaneda. At one of these events, which I attended, Castaneda explained that he and his fellow apprentices had had to decide whether to take apprentices themselves, and thus continue the lineage, or allow the lineage to come to an end. He said that they had concluded that the age of closely held esoteric teaching was over, and they had chosen to allow the lineage to end with them. However, while declining new apprentices, they decided to make certain aspects of the teaching broadly available to the general public. These public events were mostly focused on teaching a modern version of what Castaneda called shamanic magical passes. These were a complex series of physical movements that were intended to enhance the ability to perceive and reorganize energy in oneself and the external world. Castaneda labeled these exercises "Tensegrity," a term he took from architect and scientist Buckminster Fuller that alludes to interconnectivity in nature. (Castaneda, 1995; Castaneda, 1995–2012)

I attended two of these large several-day events in Anaheim. I also attended several lectures that Castaneda offered in more intimate venues, such as a small auditorium at Mills College in Oakland, California. At one of these lectures, Castaneda observed that don Juan Matus would never appear before even a small group, nor would any member of what was called the sorcerer's party, the other individuals of don Juan's generation who were within this ancient lineage. He explained that for thousands of years sorcerers had always dealt with only a few persons at a time, because in a larger group they would have been overwhelmed by the act of *seeing* so many people in the same place at the same time. Castaneda said that it had taken years for him (Castaneda himself) to develop a tolerance for such large-scale *seeing*, but that it was part of what was then required of him in the new exoteric form of the teaching.

Appendix I

Strategies in Our Neural Programming

As discussed in the Conclusion, in NLP terminology a *strategy* is a sequence of internal and external sensory representations that leads to a particular outcome. For example, everyone has a decision strategy for knowing when it is time to clean the house. We can elicit this strategy, in very rudimentary form, by asking the person, "How do you know when it is time to clean the house?" (Trigger representation) and "How do you know when the house is clean enough?" (Test and Exit representations.) If the person lacks a Trigger representation/s, the individual will not initiate house cleaning. If the person lacks Test and Exit representations, and the concurrent representational events that allow the comparisons that generate a meaning of clean enough, then he or she will never stop cleaning! (NLP practitioners are taught to consider compulsions to be the result of dysfunctional strategies, strategies that lack adequate Test and Exit operations.)

The Operate representations both lead to and are the consequence of external behavior that makes the house cleaner. Whoever or whatever determines the nature and content of the T.O.T.E. representations and sequences becomes that which determines the behavior and experience of the human. (Dr. Skinner's pigeons had Dr. Skinner to determine their T.O.T.E. representations. Humans have parents and families.)

We may imagine the simple activity of pouring water from a pitcher into an empty drinking glass in elementary T.O.T.E terms: First, there must be some kind of Triggering events, and the representations that communicate about them in the human operating system. There must be something(s) that tells us it is time to pour water into the glass. Next, we must perform an Operation that puts water into the glass. Obviously, this Operation involves massively complex perceptual and motor events that we will simply summarize with the word *pouring*. But let us consider the functioning of this simple T.O.T.E. so far: If we do not have a pitcher, a glass, and some water, or if we cannot get access to them, or if we cannot perceive their presence in the environment with sufficient accuracy, or if we cannot imagine our agency in the matter, we cannot pour water into the glass.

There are T.O.T.E.s. within T.O.T.E.s within T.O.T.E.s that operationalize the beliefs within beliefs within beliefs that generate and sustain our realities in every instant of awareness, choice, and action for all possibilities and events. For example, in very simplistic terms, a life-long, dysfunctional water pouring T.O.T.E. might lead to the belief that "there is never water for me!" Conversely, a lifelong belief that "there is never water for me!" will *require* T.O.T.E functions that produce perceptions and outcomes to confirm this belief as a condition of reality in the environment.

Having briefly noted the presence and roles of the Trigger and Operate functions within our water pouring T.O.T.E, let us now consider the all-important Test step. What lets us know when to stop pouring water into the glass? Of course, our answer will be that we will know to stop when the glass is full enough. But how do we know when the glass is "full enough?" We will, each of us, know to Operate—to pour water—until our Test tells us that we have matched the condition called enough. But how do we know that *that* really is enough? The answer is that we Test and Test and Test—compare and compare and compare—until we notice that the condition of external reality, our external visual of the state of the glass/water interaction, matches some internal representation of the outcome we are seeking to accomplish. In other words, without having to plan or think, we pour water into the glass until the level of the water in the external glass matches the amount of water in the (not very consciously present) internal picture of the outcome we are seeking. We Operate until the Test produces a match, and then we Exit from the T.O.T.E. If we cannot Trigger, Operate, Test, and Exit in functional ways, we will never begin to fill our glass, or always under-fill our glass (a condition of ongoing deprivation, perhaps!), or we will continue to fill an already full glass, which is a good way to create a mess that will require some cleaning up (another fairly common condition in life).

Our water pouring T.O.T.E. example is valid in its simplistic way, but for more significant life issues, consider these questions: How do you know when you have worked hard enough? How would you know that you were kind enough? How do you know you are loved enough? Each of these questions, and all the others like them, may serve to evoke some kind of unconscious awareness that may or may not lead to the availability of a conscious response in the form of a verbal answer. Whether the response is conscious or not, an indefinite number of T.O.T.E. operations are in play beneath all of this conscious and unconscious experience. The acquisition of the T.O.T.E model begins to code our experience into a syntax of understandable, highly generalized, yet discrete cognitive operations—the most basic of the basic building blocks of our experience of the actual moment-to-moment events of being human.

Definitions of Key Terms

As discussed above, the field of Neuro-Linguistic Programming developed from a combination of several fields of psychology (primarily humanistic psychology, cognitive psychology, gestalt therapy, and family systems therapy) as well as the discipline of linguistics (which Noam Chomsky considered a branch of psychology) and the clinical hypnotherapy of Milton Erickson. This entire intellectual construct was built on the foundation of the conceptual framework provided by Alfred Korzybski. All of these contributing fields of intellectual endeavor have their own perspectives and vocabulary that are not familiar to most people who are not in that field.

The founders of NLP utilized concepts and terms from all of these fields. After John Grinder and Richard Bandler went their separate ways, each new branch of this field developed its own vocabulary and added its new terms to the NLP lexicon. Hence, it is a daunting task to compile a comprehensive list of definitions of key terms and concepts. Nevertheless, we will attempt to provide definitions for those terms that are the most significant and relevant to this book.

Anchoring

Anchoring is the process of creating an association of one thing with another in the mind of the client, through any of the five senses. This is an application of Ivan Pavlov's classical stimulus-response conditioning process, which is the association of a particular stimulus with a highly predictable response. All humans (as well as higher animals) have naturally anchored reactions to certain visuals, sounds, tastes, or smells. These naturally acquired, automatic, relatively permanent stimulus-response associations are occasionally used as part of doing NLP change work. However, most anchoring based change work utilizes intentionally created, highly reproducible anchors associated with desired emotions, experiences, and resources in the client's neurology, so the clients can automatically access these new states of resourcefulness and capability in the appropriate situations (Bandler & Grinder, 1979; Dilts, 1999b; McClendon, 1989).

Building Rapport

In NLP, rapport building is mainly accomplished by behavioral operations and events that work beneath the level of the conscious personality. Thus, this methodology is not about becoming more likeable or charming. It most often does not even involve making adjustments at the level of the information content that is exchanged in any given human interaction. Rather, rapport is influenced through slight behavioral shifts that allow the practitioner to communicate to the client's creature neurology that it is in a safe environment. This other-than-conscious signaling supports the client's conscious self to also feel more well and safe then would be the case if the creature were in a state of even minimal fight/flight alert. This is accomplished through such techniques as mirroring, matching, and pacing (Buchheit, 1995-2016; Dilts, 1980; Lewis & Pucelik, 1982; McClendon, 1989).

Calibration

Calibration is the process of observing someone's external behavior and appearance to obtain information about the person's internal process and experience. The NLP practitioner calibrates the client by learning to observe and recognize external visual, auditory, and kinesthetic behavioral and physiological clues to the other individual's internal mental and emotional processes. Because the external physiological indicators, such as changes in breathing and skin color, almost always occur outside of conscious control, calibrated information is highly reliable. The practitioner can ask the client what s/he is experiencing, and then watch for repeating physiological indicators. The practitioner can be quite certain that the client's calibrated physiology will always coincide with the previously calibrated emotions and thoughts. For example, the client will show his or her own physiology for "sadness." If the practitioner observes the calibration for sadness, then it is extremely likely that the client is sad, whether the client is consciously aware of the emotion or not (Lewis, & Pucelik, 1982; O'Connor & Seymour, 1990).

Changing Personal History

The technique of changing personal history is not about changing the facts of one's experience; rather, it is a method of revising how one responds in the present to memories of those past facts. The goal is to integrate new resources into the memory of past situations in order to create improvement in feelings and abilities in the present. The practitioner temporarily associates or anchors two different experiences: A first anchor is used to momentarily stabilize the unwanted present feelings that are arising as an automatic response concerning a painful past experience; a second anchor is then created to momentarily stabilize a sense of resourcefulness and well-being. The practitioner then collapses the two anchors. The result is a new and permanent association between the past pain and an expanded sense of understanding or well-being about the past pain. It is an intentional, direct, structural revision in the building blocks of present experience and the consequent flow of meaning in the client's present life (Bandler & Grinder, 1979).

Collapsing Anchors

Collapsing Anchors is a technique to cause two or more experiences that have heretofore not been neurologically associated to become permanently connected or combined in the client's present and future experience. This technique uses intentionally created anchored responses to combine the states, resources, emotions, or other experiences that have been associated with these anchors. The anchors themselves are temporary—it is the result of combining them that remains permanently in the client's experience (Bandler & Grinder, 1979; Dilts, 1980; McClendon, 1989). For example, using collapsing anchors we can permanently associate an experience of enjoyable, focused attention (that one might automatically encounter when pursuing a sport or hobby) with the experience of sitting in boring meetings. Assuming that this combination was determined to be desirable and useful for the client, the result would be a greatly increased capacity to choose to participate resourcefully in previously boring meetings.

Complex Equivalence

A term carried over from linguistics, complex equivalence refers to the meaning that a person attaches to a word or action. It usually describes complexes of other people's behaviors that have an equivalence on the client's internal map (Lewis & Pucelik, 1982). For example, for some people, being left to themselves during times of upset may be a complex equivalence for being loved and respected, while for another person the very same behavior—being left to oneself during times of upset—is a complex equivalence for being disrespected and *not* cared for. Complex equivalence is usually abbreviated as CEq (pronounced "see-ee-kew").

Ecology

The notion of ecology in NLP is based on the work of the renowned epistemologist and anthropologist Gregory Bateson, who pointed out that change in the human psyche, as in all processes in nature, must be viewed in context of its environment (Bateson, 2000). He taught the founders of NLP that it is necessary to assess how the desired change might affect the client's model of the world. An "ecology objection" arises when a client is faced, often at an other-than-conscious level, with the loss of a pre-existing secondary gain associated with the problem state, or with an eruption of new difficulties that develop precisely because of the fulfillment of the desired state experience. It is the unconscious concern regarding how having the outcome may affect one's relationships, career, belief system, values, or identity (Bostic St. Clair & Grinder, 2001; Buchheit, 1995-2016; Dilts, et al.,1990).

In Transformational NLP, the concept of ecology expands to include attention to the individual's significant but unconscious concern about painful loss that "will occur" *in the past*, not only loss in the present or future. In fact, we find that the continuing hope for a better past for everyone is one of the main drivers that holds humans locked into patterns of "devotional pain."

Ericksonian Hypnosis

Milton Erickson's hypnotherapy greatly influenced the work of Grinder and Bandler. Erickson utilized a permissive hypnosis in contrast to traditional hypnosis, which most often uses direct commands. He taught that the unconscious mind usually resists authoritarian commands. Erickson's form of hypnosis interrupts unconscious patterns in thoughts and behavior by means of vague language and metaphors. Thus the Milton model, which deliberately uses ambiguous, general language, is the opposite of the Meta Model, derived from the work of Virginia Satir, which attempts to achieve greater and greater specificity (Grinder, DeLozier, & Bandler, 1977; McClendon, 1989).

Eye-Accessing Cues

Eye-accessing cues are specific, externally observable and confirmable movements of the eyes that correlate with specific internal sensory representations that are the basis of cognitive and emotional experience. The representational events that are most easily available for real-time observation by using eye-accessing cues are visual recall and construction, auditory recall and construction, internal voice, and olfactory, gustatory, and kinesthetic (feeling and emotion) events. In other words, the practitioner can observe eye movements that, in the immediate moment, correlate with internal images, sounds, smells, tastes, touch or emotions. While the representations themselves are momentary and fleeting, they arise continuously, almost always outside of conscious awareness, and are interpreted by us as reality. The eye-accessing cues tell the practitioner nothing about *what* someone is experiencing, merely about *how*, in sensory terms, the experience is being generated in the moment. Although the internal representations, such as a picture, may be about the past or future, they and the feelings associated with them are actually in the present. With NLP, the present feelings associated with representations about the past can be modified, thereby changing the meaning of the past (Buchheit, 1995-2016; Dilts, 1980; Lewis & Pucelik, 1982; McClendon, 1989).

4-Tuple

The term "4-tuple" is a term from the earliest days of NLP. It refers to the four sensory representational systems: V (visual), A (auditory), K (kinesthetic), and O/G (the elision of olfactory and gustatory into one representational system). Very early on, the NLP founders noticed that different people had dissimilar processing biases toward one or more of these representational modalities. Later, they also noticed that the feeling and meaning of any given experience is highly dependent on specific combinations of sub-modalities (representational sub-distinctions), and that these are easily changeable. For example, if a person changes an internal image from color to black and white, this will most often change the experience associated with that image, although the content of that past experience—the events that occurred—remains entirely unchanged (Dilts, 1980; Lewis & Pucelik, 1982; McClendon, 1989).

Imprint

An imprint in most animals is the triggering of an innate instinctive behavior, such as attachment to parents, during a critical time period in the young animal's development. The theory of imprinting in animals comes from the work of zoologist Konrad Lorenz, for which he received the Nobel Prize in 1973. In humans an imprint is caused by trauma, either one that is very intense or several that are less intense, usually at a very young age. A trauma creates an imprint when it threatens physical survival or the coherence of the child's still-developing identity or when it compromises the child's experience of belonging in the family. Children always seek to understand why devastating events occur, so they make decisions about why it happened, about the "rules of the world," and about what it means about themselves, and this coalesces into a stabilized, life-long belief about themselves and their relationship to the world.

Neurologically, the sense impressions of the trauma's triggering circumstances and subsequent events, along with the emotions and beliefs engendered by it, come together to stabilize a "compelling reference experience" which is "imprinted" on the nervous system. Once imprinted, the thoughts, emotions, and beliefs associated with the traumatic event are usually no longer available for further learning no matter how many experiences contradicting these beliefs are acquired in the future. We may call such beliefs and the behavior patterns that go with them "quarantined." Since quarantined patterns are directly associated in the creature brain with the survival of a life-threatening emergency, the imprint remains in the system and is easily reactivated in future situations that appear to be isomorphic (having the same shape) with the original traumatic event (Buchheit, 1995-2016; Dilts, 1990).

Intended Positive Outcomes (IPOs)

One of the original and main presuppositions of NLP is the idea that all behavior and all experience are sourced from some kind of positive intention. This model is referred to as Original Positive Intentions (Bandler, Grinder, & Satir, 1976; Dilts, 1998b, 1996a). This concept is similar to what many psychologists term "secondary gains," the possibly beneficial by-products associated with inappropriate or dysfunctional patterns of behavior. In my own work I expand on this concept, using the term IPOs to reveal to the client the validity and purposefulness of all of their experiences, however negative, painful, or limiting they may have been (Buchheit, 1995-2016).

Limiting Beliefs

Beliefs are automated, usually unconscious convictions about the nature of reality. Many beliefs are inherited as children from family and culture. Others are formed by decisions that children make about life and themselves at a very young age to explain how and why things are the way they are.

Our beliefs construct our outer as well as our inner worlds. They control the patterns we automatically use to perceive our inner and outer worlds, as well as the patterning we use to automatically make sense (meaning) out of these perceptions. Whatever we believe, we will have evidence for in our lives. (Beliefs are not the same as faith, since the whole point of faith is to believe that for which we have no evidence.) Our beliefs determine our experience, and our experience reinforces our beliefs, which determine our experiences, *ad infinitum.*

In the context of personal growth endeavors, a "limiting belief" refers to an unwanted belief that overrides current choices by imposing a reality that conflicts with what the person wants. Such beliefs usually come from decisions made by the very young child to explain traumatic events. For example, if the child spilled milk on mother's nice dress when s/he was two years old and mother got very angry and shouted that s/he was clumsy, the child might try to make sense out of it by generalizing, "I can't get anything right." If similar interactions occurred several times, and the child was made to feel tremendously ashamed or otherwise attacked because of them, this generalization might stabilize into a belief about him/herself. A person who has the belief that "I can't get anything right" will inevitably manifest this belief in his/her life. All limiting beliefs are beliefs that are no longer useful or appropriate in one's life, and they can be revised (Buchheit, 1995-2016; Dilts, 1990; Dilts, et al., 1990).

Meta Model

In NLP, being *meta* refers to the perceptual maneuver of shifting one's perspective or view of something to a position above or beyond the level at which one customarily perceives and/or thinks. A Meta Model is a higher-level perception or observation of a person's model of reality. The concept of the Meta Model is derived from the work and therapeutic style of family therapist Virginia Satir. Codifying Satir's brilliant therapeutic instincts, Grinder and Bandler elucidated and taught Meta Model "challenges" as a methodology to reveal and perhaps revise unquestioned assumptions and beliefs about reality. The Meta Model utilizes specific questions to obtain information about beliefs based on Meta Model "violations," (i.e., information that is distorted, generalized, and/or deleted. The practitioner challenges the client's words and thereby the presuppositions behind the words) (Bandler & Grinder, 1975b; Grinder & Pucelik, 2013).

Meta Programs

Meta programs are filters that determine which of our perceptions are selected for attention and represented internally. Hence, they are the keys to the way a person forms internal representations and habitually directs behavior. According to the *Encyclopedia of Systemic Neuro-Linguistic Programming and NLP New Coding,* there are seven key Meta program patterns: (1) Does the person approach problems by going *toward* a goal or *away* from the problem? (2) Does s/he focus on the past or present or future, and is s/he concerned more with short-term or long-term goals? (3) Does s/he notice the general picture more than the details? (4) Is the person's frame of reference the views of others or internal to him/herself? (5) Does s/he tend to notice similarities or differences between him/herself and others? (6) In solving problems, does s/he focus more on the choice of goal or the procedure involved in achieving the goal? Also, is the individual's main focus on self, the other, or the team? (7) Is his/her thinking style predominantly oriented toward the vision, action, logic, or emotion? (Dilts & Delozier, 2000).

Modeling

"Modeling" refers to the ability of skilled NLP practitioners to elicit and then reproduce in others the verbal, cognitive, and behavioral patterns (neuro-linguistic programs) of a specific individual, usually an exceptional person who is an exemplar of excellence. In addition to utilizing the language and key behavioral patterns, modeling makes available the "strategies" of the person who is being modeled. In NLP, "strategies" are sequences of internal and external representations (pictures, sounds, feelings, smells, and tastes) that lead to particular outcomes and experiences (Dilts, 2005).

Neuro-Linguistic Programming (NLP)

Neuro-Linguistic Programming is the study of the structure of subjective experience and the modeling of human excellence. NLP provides procedures and tools for understanding and changing human experience and behavior. It is a model (rather than a theory) of how people process information and the resulting effects on behavior, thoughts, feelings, and overall perception of the world we experience (Grinder & Bandler, 1976).

NLP is different from all other therapeutic modalities in that it can make information about certain purely internal processing events—called sensory representations and sequences—externally accessible and confirmable. NLP can reveal, in real time, the internal representational events that are generating, and that actually comprise, a person's experience in the moment. It does not matter whether that experience is understood to be about the past, present or future: it is all generated and presented now. Out-of-conscious sensory accessing cues (VAKOG), especially eye-accessing cues, are the main doorway to the revelation of these unconscious internal events. Most people can become aware of what we are feeling in the moment, but we are (almost) never conscious of the pictures and sounds that are leading to and generating those feelings.

Our internal sensory events are woven together to create our maps of reality, the internally generated and maintained constructions whereby we create and sustain our experiences of self and others, and of life itself. Because NLP provides the skilled practitioner with access to the basic source code that generates personal experience, s/he can assist the client to revise these instructions for reality. This capability, combined with the practitioner's sense of the positive purposes and intentions that were seeking fulfillment through the old, out-grown patterning, allows the practitioner to support the client to rapidly make the changes in behavior and beliefs that s/he truly wants, as well as to improve his or her ability to communicate and connect with others.

The meaning of the words in the name "Neuro-Linguistic Programming" points to the conceptual framework and goals of this new discipline. *Neuro* refers to the nervous system, the neural pathways through which our experience is received and processed via the five senses: visual, auditory, kinesthetic, olfactory, and gustatory. *Linguistic* is about the content of this experience. It includes the processes of both verbal and nonverbal signaling through which our sensory representations are coded and given meaning. This signaling consists of pictures, sounds, feelings, tastes, and smells, as well as the words that represent them. *Programming* is the way the content is organized in our minds to produce our thoughts and behaviors and our model of the world. A trained NLP practitioner can discover and adjust these programs to assist people to have new experiences in life that are more in alignment with what they want (Bandler & Thomson, 2011; Buchheit, n.d.; Buchheit, 1995-2016).

Outcome Frame

The Outcome Frame is the basis of information-gathering procedures in all schools of NLP, although each school may use a slight variation. As explained in *Encyclopedia of Systemic Neuro-Linguistic Programming and NLP New Coding,* "The basic purpose of the Outcome Frame is to establish and maintain a focus on the goal or desired state during any technique or process—that is, to be constantly 'outcome oriented.' Establishing an Outcome Frame involves evaluating any activity or information with respect to its relevance to the achievement of a particular goal or desired state" (Dilts & Delozier, 2000, p. 905). The basic questions asked in a conventional Outcome Frame are: (1) What do you want? (2) What is happening now? (3) What stops you from getting what you want? (4) What do you need in order to get what you want? (5) How would you know if you were moving adequately toward your goal? (6) Have you ever got it before? What did you do then? (Dilts, 1980, p.161).

The Outcome Frame practiced in Transformational NLP is very different from that in conventional NLP. In conventional NLP, the information that is gathered from the client is almost entirely about the content of his/her experience. In Transformational NLP, the information gathered is equally about the unconscious structure of the client's patterning. The basic TNLP Outcome Frame consists of five questions: (1) What would you like? (2) What will having that do for you? (3) How will you know when you have it? (4) Where, when, and with whom would you like it? (5) How will having this outcome affect other significant aspects and people in your life? What might you lose that you value, when you can have this desired outcome? (Buchheit, 1995-2016).

In Transformational NLP, an Outcome Frame interaction is an exploration of the client's life, not merely the rote execution of five questions. As such, a skillful Outcome Frame interaction can last for hours and is a significant intervention in itself. It changes the clients' relationship with themselves, and with their past, present, and future.

Also, in TNLP the Outcome Frame is as much about gathering structural information as it is about collecting content. We are almost more interested in the VAKOG structural information that any person will continually offer, outside conscious awareness, as they talk about their experience. For example, if a person is about to say something about a topic that carries a strong charge of jeopardy or lack of safety, s/he will almost always "check in" with internal pictures or soundtracks having to do with the original persons and events in relation to which the fear patterning was originally established. These eye-accessing cues are likely to be the keys to making specific revisions in safety patterning later in the session (Buchheit, 1995-2016).

Reframing

A frame refers to the context of an event that provides the event with its meaning. The frame is formed by one's map of the world and his/her beliefs surrounding the event. Reframing is the art of changing the client's view of the meaning of the event. It includes viewing the event from a different perspective. While the facts remain unchanged, what these facts mean is now different (Bandler & Grinder, 1979).

Re-imprinting

Re-imprinting is the theory and methodology evolved separately by Robert Dilts and Jonathan Rice to re-organize information processing in the human nervous system. Re-imprinting is a procedure to alter significant imprinted representations that form the basis of one's beliefs and identity. The techniques of re-imprinting are based on a simpler methodology called Changing Personal History, which utilizes a change format known as Collapsing Anchors. However, the technique of Changing Personal History seeks only to add a resource that will make the painful feelings about a past event feel better in the present. Re-imprinting is not an attempt to make the client feel better immediately. Instead, it seeks to revise whole clusters of meanings that produce unwanted limitations concerning the client's identity, beliefs, and behavior (Dilts, 1996b; J. Rice, personal communication, November 2011).

Transferring Resources

A resource (or a resource state) is a belief, skill, behavior, knowledge, sensation, person, object, or awareness that supports or contributes to the fulfillment of a desired outcome. The NLP technique for transferring resources makes it possible to achieve immediate cross-contextual learning through direct representational intervention. For example, a resource state called "confidence," which is already associated with and is part of a person's successful athletic activity can be transferred to—made available within—the unrelated context of office meetings. Since it involves direct duplication and transfer of a previously stabilized capability, this method operates in strong contrast to only talking about obtaining access to new learning and capability. If a person does not himself or herself already have the particular desired resource available in any context of his or her life, then the same good effect may be accomplished be asking the person to simply imagine the experience of someone else who does appear to possess the desired resource. Once the person steps into the desired experience, with all its representational components, the practitioner can collapse this resourcefulness of the other person into the client's own patterning, where it becomes permanently available as a natural aspect of life. This variation of transferring resources is called the New Behavior Generator (Grinder et al., 1977).

Walking Timeline

A walking timeline is a format used by most schools of NLP to accomplish the re-imprinting of belief and identity issues. A "timeline" is most often a simple marking out of external spatial anchors on the floor. One simply imagines a line on the floor that runs from the past through the present to the future. Simple, explicit markers are often used—index cards, for example—to indicate the place in time of one's birth, the present moment, and the process of an unfolding future. Various other specific points on the external timeline are then associated with the particular life events that are of interest, such as moments of past trauma, the present state (how things are now), and the future or desired state (how things will be after the changes will be integrated). By having the client figuratively walk through time by literally, physically walking backward and forward on the marked out, external representation of the process of time—the timeline—the NLP practitioner is able to re-imprint the client's experience (Dilts, 1990). This method is an alternative to re-imprinting by using visual, auditory, and kinesthetic anchors in a format that looks like (although it is far from) conventional sitting psychotherapy.

Notes

INTRODUCTION

1. Recently, a growing number of NLP practitioners are finding clients who are disenchanted with the traditional talk psychotherapies. The relatively few NLP practitioners who work in a manner resembling psychotherapy do not focus on diagnosis and treatment of mental illness with either drugs or counseling. Rather, their preferred approach is to help clients overcome their self-perceived problems through the application of specific NLP techniques that challenge existing language and thought patterns and re-imprint new ones. Also, a small number of licensed psychotherapists, most of them located in the United Kingdom, are beginning to be more open to using NLP as an adjunct to their main approach in their practices, especially in the relatively new field of Brief Psychotherapy. They are finding that NLP can often greatly improve the effectiveness of psychotherapeutic practices (Wake, 2008).

CHAPTER I

1. MacLean's conceptualization of the several-in-one structure of the brain continues to predominate in the field of neuroscience. Despite some controversy regarding the range, extent, and interaction of the roles played by each structure, MacLean's work remains the basis for much of the current research in the field (Dalgleish, 2004; Joseph, 2001; LeDoux, 1998, 2003).
2. The date given for the extremely rapid development of what is known as the Fourth Brain varies according to different sources from 30,000 to 50,000 BP.
3. Another recent theory is that when humans migrated from Africa to Europe, they were forced to adapt to the cold weather by creating technologies for clothing that would keep them warm. The Neanderthals had already adapted to the cold by having stockier bodies. When the climate became extremely cold around 30,000 years ago, the Homo sapiens already had the technology to create warmer clothing. The Neanderthals did not have the ability to adapt fast enough, so they became extinct (Gilligan, 2007; Collard et al, 2016).

4. Neuroscientist Regina Sullivan's research supports this view of what I call "survival equivalence." See the transcript of her talk at Tufts University in February 2014 (Sullivan, 2014). It is also supported by the work of psychiatrist Bessel van der Kolk, (Van der Kolk, 2014).
5. A "limiting belief" refers to an *unwanted* belief that overrides current choices by imposing a reality that conflicts with what the person wants. Such beliefs usually come from decisions made by the individual when s/he was a very young child to explain traumatic events. Our beliefs determine our experience, and our experience reinforces our beliefs, which determine our experiences, and so on in a never-ending cycle.

CHAPTER 2

1. The term "cognitive psychology" was popularized in 1967 by American psychologist Ulric Neisser when he published his landmark book on the subject entitled *Cognitive Psychology*. However, a work called *Cognitive Psychology* had already been published by Thomas Vener Moore in 1939.
2. For example, see the one-sentence mention of Korzybski in *Structure* II, p. 25 (Grinder & Bandler, 1976).
3. For an example of the controversy regarding the Sapir-Whorf Hypothesis, see the article by Ash (1999) "The Sapir-Whorf Hypothesis."

CHAPTER 3

1. In 1971, Richard Bandler led gestalt therapy groups with Frank Pucelik, a 27-year-old student who had returned from service in Vietnam and worked with local troubled and drug-addicted youth. The two young men ran two or three therapy sessions a week. Bandler met Grinder in September 1971, in a university-mandated sensitivity training (encounter) group for which Grinder was the faculty sponsor. In 1972, Bandler asked Grinder to observe what they were doing in the groups. The three young men experimented with the encounter group format and began to develop the Meta Model. Under Grinder's influence, from 1972 to 1974 they used Noam Chomsky's transformational grammar to model the language patterns of Perls and Satir. According to Pucelik, by the middle of 1973 Bandler and Grinder became the main leaders of what became the Metal Model group, and Pucelik was relegated to the role of leader of the students (Grinder & Pucelik, 2013).
2. It is important to understand that, negative though they sound, the terms "deletion," "distortion," and "generalization" are not indications

of the client's cognitive errors or flaws of character. Rather, they are the essential universal modeling processes by which a human being converts lived experience into language *about* that experience. In turn, these habituated patterns of language support specific cognitive, perceptual, and belief biases that then determine which realities will be available to (perceived by) the client. Thus, the cycle of experience giving rise to language, and language then binding the possibilities of experience, continues.

3. The term Meta Model "challenges" is somewhat misleading. To challenge a Meta Model "violation" is not to be confrontational or aggressive. It is merely to ask for more specific information or to otherwise induce the speaker to reconsider what has just been said. This process is both subtle and direct. It calls the client's attention to limitations that are both revealed and sustained by structural patterns in his or her spoken language (Bandler & Grinder, 1975b).
4. In *Frogs into Princes* (1979), Bandler and Grinder provide a much more clearly written discussion of the content of *Structure* I. Also, Bandler, in his more recent work, *Guide to Trance Formation* (2008), explains these concepts more lucidly.
5. In actuality, Sigmund Freud had developed the theory of brain plasticity sixty years before Hebb. In 1888 Freud wrote that when two neurons fire simultaneously, this firing facilitates their ongoing association. In 1891, in his book *On Aphasia*, he stated that the brain is plastic and can reorganize itself, and in 1895, in *Project for a Scientific Psychology*, he described how synapses can be changed by what we learn. Also Ivan Pavlov, in his later years, argued that the brain is plastic. The discovery that thoughts can change brain structure overturns Descartes' view of the immutable duality between the mind and the brain that has dominated Western thinking for several centuries (Doidge, 2007).

CHAPTER 4

1. The strategy model elucidated by Robert Dilts in *Neuro-Linguistic Programming: The Study of the Structure of Subjective Experience. NLP* Vol. I (1980) is based on the work done by George Miller, Eugene Galanter, and Karl Pribram in *Plans and the Structure of Behavior* (Holt, Rinehart and Winston, 1960). In this work, these scholars outline the T.O.T.E. (test-operate-test-exit) model. The chapter on "Plans for Speaking" reveals the authors' intellectual agreement with the ideas of Noam Chomsky, which in turn strongly influenced John Grinder.

2. Leslie Cameron Bandler divorced Richard and teamed up with Michael Lebeau (who later became her husband) and David Gordon. They set up an organization in Larkspur, California called The NLP Center for Advanced Studies. The three of them developed and promoted Leslie's model of NLP (McClendon, 1989).
3. Steven Andreas wrote a brilliant, comprehensive review of *Whispering in the Wind* in 2003, which can be accessed at his website: *www.steveandreas.com/Articles/whispering.html.*
4. Dilts had first consciously recognized and formalized these patterns in 1980 when he witnessed Richard Bandler use them during a seminar. Listening to the verbal reframes created spontaneously by Bandler, Dilts recognized that they had the same structures as those used by other effective leaders and teachers (Dilts, 1999a, p. x). He took the term *sleight of mouth* from the notion of sleight of hand, which is a type of magic done by close-up card magicians. "The verbal patterns of Sleight of Mouth have a similar sort of 'magical' quality because they can often create dramatic shifts in perception and the assumptions upon which particular perceptions are based" (Dilts, 1999a, pp. 6–7).

CHAPTER 5

1. Psychotherapy is based on the understanding that all behaviors—whether physical, emotional, or psychological, and whether interpreted as positive or negative—are the manifestations of the entire psyche as an organic unit rather than exist as independent and isolated phenomena. As Sigmund Freud, the father of psychoanalysis, explains in *Studies in Hysteria* (1895), both physical and psychological self-defeating behaviors are often symptoms of repressed traumatic events. If the symptom is changed without addressing the trauma that caused this manifestation, the client will often simply develop another symptom. An example is the person who stops smoking and soon after starts overeating. The goal of psychoanalysis and most psychotherapy is to find the trauma that was buried in the unconscious mind of the client and continues to cause the symptom. The theory is that when the trauma is brought to the conscious mind, its impact will dissipate and the client will have more choice.

   Mainstream NLP practitioners tend to disregard this model and instead focus on the unwanted behavior itself. While the specific behavior may change, there may be unwanted consequences if the reason this behavior developed in the first place is not addressed. Transformational

NLP practitioners use the half-second eye access to bring to conscious awareness the childhood trauma that resulted in the unwanted patterning, and employ the method of re-imprinting to dissipate its emotional and psychological impact. Then the limiting pattern of behavior can be changed without being converted to another unwanted symptom.

2. Tim Hallbom, one of the most popular contemporary teachers of mainstream NLP, explains that in his experience, the neurology is more available for change when the person is standing or walking rather than sitting. Also, he believes that it is easier to add a touch anchor if necessary when the practitioner stands next to the client (T. Hallbom, personal communications, August 2014).
3. Doing experiments with electrodes in the brains of nearly a hundred patients who were undergoing brain surgery under the supervision of neurosurgeon Bertram Feinstein, neuroscientist Benjamin Libet spent nearly five years researching the connection between brains and conscious states. He found that it normally took about half a second before the patients noticed and reported a sensation as being in conscious awareness. Libet published the results of these experiments in the Journal of Neurophysiology in 1964 (McCrone, 2006).

   In 1983, Libet discovered that the awareness of a decision to act was consciously perceived as an intention about a third of a second *after* the impulse to act was noted in the brain's motor planning areas. A decision to act is made by unconscious neuronal processes in the brain and precedes the conscious choice to perform the action. In other words, our decisions occur before we are aware of them and they are outside our control. Our thoughts, desires, impulses, and intentions are concealed from our experiencing selves until after the fact! Hence, much of our mental lives are driven by subconscious or preconscious drives. This experiment caused a great deal of controversy when it was published during the early 1980s, since it seemed to imply that there is no free will. Libet addressed this concern by demonstrating that a person had the free will to block the action *after* the impulse was generated when s/he became aware of it (McCrone, 2006; Schwartz & Gladding, 2012).
4. Robert Dilts explains that "The half-second rule was the basis for my biofeedback patent, filed in 1983, in which I demonstrated that giving feedback on the rate of change (first derivative) of an autonomic reaction (i.e., galvanic skin response, heart rate, body temperature, etc.) accelerated a person's sense of control because it moved the perception

of the change into the half-second window. Most biofeedback displays changes in the absolute value of the responses, which (depending on the type of response) can take up to two seconds to manifest. The rate of change, however, happens within the first half second" (R. Dilts, personal communication, October 2014).

5. Dr. Rice described to Carl how he developed the Core Sorting questions: He and a colleague, psychotherapist Susan Mehra, PhD, were watching a videotape of Leslie Cameron demonstrating how to work with a client.

> She [Leslie] had been gathering information [from the client]. . . . Visibly getting fed up with the client's storytelling, she burst out with a demand:
>
> "I know what you want but what stops you from getting it?"
>
> Now, to place this in context, Susan and I had spent many hours practicing seeing and hearing sensory states and state changes so we were pretty finally tuned to changes . . . especially to age regression.
>
> In the second or two after Leslie made her demand [on the video tape] Susan reached out and pushed pause on the tape machine.
>
> She asked, "Did you see that profound age regression?" I said, "I saw something—run it back." So we spent the next hour or two checking the tape and trying out "What do you want? What stops you?" on each other. Leslie eventually got into the woman's age regression by other means, but [Susan and I] left our practice session realizing we had something new that was worth exploring.
>
> As a clinical psychologist in daily practice, I immediately saw the usefulness of noticing and unpacking the eye access of the first half second after asking the two questions (What would you like? What stops you?) as a way to get directly to the source of the client's issue. (J. Rice, personal communication, August 2014)

6. In the Patrick Video, Jonathan Rice asks the Core Sorting questions:

   1. What would you like?
   2. Do you have a way of knowing when you have it?
   3. What stops you?

Patrick first looks down and to his right, into the classic kinesthetic quadrant. He is experiencing a visual/kinesthetic synesthesia—a combination of nearly simultaneous picture and feeling, with the feeling being mostly predominant in Patrick's conscious awareness. In other words, Patrick suddenly feels something when his eyes involuntarily move down and right in response to Rice's question; the visual representation is secondary. Then Patrick's eyes automatically move up and right, which has the effect of making the picture part of the experience more available (although it is not consciously perceived until Rice elicits the memory behind the image of the Mickey Mouse ears that Patrick sees).

Patrick's brain is reacting in two movements. Sometimes there are more than two. The important access or accesses usually occur in the first one-quarter to one-half second after the triggering question—"What stops you?"—is asked. However, sometimes the only physiology visible in the first half second is that of surprise or confusion. Then, after another second or two, another kind of involuntary reaction occurs—the eye movements that reveal the quadrant(s) in which the relevant past traumatic events have been stored.

So, there are two kinds of events that can occur immediately after "What stops you?"—immediate access to relevant past experience, or a second of surprise or confusion that is immediately followed by the valuable accessing that the practitioner is watching for. The client's system will always react either immediately or almost immediately. The experienced practitioner can tell the difference between the two types of reaction by calibrating the physiology. If the client's eyes stay in the visual/kinesthetic synesthesia, which usually looks like a blank stare, the practitioner can manually "raise" the bubble containing the image until the client can see it.

CHAPTER 6

1. The term "safety patterning" is another label for "survival patterning" or "survival programming." Paradoxically, "safety patterning" puts the human whom it serves into situations that are actually unsafe again and again, because these situations are isomorphic to (have the same shape as) experiences that were survived in childhood. So, "safety patterning" may not the best way for the human to be actually safe, but is a 100 percent effective means of ensuring that we will not die in the past!
2. Most NLP practitioners use a version of the question, "What will you have to give up in order to have what you want?" However, I prefer to ask, "What might you lose, that you value, when you can have what you

want?" The questions are similar, but each evokes different responses. It seems that the conventional "What will you have to give up?" formulation asks the client to sort for baleful evidence of previous excess and bad decision-making. The question "What might you lose, that you value?" seems to be less blaming or accusing.

CHAPTER 7

1. I attended a number of workshops with Bert Hellinger during the period 1997–2007 during which he talked about the concept of weight as a function of a person's life experience. Hellinger did not write about this model in any of his books or articles, but I found this theory very useful in my own work and elaborated upon it as it pertains to the practitioner stance.
2. I first heard this phrase in 1977 from a channeled master named Kaskafayet, whose teachings greatly influenced my work. This influence is described further in Chapter 9 and in Appendix G.
3. In his brilliant work *The Road Less Traveled* (1978), M. Scott Peck illustrates a similar concept through the ancient Greek myth of Orestes and the Furies (as dramatized in the trilogy *Oresteia* written by Aeschylus in the fifth century B.C.E.). It is when Orestes took total responsibility for his actions, instead of blaming his family background or the gods (fate), that he was able to heal from his mental illness.

CHAPTER 10

1. Amy Wallace, who wrote *Sorcerer's Apprentice: My Life with Carlos Castaneda* (2003), was a member of the group around Carlos Castaneda for seven years. After he died in 1998 she claimed that she had been his wife, that he was a fraud and his books were fiction, and that he had never been an apprentice of a shaman named don Juan Matus.

    I have seen nothing in her book that indicates that the Castaneda books are not truthful, whether in fact or (in places) in metaphor. According to what Wallace wrote in her book, she was not his wife, nor even in the innermost circle. As one of his followers, she was part of what she herself describes as the "harem" of women with whom Carlos had sex.

    Wallace complains of the terrible way Castaneda treated his disciples. It seems that either he let power go to his head and became almost psychopathic in his cruelty, or he was doing things that he thought would help his disciples become enlightened. For example, sleeping with female followers is something that gurus from many traditions do with the idea that it will help the evolution of the women by receiving their (the gurus') energy—although this practice can easily turn into very self-serving activity.

It seems to me that the jury is still out regarding whether the books by Carlos Castaneda are factual accounts of his experiences with a shaman named don Juan, or metaphorical analogies, or simply fictional flights of his imagination to provide context for his many pearls of mystical wisdom. Whether they are true or not, or how much is true either factually or metaphorically, there is much material drawn from the eastern and western as well as indigenous wisdom traditions that has greatly influenced our culture from the late 1960s to the present day.

CHAPTER 11

1. Deepak Chopra's teacher, Maharishi Mahesh Yogi, talked about his own teacher's search, when he was a youth, for a teacher who was not only enlightened but also did not have what he viewed as negative personality traits such as a tendency toward anger and jealousy. Maharishi also cautioned his students that one cannot assess people's state of consciousness by their external behavior. Ellie Schamber was in the presence of Maharishi Mahesh Yogi several times during the period of 1972–1976 when the great teacher discussed these topics (E. Schamber, personal communications, 1972-1976). In another tradition, David Bohm was distressed to discover that his teacher, Krishnamurti, despite all his discussion about this topic, had not been able to change his own conditioning and behavior (Peat, 1997).

References

Ash, R. (1999). The Sapir-Whorf hypothesis. Retrieved from http://www.angelfire.com/journal/worldtour99/sapirwhorf.html.

American Institute of Physics. (1997–2014). Discovery of the electron. Retrieved from http://www.aip.org/history/electron/.

Andreas, S. (2003). Whispering in the Wind. [Review of the book *Whispering in the Wind* by C. B. Bostic St. Clair & J. Grinder, J.]. Retrieved from http://www.steveandreas.com/Articles/whispering.html.

Association for NLP. (n.d.). See what ANLP can do for you. Retrieved from http://www.anlp.org/anlp-history.

Bandler, R. (1984). *Magic in action.* Cupertino, CA: Meta Publications.

Bandler, R. (1985). *Using your brain for a change.* Moab, UT: Real People Press.

Bandler, R. (2008). *Guide to trance-formation: How to handle the power of hypnosis to ignite effortless and lasting change.* Deerfield, FL: Health Communications.

Bandler, R., & Grinder, J. (1975a). *Patterns of the hypnotic techniques of Milton H. Erickson, M.D.* (Vol. 1). Cupertino, CA: Meta Publications.

Bandler, R., & Grinder, J. (1975b). *The structure of magic: A book about language and therapy* (Vol. 1). Palo Alto, CA: Science and Behavior Books.

Bandler, R., Grinder, J., & Satir, V. (1976). *Changing with families: A book about further education for being human.* Palo Alto, CA: Science and Behavior Books, Inc.

Bandler, R., & Grinder, J. (1979). *Frogs into princes* (Andreas, S., Ed). Moah, UT: Real People Press.

Bandler, R., & Thomson, G. (2011). *The secrets of being happy.* Devon, UK: I. M. Press, Inc.

Bateson, G. (2000). *Steps to an ecology of mind.* Chicago: University of Chicago Press.

Beck, C. E., & Beck, E. A. (1984). Test of the eye-movement hypothesis of Neurolinguistic Programming: A rebuttal of conclusions. *Perceptual and Motor Skills 58*, pp. 175–176.

Beck, S. (Trans.). (2001). Bhagavad gita. Retrieved from http://www.san.beck.org/Gita.hml.

Beyerstein, B. (1995). Distinguishing science from pseudoscience. Retrieved from http://www.dcscience.net/beyerstein_science_vs_pseudoscience.pdf.

Boas, F. (1862–1942). *Franz Boas papers.* Retrieved from www.amphilsoc.org/mole/view?docId=ead/Mss.B.B61-ead.xml .

Bostic St. Clair, C. B., & Grinder, J. (2001). *Whispering in the wind.* Scotts Valley, CA: J & C Enterprises.

Bourke, F. (2015). Bibliography of NLP research. Retrieved from http://www.researchandrecognition.org/#!bibliography/cuks.

Bowman, C. & Brownell, P. (n.d.). Prelude to contemporary gestalt therapy. *Gestalt! 4*(3). Retrieved from http://archive.today/4iVd.

Buchheit, C. (2006). *Using our brains for a change.* Retrieved from http://nlpmarin.com/using-our-brains-for-a-change-2/.

Buchheit, C. (1995-2016). *NLP Marin Master Practitioner Certification Training Manual.* San Rafael, CA: NLP Marin.

Buchheit, C. (n.d.). *What is NLP*? Retrieved from http://nlpmarin.com/what-is-nlp/.

Castaneda, C. (1972). *Journey to Ixtlan: The lessons of Don Juan.* New York: Simon & Schuster.

Castaneda, C. (1995). *Carlos Castaneda's Tensegrity: Redistributing dispersed energy 2* [Video]. Beverly Hills, CA: Laugan Productions.

Castaneda, C. (1995–2012). Carlos Castaneda's tensegrity: The contemporary expression of the practical wisdom of the shamans of ancient Mexico. Retrieved from http://www.cleargreen.com.

Chomsky, N. (1957). *Syntactic structures.* The Hague: Mouton & Co.

Chopra, D. (1991). *Perfect health: The complete mind/body guide.* New York: Harmony Books.

Chopra, D. (1993) *Ageless body, timeless mind.* New York: Harmony Books.

Collard, M., Tarle, L., Sandgathe, D., Allan, A. (2016, August 3). Faunal evidence for a difference in clothing use between Neanderthals and early modern humans in Europe. Jou*rnal of Anthropological Archaeology.* Retrieved from http://www.sciencedirect.com/science/article/pii/S0278416516300757.

Collingwood, C and J. (1996). An interview with John Grinder 1996. *Inspiritive.* Retrieved from http://www.inspiritive.com.au/interview-john-grinder-1996/.

Cummings, J. L., & Miller, B. L. (2007). Conceptual and clinical aspects of the frontal lobes. In B. L. Miller and J. L. Cummings (Eds.), *The human frontal lobes: Functions and disorders*, 2nd ed. (pp. 12-24). New York: Guilford Press.

Damasio, A. R. (1994). *Descartes' error: Emotion, reason, and the human brain.* New York: Avon Books, Inc.

Darnell, R., & Irvine, J. T. (1997). Edward Sapir. Retrieved from http://www.nap.edu/readingroom/books/biomems/esapir.html.

Dediu, D. & Levinson, S. (2013). On the antiquity of language: the interpretation of Neandertal linguistic capacities and its consequences. *Frontiers in Psychology 4*(397).

Devilly, G. J. (2005). Power therapies and possible threats to the science of psychology and psychiatry. *Australian and New Zealand Journal of Psychiatry 39*, pp. 437–459.

Diamond, S. (2009, September 27). Anger and catharsis: Myth, metaphor or reality? Retrieved from http://www.psychologytoday.com/blog/evil-deeds/200909/anger-and-catharsis-myth-metaphor-or-reality.

Dilts, R. (1980). *Neurolinguistic programming: The study of the structure of subjective experience* (Vol. 1). Cupertino, CA: Meta Publications.

Dilts, R. (1983). *Applications of neurolinguistic programming.* Capitola, CA: Meta Publications.

Dilts, R. (1990). *Changing belief systems with NLP.* Capitola, CA: Meta Publications.

Dilts, R. (1991). *Tools for dreamers.* Capitola, CA: Meta Publications.

Dilts, R. (1993). *Skills for the future.* Capitola, CA: Meta Publications.

Dilts, R. (1994). *Strategies of genius* (Vols. I–III). Capitola, CA: Meta Publications.

Dilts, R. (1996a). Bringing light into the darkness: The principle of positive intention. Retrieved from http://www.nlpu.com/Articles/article2.htm.

Dilts, R. (1996b). The influence of Timothy Leary on re-imprinting. Retrieved from http://www.nlpu.com/Articles/article4.htm.

Dilts, R. (1996c). *Visionary leadership skills.* Capitola, CA: Meta Publications.

Dilts, R. (1998a). *Modeling with NLP.* Capitola, CA: Meta Publications.

Dilts, R. (1998b). Reframing: The principle of 'positive intention.' Retrieved from http://www.nlpu.com/Patterns/pattern2.htm.

Dilts, R. (1999a). *Sleight of mouth: The magic of conversational belief change.* Capitola, CA: Meta Publications.

Dilts, R. (1999b). Anchoring. Retrieved from http://www.nlpu.com/Articles/artic28.htm.

Dilts, R. (2003). *From coach to awakener.* Capitola, CA: Meta Publications.

Dilts, R. (2005). Introduction to: A proposed distinction for neuro-linguistic programming. Retrieved from http://www.nlpu.com/Articles/essarticle.htm.

Dilts, R. (2008). The discovery of eye accessing cues. Retrieved from www.nlpiash.org/Conferences/2008Conference/Ebulletins/tabid/248/EntryID/10/Default.aspx.

Dilts, R., & Hallbom, T. (2009). *Early days of NLP* [DVD]. San Francisco, CA: NLPCA.

Dilts, R. & Delozier, J. (2000). *Encyclopedia of systemic neuro-linguistic programming and NLP new coding.* Retrieved from http://nlpuniversitypress.com/.

Dilts, R., Hallbom, T., Smith, S. (1990). *Beliefs: Pathways to health and well-being.* Portland, OR: Metamorphous Press.

Dirac, P. (1933). Theory of electrons and positrons. Nobel Lecture, December 12, 1933. Retrieved from http://www.nobelprize.org/nobel_prizes/physics/laureates/1933/dirac-lecture.pdf

Doidge, N. (2007). The brain that changes itself. New York: Viking Penguin. Retrieved from http://www.stellarpoint.com.au/wp-content/uploads/2013/01/The-Brain-That-Changes-Itself.pdf.

Druckman, D. & Swets, J. A. (Eds.). (1988). Enhancing human performance: Issues, theories, and techniques. Atlanta, GA: National Academy Press.

Eakin, P. J. (2000). Autobiography, identity, and the fictions of memory. In D. L. Schacter (Ed). *Memory, brain, and belief* (pp. 293–294). Cambridge, MA: Harvard University Press.

Einspruch, E. L., & Forman, B. D. (1985). Observations concerning research literature on neuro-linguistic programming. *Journal of Counseling Psychology, 32*(4), pp. 589–596.

Feynman, R. P. (1965). *The development of the space-time view of quantum electrodynamics.* Nobel Lecture, December 11, 1965. Retrieved from http://www.nobelprize.org/nobel_prizes/physics/laureates/1965/feynman-lecture.html.

Friedman, N. (1997). *The hidden domain.* Eugene, OR: The Woodbridge Group.

Gilligan, I. (2007, December). Neanderthal extinction and modern human behaviour: The role of climate change and clothing. *World Archaeology* 39, 4, 499-514. Retrieved from http://www.jstor.org/stable/40026145?seq=1#page_scan_tab_contents.

Goleman, D. (1995). *Emotional intelligence.* New York: Bantam Books.

Goswami, A. (1993). *The self-aware universe.* New York: Penguin Putnam, Inc.

Gray, R., Liotta, R., & Cheal, J. (2012). Research and the history of methodological flaws. In L. Wake, R. Gray, & F. Bourke (Eds.), *The clinical effi-*

cacy of NLP: A critical appraisal (pp. 194–216). London: Routledge. As cited in: Gray, R. M., 35 years revisited: Conceptual errors in scientific inquiry, a case study. Retrieved from http://nlpwiki.org/35-years-revisited-3.

Grinder, J., & Delozier, J. (1987). *Turtles all the way down: Prerequisites to personal genius.* Scotts Valley, CA: Grinder & Associates.

Grinder, J., & Bandler, R. (1976). *The structure of magic: A book about communication and change* (Vol. 2). Palo Alto, CA: Science and Behavior Books.

Grinder, J., & Pucelik, R. F. (Eds.). (2013). *The origins of neuro-linguistic programming.* Bethel, CT: Crown House Publishing.

Grinder, J., Delozier, J., & Bandler, R. (1977). *Patterns of the hypnotic techniques of Milton H. Erickson, M.D* (Vol. 2). Cupertino, CA: Meta Publications.

Hagelin, J. (2006). Consciousness is the unified field. *Light of Consciousness: Journal of Spiritual Awakening, 18*(1), 11–15.

Hall, L. M. (2007a). Neuro-semantics: Not quite everything about everything you want to know about the new field. Retrieved from http://www.neurosemantics.com/ns-writings/introducing-neuro-semantics-2.

Hall, L. M. (2007b). The newest code of NLP. Retrieved from http://www.neurosemantics.com/nlp-critiques/the-newest-code-of-nlp.

Hall, L. M. (2010a). The invigorating 1970s. Retrieved from http://www.neurosemantics.com/nlp/the-history-of-nlp/the-invigorating-1970s.

Hall, L. M. (2010b). NLP and the human potential movement. Retrieved from http://www.neurosemantics.com/nlp-advanced/nlp-and-the-human-potential-movement.

Hall, L. M., & Bodenhamer, B. G. (1997). *Mindlines: Lines that change minds.* Grand Junction, CO: E. T. Publications.

Hanson, R. (2013). *Hardwiring happiness: The new brain science of contentment, calm, and confidence.* New York: Harmony Books.

Heap. M. (1988). Neurolinguistic programming: An interim verdict. In M. Heap (Ed.), *Hypnosis: Current clinical, experimental and forensic practices* (pp. 268–270). London: Croom Helm.

Hellinger, B. (1998). *Love's hidden symmetry.* Phoenix, AZ: Zeig, Tucker & Co., Inc.

Hellinger, B. (1999). *Acknowledging what is.* Phoenix, AZ: Zeig, Tucker & Co., Inc.

Hellinger. B. (2006, July). *Bert Hellinger demonstrates movements of the spirit mind* [DVD]. Presentation at workshop in Washington, DC. Retrieved from www.hellingerdc.com/store_videos.php.

Hellinger, B., & Beaumont, H. (1999). *Touching love* (Vol. 2). Heidelberg, Germany: Carl-Auer-Systeme Verlag.

Hellinger. B., Schutzenberger, A., & Sheldrake, R. (1999). *Reviewing assumptions* [Video]. Phoenix, AZ: Zeig, Tucker, & Theisen, Inc.

Hestenes, D. (1983). Quantum mechanics from self-interaction. *Found Physics 15*(1), 63–87. Retrieved from http://geocalc.clas.asu.edu/pdf-preAdobe8/QMfromSI.pdf.

Huxley, A. (2009). *The perennial philosophy.* New York: Harper Perennial Modern Classics.

James, T., & Woodsmall, W. (1988). *Time line therapy and the basis of personality.* Cupertino, CA: Meta Publications.

Joseph, R. (1996). *Neuropsychiatry, neuropsychology, and clinical neuroscience* (2nd ed.). Baltimore, MD: Williams and Wilkins.

Kahneman, D. (2010). *The riddle of experience vs. memory* [Video]. Retrieved from http://www.ted.com/talks/daniel_kahneman_the_riddle_of_experience_vs_memory.html.

Kammer, D. (Ed.). (2016). *Neuro-linguistic programming research data base.* Retrieved from http://www.nlp.de/cgi-bin/research/nlp-rdb.cgi.

Keen, S. (1972). Seeing Castaneda. *Psychology Today.* Retrieved from http://www.nagualism.com/carlos-castaneda-interview-psychology-today.html.

Kemmer, S. (2008a). Biographical sketch of Edward Sapir. Retrieved from http://www.ruf.rice.edu/`kemmer/Found/sapirbio.html.

Kihlstorm, J. F., Beer, J. S., & Klein, S. B. (2001). *Self and identity as memory.* Retrieved from http://socrates.berkeley.edu/~kihlstrm/SelfIdentityMemory.htm.

Klein, S. B. (2001). A self to remember: A cognitive neuropsychological perspective on how self creates memory and memory creates self. In C. Sedikides & M. Brewer (Eds.), *Individual self, relational self, collective self* (pp. 25–46). Philadelphia, PA: Psychology Press/Taylor & Francis. Retrieved from http://socrates.berkeley.edu/~kihlstrm/SelfIdentityMemory.htm.

Korzybski, A. (1994). *Science and sanity: An introduction to non-Aristotelian systems and general semantics* (5th ed.). Englewood, NJ: Institute of General Semantics.

Krauss, L. M. (2012, July 6). Higgs and the holy grail of physics. Retrieved from http://www.cnn.com/2012/07/06/opinion/krauss-higgs-particle/ *CNN.*

Krishnamurti, J., & Bohm, D. (1999). *The limits of thought.* London: Routledge.

Laszlo, E. (2004). *Science and the akashic field.* Rochester, VT: Inner Traditions.

LeDoux, J. (1998). The emotional brain: The mysterious underpinnings of emotional life. New York: Touchstone.

LeDoux, J. (2003, October). The emotional brain, fear, and the amygdala. *Cellular and Molecular Neurobiology, 23(*4/5). Retrieved from http://www.ekmaninternational.com/media/4634/fearbrain%20amygdala%20joe%20ledoux.pdf.

Lewis, B. A., & Pucelik, F. R. (1982). *Magic demystified: An introduction to NLP.* Lake Oswego, OR: Metamorphous Press.

Lilienfeld, S. O., Lynn, S. J., & Lohr, J. M. (Eds.). (2003). *Science and pseudoscience in clinical psychology.* New York: Guilford.

Lipton, B. (2005). *Biology of belief.* Santa Rosa, CA: Mountain of Love/Elite Books.

Maharishi Mahesh Yogi (Trans.). (1990). *Bhagavad gita.* New York: Penguin Arkana Books.

McCall, G. J. (2006). Symbolic interaction. In P. J. Burke (Ed.), *Contemporary social psychological theories* (pp. 1–4). Palo Alto, CA: Stanford University Press.

MacLean, P. D. (1990). *The triune brain in evolution: Role in paleocerebral functions.* New York: Plenum Press.

McClendon, T. L. (1989). *The wild days: NLP 1972–1981.* Cupertino, CA: Meta Publications.

McCrone, J. (2006). Dichotomistic: Benjamin Libet's half second. Retrieved from http://www.dichotomistic.com/mind_readings_chapter on libet.html.

McDonald, L. (2001). Neurolinguistic programming in mental health. In J. France & S. Kramer (Eds.), *Communication and mental illness* (pp. 297–302). London: Jessica Kingsley Publishers.

McMaster, M., & Grinder, J. (1980). *Precision: A new approach to communication.* Beverly Hills, CA: Precision Models.

Massey, D. S. (2001). A brief history of human society: The origin and role of emotion in social life. Retrieved from http://wwvv.asanet.org/images/members/docs/pdf/featured/masseyaddress.pdf.

Medicine Eagle, B. (1991). *Buffalo woman comes singing.* New York: Ballantine Books.

Miller, B. L. (2007). The human frontal lobes: An introduction. In B. L. Miller and J. L. Cummings (Eds.). *The human frontal lobes: Functions and disorders* (2nd ed.) (pp. 3-11). New York: Guilford Press.

Miller, G. A. (2003, March). The cognitive revolution: A historical perspective. *TRENDS in Cognitive Sciences 7*(3), p. 141. Retrieved from http://www.cs.princeton.edu/~rit/geo/Miller.pdf.

Miller, G., Galanter, E., & Pribram, K. (1960). *Plans and the structure of behavior.* New York: Holt, Rinehart and Winston, Inc.

Moore, T. V. (1939). *Cognitive psychology.* Chicago: Lippincott.

Nave, C. R. (2012). Lamb shift. Retrieved from http://hyperphysics.phy-astr.gsu.edu/hbase/quantum/lamb.html.

Neisser, U. (1967). *Cognitive psychology*. New York: Meredith.

National Geographic Society. (2016). *Geonographic project*. Retrieved from https://genographic.nationalgeographic.com/neanderthal/.

Neurolinguistic Psychotherapy and Counselling Association. (2014). See what ANLP can do for you. Retrieved from http://www.anlp.org/anlp-history.

Nowell, A.; Walker, C.; Cordova, C.E.; Ames, C.J.H.; Pokines, J.T.; Stueber, D.; DeWitt, R.; and al-Souliman, A.S.A. (2016). Middle Pleistocene subsistence in the Azraq Oasis, Jordan: Protein residue and other proxies. *Journal of Archaeological Science 73*, 36-44.

O'Connor, J., & Seymour, J. (1990). *Introducing neuro-linguistic programming*. London: Thorsons (Harper Collins).

Pais, A., Weinberg, S., & Quigg, C. (1997). 100 years of elementary particles. *Beam Line 27*(1). Retrieved from http://www.slac.stanford.edu/pubs/beamline/pdf/97i.pdf.

Peat, D. F. (1997). *Infinite potential: The life and times of David Bohm*. Reading, MA: Addison-Wesley Publishing Company, Inc.

Peck, M. S. (1978). *The road less traveled*. New York: Simon and Schuster.

Read, A. W. (1990). Formative influences on Korzybski's general semantics. In M. Kendig (Ed), *Alfred Korzybski: Collected writings, 1920–1950* (pp. xxiii–xxiv). Pittsboro, NC: Town House Press, Inc.

Rincon, P. (2016). *DNA hints at earlier human exodus from Africa*. BBC News website. Retrieved from www.bbc.com/news/science-environment-37408014

Rosenblum, B., & Kuttner, F. (2006). *Quantum enigma*. Oxford: Oxford University Press.

Satinover, J. (2001). *The quantum brain: The search for freedom and the next generation of man*. New York: John Wiley & Sons.

Schenk, A. (2004a). *Movements of the soul*. Interview with Angela Schenk in Bert Hellinger's Spiritual Family-Constellations [website]. Retrieved from http://www.family-constellations.org/index.html.

Schenk, A. (2004b). *Moving with spirit*. Interview with Angela Schenk in Bert Hellinger's Family-Constellations [website]. Retrieved from http://www.family-constellations.org/moving_with_spirit.htm.

Schutzenberger, A. A. (1998). *The ancestor syndrome*. London: Routledge.

Schwartz, J.M. & Gladding, R. (2012). *You are not your brain*. New York: Avery.

Seung, S. (2012). *Connectome: How the brain's wiring makes us who we are*. New York: Houghton Mifflin Harcourt.

Sharpley, C. F. (1984). Predicate matching in NLP: A review of research on the preferred representational system. *Journal of Counseling Psychology 31*(2), pp. 238–248.

Sharpley C. F. (1987). Research findings on neuro-linguistic programming: Non-supportive data or an un-testable theory. *Communication and Cognitio 34*(1), pp. 103–107.

Sheldrake, R. (1995a). *A new science of life: Morphic resonance.* Rochester, VT: Park Street Press.

Sheldrake, R. (1995b). *The presence of the past.* Rochester, VT: Park Street Press.

Sheldrake, R. (2005). *Morphic resonance and morphic fields: An introduction.* Retrieved from http://www.sheldrake.org/Articles&Papers/papers/morphic/morphic_intro.html.

Sheldrake, R., McKenna, T., & Abraham, R. (1992). *Chaos, creativity and cosmic consciousness.* Rochester, VT: Park Street Press.

Stapp, H.P. (2011). *Mindful universe: Quantum mechanics and the participating observer* (2nd ed.). New York: Springer.

Thornton, S.P. (nd). Sigmund Freud (1856-1939). In J. Fieser & B. Dowden (Eds), *Internet encyclopedia of philosophy: A peer-reviewed academic resource.* Retrieved from http://www.iep.utm.edu/freud.

Tolle, E. (1999). *The power of now: A guide to spiritual enlightenment.* Novato, CA: New World Library.

Tosey P. & Mathison, J. (2007). *Fabulous creatures of HRD: A critical natural history of neuro-linguistic programming.* University of Surrey paper presented at the 8th International Conference on Human Resource Development Research & Practice Across Europe. Oxford Brookes Business School, June 26–28, 2007.

Van der Kolk, B. (2014). *The body keeps the score: Brain, mind, and body in the healing of trauma.* New York, NY: Viking.

Wake, L. (2008). *Neurolistic psychotherapy: A postmodern perspective.* London & New York: Routledge.

Wallace, A. (2003). *Sorcerer's Apprentice: My life with Carlos Castaneda.* Berkeley, CA: Frog, Ltd.

Whorf, B. L. (2012). *Language, thought & reality* (2nd ed.). Cambridge, MA: MIT Press.

Wolfe, F. A. (1985). Continuum: Quantum consciousness. *OMNI 7*(12), pp. 1–2. Retrieved from http://www.fredalanwolf.com/myarticles/omni%20continuum.pdf.

Wysong, J. (n.d.). Alfred Korzybski and gestalt therapy. Retrieved from http://www.gestalt.org/alfred.htm.

Zimbardo, P., & Boyd, J. (2008). *The time paradox.* New York: Free Press.

About the Authors

Carl Buchheit has a Ph.D. in Transpersonal Psychology from the International University of Professional Studies. Carl began studying Neuro-Linguistic Programming in 1979, and he studied closely with Jonathan Rice from 1984 to 1995. His career in NLP began at the NLP Center for Advanced Studies, where from 1984 to 1989 he was an NLP trainer and from 1986 to 1989 the Center's owner. He received an NLP Master Trainer Certification at the Institute of NLP in Austin, Texas in 1991. From 1993 to the present Carl has been the owner and director of training at NLP Marin in San Rafael, California. Currently he teaches thirty-five three-day training weekends per year, and on weekdays he works with individuals or couples in his private practice. Since 2005, Carl has also been facilitating bi-weekly Systemic Constellation Evenings. Carl travels globally and lectures frequently about his methodology, which he calls Transformational NLP.

Ellie Schamber has a Ph.D. in European Intellectual and Cultural History from the University of California at Berkeley. She was a teaching assistant in History at U.C. Berkeley in the late 1960s, and an instructor in Western Civilizations at Lone Mountain College in the early 1970s. She revised her Ph.D. dissertation into a book that was published by the University Press in 1984. She later taught at the University of Arizona, Mississippi State University, and Southeastern Louisiana University. She now lives in Mill Valley, California, where she has taught in the distance education (online) departments of the University of Phoenix, Kaplan University, and Boston University.

Ellie continues to facilitate courses at Boston University as well as works as an SAT prep tutor and an editor for professionals and university students. She became a student of Carl's at NLP Marin in 2000, and has continued to study and practice Transformative NLP since then. She currently resides and works in Mill Valley, California. She regularly lectures to the public about spiritual topics.

Printed in Dunstable, United Kingdom

65671027R00131